Current Practices
in Public Libraries

Current Practices in Public Libraries has been co-published simultaneously as *Public Library Quarterly*, Volume 25, Numbers 1/2 2006.

> **Monographic Separates from *Public Library Quarterly*®**
>
> For additional information on these and other Haworth Press titles, including descriptions, tables of contents, reviews, and prices, use the QuickSearch catalog at http://www.HaworthPress.com.

Current Practices in Public Libraries, edited by William Miller and Rita M. Pellen (Vol. 25, No. 1/2, 2006). *Examines a variety of current trends, issues, and practices in public library administration.*

Current Practices in Public Libraries

William Miller
Rita M. Pellen
Editors

Current Practices in Public Libraries has been co-published simultaneously as *Public Library Quarterly*, Volume 25, Numbers 1/2 2006.

LONDON AND NEW YORK

First Published 2006 by
The Haworth Information Press®

2 Park Square, Milton Park, Abingdon, Oxon OX14 4RN
711 Third Avenue, New York, NY 10017, USA

Routledge is an imprint of the Taylor & Francis Group, an informa business

First issued in paperback 2016

Current Practices in Public Libraries has been co-published simultaneously as *Public Library Quarterly*, Volume 25, Numbers 1/2 2006.

Copyright © 2006 Taylor & Francis.

All rights reserved. No part of this book may be reprinted or reproduced or utilised in any form or by any electronic, mechanical, or other means, now known or hereafter invented, including photocopying and recording, or in any information storage or retrieval system, without permission in writing from the publishers.

Notice:
Product or corporate names may be trademarks or registered trademarks, and are used only for identification and explanation without intent to infringe.

Photographs© Peter Aaron/Esto. All rights reserved.

Library of Congress Cataloging-in-Publication Data

Current practices in public libraries / William Miller, Rita M. Pellen, editors.
    p. cm.
    "Co-published simultaneously as Public library quarterly, volume 25, numbers 1/2."
    Includes bibliographical references and index.
    1. Public libraries–United States. I. Miller, William, 1947- II. Pellen, Rita M. III. Public library quarterly.
Z731.C89 2007
027.4730973–dc22

                                              2007026938

ISBN 13: 978-0-7890-3607-0 (hbk)
ISBN 13: 978-1-138-99056-2 (pbk)

The HAWORTH PRESS, Inc.
Abstracting, Indexing & Outward Linking
PRINT and ELECTRONIC BOOKS & JOURNALS

This section provides you with a list of major indexing & abstracting services and other tools for bibliographic access. That is to say, each service began covering this periodical during the year noted in the right column. Most Websites which are listed below have indicated that they will either post, disseminate, compile, archive, cite or alert their own Website users with research-based content from this work. (This list is as current as the copyright date of this publication.)

Abstracting, Website/Indexing Coverage . . . . Year When Coverage Began

- *International Bibliography of Book Reviews on the Humanities and Social Sciences (IBR) (Thomson)* <http://www.saur.de> . . . 2006

- ***Academic Search Premier (EBSCO)****
  <http://search.ebscohost.com> 2006

- ***LISA: Library and Information Science Abstracts (ProQuest CSA)**** <http://www.csa.com/factsheets/list-set-c.php> . . 1992

- ***MasterFILE Premier (EBSCO)****
  <http://search.ebscohost.com> 2006

- *Academic Source Premier (EBSCO)*
  <http://search.ebscohost.com> 2007

- *Advanced Polymers Abstracts (ProQuest CSA)*
  <http://www.csa.com/factsheets/ema-polymers-set-c.php> 2006

- *Aluminium Industry Abstracts (ProQuest CSA)*
  <http://www.csa.com/factsheets/aia-set-c.php> 2006

- *British Library Inside (The British Library)*
  <http://www.bl.uk/services/current/inside.html> 2006

(continued)

- *Cabell's Directory of Publishing Opportunities in Educational Technology & Library Science* <http://www.cabells.com> 2006
- *Cambridge Scientific Abstracts (now ProQuest CSA)* <http://www.csa.com> 2006
- *Ceramic Abstracts (ProQuest CSA)* <http://www.csa.com/factsheets/wca-set-c.php>............. 2006
- *Composites Industry Abstracts (ProQuest CSA)* <http://www.csa.com/factsheets/ema-composites-set-c.php>... 2006
- *Computer and Information Systems Abstracts (ProQuest CSA)* <http://www.csa.com/factsheets/computer-set-c.php> 2004
- *Corrosion Abstracts (ProQuest CSA)* <http://www.csa.com/factsheets/corrosion-set-c.php> 2006
- *CSA Engineering Research Database (ProQuest CSA)* <http://www.csa.com/factsheets/engineering-set-c.php> 2006
- *CSA High Technology Research Database With Aerospace (ProQuest CSA)* <http://www.csa.com/factsheets/hightech-set-c.php>........ 2006
- *CSA Technology Research Database (ProQuest CSA)* <http://www.csa.com/factsheets/techresearch-set-c.php> 2006
- *CSA/ASCE Civil Engineering Abstracts (Cambridge Scientific Abstracts)* <http://www.csa.com/factsheets/civil-set-c.php> 2006
- *Current Abstracts (EBSCO)* <http://search.ebscohost.com> 2007
- *Current Citations Express (EBSCO)* <http://search.ebscohost.com>............................. 2007
- *EBSCOhost Electronic Journals Service (EJS)* <http://search.ebscohost.com> 2001
- *Electronic Collections Online (OCLC)* <http://www.oclc.org/electroniccollections/> 2006
- *Electronics and Communications Abstracts (ProQuest CSA)* <http://www.csa.com/factsheets/electronics-set-c.php> 2006
- *Elsevier Eflow-D* <http://www.elsevier.com> 2006
- *Elsevier Scopus* <http://www.info.scopus.com> 2005
- *Engineered Materials Abstracts (ProQuest CSA)* <http://www.csa.com/factsheets/emaclust-set-c.php> 2006

(continued)

- *Google <http://www.google.com>*............................ 2004
- *Google Scholar <http://scholar.google.com>*.................. 2004
- *Haworth Document Delivery Center*
  <http://www.HaworthPress.com/journals/dds.asp>.......... 1979
- *Index Guide to College Journals*............................ 1999
- *Index to Periodical Articles Related to Law*
  <http://www.law.utexas.edu>............................ 1992
- *Informed Librarian, The <http://www.informedlibrarian.com>*... 1993
- *INIST-CNRS <http://www.inist.fr>*.......................... 2000
- *International Bibliography of Periodical Literature
  on the Humanities and Social Sciences (IBZ) (Thomson)
  <http://www.saur.de>*............................... 2001
- *Internationale Bibliographie der geistes- und
  sozialwissenschaftlichen Zeitschriftenliteratur ... See IBZ
  <http://www.saur.de>*................................ 2001
- *Journal of Academic Librarianship: Guide to Professional
  Literature, The*... 2006
- *JournalSeek <http://www.journalseek.net>*.................... 2006
- *Konyvtari Figyelo (Library Review)
  <http://www.oszk.hu/index_en.htm>*...................... 1997
- *Library Literature & Information Science Index / Full Text
  (H.W. Wilson) <http://www.hwwilson.com>*................. 1984
- *Library, Information Science & Technology Abstracts
  (EBSCO) <http://search.ebscohost.com>*................... 2006
- *Library, Information Science & Technology Abstracts
  with Full Text (EBSCO) <http://search.ebscohost.com>*....... 2007
- *Links@Ovid (via CrossRef targeted DOI links)
  <http://www.ovid.com>*................................. 2005
- *Materials Business File (ProQuest CSA)
  <http://www.csa.com/factsheets/mbf-set-c.php>*............ 2006
- *Materials Research Database with METADEX
  (ProQuest CSA)
  <http://www.csa.com/factsheets/materials-set-c.php>*........ 2006
- *Mechanical & Transportation Engineering Abstracts
  (ProQuest CSA)
  <http://www.csa.com/factsheets/mechtrans-set-c.php>*....... 2006
- *METADEX (ProQuest CSA)
  <http://www.csa.com/factsheets/metadex-set-c.php>*......... 2006

(continued)

- *NewJour (Electronic Journals & Newsletters)*
  <http://gort.ucsd.edu/newjour/> 2006
- *OCLC ArticleFirst* <http://www.oclc.org/services/databases/> 2007
- *Ovid Linksolver (OpenURL link resolver via CrossRef targeted DOI links)* <http://www.linksolver.com> 2005
- *Scopus (See instead Elsevier Scopus)*
  <http://www.info.scopus.com> 2005
- *Solid State and Superconductivity Abstracts (ProQuest CSA)*
  <http://www.csa.com/factsheets/solid-state-set-c.php> 2006
- *SwetsWise* <http://www.swets.com> 2000
- *TOC Premier (EBSCO)* <http://search.ebscohost.com> 2007
- *WilsonWeb* <http://vnweb.hwwilsonweb.com/hww/Journals/> 2005
- *zetoc (The British Library)* <http://www.bl.uk> 2004

Bibliographic Access

- *Cabell's Directory of Publishing Opportunities in Educational Curriculum and Methods* <http://www.cabells.com/>
- *MediaFinder* <http://www.mediafinder.com/>
- *Ulrich's Periodicals Directory: The Global Source for Periodicals Information Since 1932* <http://www. bowkerlink.com>

Special Bibliographic Notes related to special journal issues (separates) and indexing/abstracting:

- indexing/abstracting services in this list will also cover material in any "separate" that is co-published simultaneously with Haworth's special thematic journal issue or DocuSerial. Indexing/abstracting usually covers material at the article/chapter level.
- monographic co-editions are intended for either non-subscribers or libraries which intend to purchase a second copy for their circulating collections.
- monographic co-editions are reported to all jobbers/wholesalers/approval plans. The source journal is listed as the "series" to assist the prevention of duplicate purchasing in the same manner utilized for books-in-series.
- to facilitate user/access services all indexing/abstracting services are encouraged to utilize the co-indexing entry note indicated at the bottom of the first page of each article/chapter/contribution.
- this is intended to assist a library user of any reference tool (whether print, electronic, online, or CD-ROM) to locate the monographic version if the library has purchased this version but not a subscription to the source journal.
- individual articles/chapters in any Haworth publication are also available through the Haworth Document Delivery Service (HDDS).

As part of Haworth's continuing commitment to better serve our library patrons, we are proud to be working with the following electronic services:

AGGREGATOR SERVICES

Service	
EBSCOhost	
Ingenta	
J-Gate	
Minerva	
OCLC FirstSearch	FirstSearch
Oxmill	 Oxmill Publishing
SwetsWise	SwetsWise

LINK RESOLVER SERVICES

Service	
1Cate (Openly Informatics)	1cate
ChemPort (American Chemical Society)	ChemPort
CrossRef	
Gold Rush (Coalliance)	 Gold Rush
LinkOut (PubMed)	LinkOut LINKING TO A WORLD OF RESOURCES
LINKplus (Atypon)	 atypon
LinkSolver (Ovid)	OVID LinkSolver
LinkSource with A-to-Z (EBSCO)	
Resource Linker (Ulrich)	ULRICH'S RESOURCE LINKER
SerialsSolutions (ProQuest)	SerialsSolutions
SFX (Ex Libris)	S·F·X
Sirsi Resolver (SirsiDynix)	SirsiDynix
Tour (TDnet)	TOUR
Vlink (Extensity, formerly Geac)	extensity
WebBridge (Innovative Interfaces)	WebBridge

Current Practices in Public Libraries

CONTENTS

Introduction: Public Libraries Today   1
    William Miller

The Status of Public Library Funding 2003-2005:
   Impact of Local Operating Revenue Fluctuations   5
    Denise M. Davis

Public Library Public Access Computing and Internet Access:
   Factors Which Contribute to Quality Services and Resources   27
    John Carlo Bertot
    Denise M. Davis

Public Library Facility Closure:
   How Research Can Better Facilitate Proactive Management   43
    Christie M. Koontz
    Dean K. Jue

Public Libraries and Human Rights   57
    Kathleen de la Pena McCook
    Katharine J. Phenix

Open for Business: The NYPL Science, Industry,
   and Business Library Takes Stock   75
    Kristin McDonough
    Madeleine Cohen

Effect of Multiculturalism and Automation
   on Public Library Collection Development
   and Technical Services   91
    Phyllis Sue Alpert

Swimming Upstream 105
   Linda J. Mielke
   Paula M. Singer
   Gail L. Griffith

Marketing and Advocacy:
   Collaboration in Principle and Practice 117
   James A. Nelson

Politics and Advocacy: The Role of Networking
   in Selling the Library to Your Community 137
   Charles R. McClure
   Sari Feldman
   Joe Ryan

Creating Advocates for Public Libraries 155
   Kathleen R. T. Imhoff

Developing an Outreach Program
   Based on Freedom Songs 171
   Leslie A. Acevedo

From Literate to Information Literate
   Communities Through Advocacy 181
   Carol A. Brey-Casiano

A Literacy Center Where? A Public Library Finds Space
   to Promote and Provide Family Learning Activities 191
   Tony Petruzzi
   Mary Frances Burns

The Personal Touch: A Case for a Small, Independent Library 199
   L. Susan Hayes

Mentoring GenX for Leadership
   in the Public Library 205
   Gail Doherty

Index 219

ABOUT THE EDITORS

William Miller, PhD, MLS, is Director of Libraries at Florida Atlantic University. He formerly served as Head of Reference at Michigan State University, and as Associate Dean of Libraries at Bowling Green State University (Ohio). Dr. Miller has a PhD from the University of Rochester and an MLS from the University of Toronto. He is Past-President of the Association of College and Research Libraries, has served as Chair of the *Choice* Editorial Board, and is a frequent contributor to professional journals, as well as being a contributing editor of *Library Issues*. Dr. Miller teaches courses in English Literature and Library Science. He was named Instruction Librarian of the Year in 2004 by the ACRL Instruction Section.

Rita M. Pellen, MLS, BA, is the Associate Director of Libraries at Florida Atlantic University. Previously she was Assistant Director of Public Services and Head of the Reference Department at Florida Atlantic. Ms. Pellen has a B.A. from Pennsylvania State University and an MLS from the University of Pittsburgh. In 1993, she received the Gabor Exemplary Employee Award in recognition for outstanding service to FAU, and in 1997, the "Literati Club Award for Excellence" for the outstanding paper in *The Bottom Line*. She has served on committees in LAMA, ACRL and ALCTS, as well as the Southeast Florida Library Information Network, SEFLIN, a multi-type library cooperative in South Florida. Honor society memberships include Beta Phi Mu and Phi Kappa Phi.

Introduction: Public Libraries Today

How can we really know the state of public libraries today? The articles in this collection approach this question through both research methodologies and personal experience, and provide a broad-ranging overview of where public libraries stand with respect to their communities, their goals, and their activities. Denise Davis, Director of ALA's Office for Research and Statistics, conducted an extensive survey to provide an overview of "The Status of Public Library Funding 2003-2005." Her objective investigation reveals mixed results, with most libraries experiencing steady-state funding over the three year period she studied, and with increases, where they occur, being targeted at required expenditures such as higher salary and utility costs, so that the overall situation of the libraries was not improved.

John Carlo Bertot, the Associate Director of Florida State University's Information Use Management and Policy Institute, in its College of Information, teams up with Davis to study "Public Library Public Access Computing and Internet Access: Factors Which Contribute to Quality Services and Resources." Bertot and Davis combined data from three major public library datasets to analyze a variety of key demographic, technology, and budgetary variables to develop a profile of public access to public library computing and determine the factors which contribute most to high levels of connectivity and access, primarily at smaller public libraries. They offer recommendations for policymakers, practitioners, and researchers.

[Haworth co-indexing entry note]: "Introduction: Public Libraries Today." Miller, William. Co-published simultaneously in *Public Library Quarterly* (The Haworth Press, Inc.) Vol. 25, No. 1/2, 2006, pp. 1-4; and: *Current Practices in Public Libraries* (ed: William Miller, and Rita M. Pellen) The Haworth Press, Inc., 2006, pp. 1-4. Single or multiple copies of this article are available for a fee from The Haworth Document Delivery Service [1-800-HAWORTH, 9:00 a.m. - 5:00 p.m. (EST). E-mail address: docdelivery@haworthpress.com].

Available online at http://plq.haworthpress.com
© 2006 by The Haworth Press, Inc. All rights reserved.
doi:10.1300/J118v25n01_01

Also offering basic research are Christie M. Koontz, Director of the GeoLib Program at FSU's College of Information, and Dean K. Jue, Director of Technical Assistance at FSU's Florida Resources and Environmental Analysis Center. In "Public Library Facility Closure: How Research Can Better Facilitate Proactive Management," they analyzed data from the Federal-State Cooperative System (FSCS) including information on 438 closed library outlets to provide a base upon which to build research about public library facility closures and their potential impacts on the public. Preliminary observations include the fact that while funding cuts are sometimes the impetus for closing a location, others include changing demographics and the physical attractiveness of the outlet in question.

Kathleen de la Pena McCook, a professor at the University of South Florida's School of Library and Information Science, joined with Katharine J. Phenix, Adult Services Librarian at the Rangeview Library District (Colorado) to detail the legal and philosophical basis for "Public Libraries and Human Rights." Drawing extensively on documents such as the Universal Declaration of Human Rights, McCook and Phenix make the case for libraries as agencies that support human rights, and also discuss situations in which libraries have failed in their responsibilities, including exclusion of the homeless, refusal to purchase foreign language materials, and filtering.

Kristin McDonough, Director of the New York Public Library's Science, Industry, and Business Library (SIBL) and Madeleine Cohen, Assistant Director for Electronic Resources, SIBL, give an overview of the changes that have occurred in the ten years since the founding of this premier library. The article, "Open for Business: The NYPL Science, Industry, and Business Library Takes Stock," tracks the growth and evolution of the library, and the new strategies it has evolved to meet the needs of the local and small business communities, and penetrate their target market more fully. The experiences and success of SIBL can serve as a model for public library initiatives in all fields.

In "Effect of Multiculturalism and Automation on Collection Development and Technical Services," Phyllis Sue Alpert, Assistant Director at the Miami-Dade Public Library System, discusses the changes that automation has created in the collection development and acquisitions processes, with particular attention to the acquisition of non-English language materials. And in "Swimming Upstream" Linda Mielke, CEO of the Indianapolis Marion County Public Library, along with her colleagues Paula M. Singer (Principal Consultant of The Singer Group) and Gail L. Griffith, Deputy Director of the Indianapolis Marion County Public

Library, discuss the challenges of leadership in an era of increasing chaos, change, and complexity.

Several pieces in this collection examine the processes of advocacy. James A. Nelson, recently retired as State Librarian and Commissioner of the Kentucky Department for Libraries and Archives, describes advocacy at a state-wide level in "Marketing and Advocacy: Collaboration in Principle and Practice." Nelson describes how the state library, the state library association, and others have worked together in a thoroughgoing way to secure strong support for public libraries throughout the state. In "Politics and Advocacy: The Role of Networking in Selling the Library to Your Community," three authors–Charles R. McClure and Joe Ryan, both of the Florida State University College of Information's Information Institute, and Sari Feldman, Executive Director of the Cuyahoga County Public Library, explore the nexus between politics and advocacy, and cite political action and advocacy as the key factors that can determine the overall success of today's public library. They postulate the concept of the "Successfully Networked Public Library," and cite the Cuyahoga County Public Library as an example.

In "Creating Advocates for Public Libraries," Kathleen Imhoff, Executive Director of the Lexington Public Library, defines the attributes of a successful advocate for public libraries, and cites numerous examples of situations in which Friends groups and other advocates have been crucial to the success of library initiatives. In yet another article that focuses on advocacy, "From Literate to Information Literate Communities Through Advocacy," Carol A. Brey-Casiano, Director of the El Paso Public Library and a former president of the American Library Association, makes the connections between the public library's roles in literacy and information literacy, and then underscores the necessity for advocacy in order to secure the support for such efforts.

Three other articles in this collection emphasize the need for public outreach. Leslie Acevedo, of the Flint Public Library, describes an innovative music and history program in "Developing an Outreach Program Based on Freedom Songs." In this program, school children are taught about the Civil Rights Movement through participation in a community concert and study of the movement's history and song. In "A Literacy Center Where? A Public Library Finds Space to Promote and Provide Family Learning Activities," Tony Petruzzi and Mary Frances Burns, librarians at the Morley Library in Painesville, Ohio, describe the genesis and operation of a family learning center, a non-traditional service that meets the needs of a community where literacy and lifelong learning are a challenge. In "The Personal Touch: A Case for a

Small, Independent Library," L. Susan Hayes, library director at the Parkland city library in Florida, makes the case that "small is beautiful," and discusses the advantages in terms of flexibility which a small community library can exercise, advantages which, she feels, outweigh the greater resources available to the larger institutions.

Rounding out this volume is a piece by Gail Doherty, Coordinator of Library Information Services and New Initiatives at the Winnipeg Public Library, entitled "Mentoring GenX for Leadership in the Public Library." As its title implies, this article discusses the importance of mentoring a new generation of librarians, who may have values and expectations that differ from that of the current generation of librarians.

Taken together, the articles in this collection show the range of interests of public librarians, and those who study public libraries today. There is some anxiety about the present, and concern to secure and increase the resources necessary to do the job, but there is also guarded optimism and hope for the future, and an admirable devotion to serving the public in whatever ways seem most relevant and useful to the communities being served. Those on the academic side are determined to provide a sound factual basis for the study of these libraries, and those on the practitioner side are equally determined to keep their libraries vibrant and relevant to their communities; all this bodes well for the future.

William Miller
Director of Libraries
Florida Atlantic University

The Status of Public Library Funding 2003-2005: Impact of Local Operating Revenue Fluctuations

Denise M. Davis

SUMMARY. There has long been concern about the status of public library funding. Although libraries annually report revenue and expenditures to State Libraries, and to a federal library system for public library data, it was difficult to ascertain the extent of mid-year increases and reductions. Also, lags in access to national data about the condition of public libraries increased the need for this study. The preliminary findings of a national study of funding issues in U.S. public libraries during fiscal years 2003-2005, and expectations for funding in fiscal year 2006 are presented here. The complete report, released by ALA in spring 2006 (ISBN 0-8389-8372-3), is available by contacting the author. doi:10.1300/J118v25n01_02 *[Article copies available for a fee from The Haworth Document Delivery Service: 1-800-HAWORTH. E-mail address: <docdelivery@haworthpress.com> Website: <http://www.HaworthPress.com> © 2006 by The Haworth Press, Inc. All rights reserved.]*

Denise M. Davis, MLS, is Director, Office for Research and Statistics, The American Library Association, 50 East Huron St., Chicago, IL 60611 (E-mail: dmdavis@ala.org).

[Haworth co-indexing entry note]: "The Status of Public Library Funding 2003-2005: Impact of Local Operating Revenue Fluctuations." Davis, Denise M. Co-published simultaneously in *Public Library Quarterly* (The Haworth Press, Inc.) Vol. 25, No. 1/2, 2006, pp. 5-26; and: *Current Practices in Public Libraries* (ed: William Miller, and Rita M. Pellen) The Haworth Press, Inc., 2006, pp. 5-26. Single or multiple copies of this article are available for a fee from The Haworth Document Delivery Service [1-800-HAWORTH, 9:00 a.m. - 5:00 p.m. (EST). E-mail address: docdelivery@haworthpress.com].

Available online at http://plq.haworthpress.com
© 2006 by The Haworth Press, Inc. All rights reserved.
doi:10.1300/J118v25n01_02

KEYWORDS. Library funding, library expenditures, budget shortfall, fiscal planning

EXECUTIVE SUMMARY

There has long been concern at the American Library Association (ALA) about the status of public library funding. In a study conducted in fall 2005 it was determined that, although it is not all doom and gloom, libraries experienced significant reductions in fiscal years 2003, 2004, and 2005. During this period U.S. public libraries have managed to maintain, and in some cases increase, services despite flat or reduced budgets. The study found that libraries serving more than 500,000 and fewer than 25,000 people saw the greatest midyear funding cuts. Libraries in the West and Midwest sustained greater cuts than their counterparts in the South and East.

Revenue reductions findings were balanced by public libraries reporting revenue increases during these fiscal years, although only slightly higher than those reporting decreases. An equal number of respondents reported level funding for all fiscal years–between 77% and 82% of all libraries responding–resulting in a net decrease in local revenue for these libraries. The reality was that a vast majority of U.S. public libraries had stagnated buying power as a result of the level funding during these fiscal years.

Overall, the increases clustered in the 1% to 4% ranges for all fiscal years studied, with approximately 18% of libraries surveyed reporting in these ranges for each fiscal year. Libraries more frequently attributed local tax revenue increases or decreases to levies or other tax measures (19.3% and 15%, respectively). The second most frequent response was budget shortfalls (10.4%), and the third budget surpluses (6.3%).

There clearly were differences in funding changes, with little relief anticipated for our smallest public libraries in the West and Midwest– 48% experienced reductions in fiscal year 2003, 35.8% in fiscal year 2004, and 34.5% in fiscal year 2005. Nearly 20% of Northeast libraries indicated budget reductions in fiscal year 2004, up from 12% in fiscal year 2003.

The reductions for all respondents clustered in the 1% to 2% and 11% or more ranges, with fairly even distribution in the 3% to 4% and 8% to 10% categories. There appears to be continued reductions in the 1% to 6% ranges for all fiscal years, with some relief in the 7% to 10% range in fiscal years 2004 and 2005.

Anticipating revenue for fiscal year 2006, 58.2% of public libraries anticipated things to remain about the same and about 32.4% anticipated some improvement in local tax revenue. Approximately 9.4% of libraries anticipated more reductions.

INTRODUCTION

The status of public library funding has been a long-standing concern of the profession, and of the American Library Association (ALA). Although libraries annually report revenue and expenditures to State Libraries, and to a federal library system for public library data, it was difficult to ascertain the extent of mid-year increases and reductions versus start of fiscal year reductions. Media attention in 2004 and 2005 was focused on library budgets being reduced during the course of a fiscal year due to local revenue shortfalls in communities. Libraries were reporting such changes, but no data existed to document in any comprehensive way the extent of such funding changes. Lags in access to national data about the condition of public libraries further complicated ALA's ability to evaluate the extent of the problem.

This report presents summary discussion and the preliminary findings of a national study conducted in fall 2005 of funding issues in U.S. public libraries during fiscal years 2003-2005, and expectations for funding in fiscal year 2006. This is the first such study by the ALA Office for Research & Statistics and launches a study methodology that supports "fast response" opportunities for ALA to respond to policy issues presented by its members.

Overall, the findings show that a majority of libraries did not sustain significant funding increases or decreases during a fiscal year, but did incur reductions and increases between fiscal years. This is not an unexpected finding. However, the percent range of mid-year reductions and the geographic region and populations served of those libraries proved meaningful.

This study determined that, although it is not all doom and gloom, libraries experienced significant reductions in fiscal years 2003, 2004, and 2005. This was balanced by public libraries reporting revenue increases during these fiscal years, although only slightly higher than those reporting decreases. An equal number of respondents reported level funding for all fiscal years–resulting in a net decrease in local revenue for these libraries. Many U.S. public libraries were doing the same or more with less real dollars.

This study lays the groundwork for follow-up studies to understand more specifically those factors impacting funding increases and decreases, and why particular communities were more affected than others. The differences are not fully explained by the diversified funding models represented in legal basis codes[1] and funding source data reported by the Federal State Cooperative System of Library Data (FSCS), nor by the numerous comments provided by respondents. Additional research is needed to understand what contributing factors impacted particular libraries.

Objectives of Study

The primary objectives of this study were to provide preliminary data that would highlight the extent of funding increases and decreases during a fiscal year. Such changes more dramatically impact a library's ability to provide core services to its patrons by removing the planning opportunity available during a normal budget process. In addition to understanding increases or decreases in local operating revenue during a fiscal year, the study asked about specific services impacted by the change. These included:

- Materials
- Staffing
- Hours open, and
- Electronic access

High-level findings address these objectives, as do some key commentary from respondents appearing at the end of this paper.

Increases in Funding

Overall, funding increases clustered in the 1% to 4% ranges for all fiscal years studied, with approximately 18% of libraries surveyed reporting in these ranges for each fiscal year. Unlike revenue decreases, increases reported regardless of population served were fairly stable within each category for all fiscal years. For instance, libraries serving populations between 25,000 and 99,999 reported slow, but steady, increases in local funding for the fiscal years reported (21.8%, 24.6% and 26.8%, respectively). Special funding was often reported as the reason for a mid-year increase (see the respondent comments section of this paper). Table 1-1 presents total findings, and Tables 1-2 through 1-5 present findings by population of legal service area.

TABLE 1-1. U.S. Public Libraries That Experienced Operating Revenue Increases, FY 2003-05

Year	Number	Percent
FY 2003	84	18.0%
FY 2004	111	23.7%
FY 2005	120	25.7%

N = 468 (100%)

TABLE 1-2. U.S. Public Libraries Serving Less Than 25,000 That Experienced Operating Revenue Increases, FY 2003-05

Year	Number	Percent
FY 2003	32	17.0%
FY 2004	44	23.4%
FY 2005	48	25.5%

N = 188 (100%)

TABLE 1-3. U.S. Public Libraries Serving 25,000-99,999 That Experienced Operating Revenue Increases, FY 2003-05

Year	Number	Percent
FY 2003	31	21.8%
FY 2004	35	24.6%
FY 2005	38	26.8%

N = 142 (100%)

TABLE 1-4. U.S. Public Libraries Serving 100,000-499,999 That Experienced Operating Revenue Increases, FY 2003-05

Year	Number	Percent
FY 2003	23	21.3%
FY 2004	27	25.0%
FY 2005	27	25.0%

N = 108 (100%)

TABLE 1-5. U.S. Public Libraries Serving 500,000 or More That Experienced Operating Revenue Increases, FY 2003-05

Year	Number	Percent
FY 2003	6	20.0%
FY 2004	7	23.3%
FY 2005	8	26.7%

N = 30 (100%)

TABLE 2-1. Size of Operating Revenue Increases Experienced by U.S. Public Libraries, by Region, FY 2003

	Region				
Size of Revenue Increases	Midwest	Northeast	South	West	Total
1-2%	19	2	3	10	34
Percent of libraries in region	15.3%	1.9%	2.2%	10.1%	7.3%
3-4%	8	1	2	1	12
Percent of libraries in region	6.5%	0.9%	1.4%	1.0%	2.6%
5-6%	4	3	4	2	13
Percent of libraries in region	3.2%	2.8%	2.9%	2.0%	2.8%
7-8%	4	0	0	1	5
Percent of libraries in region	0.9%	0.0%	0.0%	0.2%	1.1%
9-10%	1	1	1	3	6
Percent of libraries in region	0.8%	0.9%	0.7%	3.0%	1.3%
11% or more	4	6	3	3	16
Percent of libraries in region	3.2%	5.6%	2.2%	3.0%	3.4%

N = 468 (100%)
Chi-square = 49.760, p = .000
Note: Increases by region for FY2004 were statistically insignificant.

Libraries serving populations below 25,000 experienced slightly smaller increases compared with libraries serving larger population groups (Table 1-3). Looking at the data regionally, Midwest libraries sustained higher increases in all fiscal years studied, with the West running a close second for increases in the 1% to 2% range. In fiscal year 2005 libraries in the South experienced larger increases than other regions, and the Northeast reported its largest increase for any fiscal year studied. The Northeast reported the highest increases (11% or more) in both fiscal years 2004 and 2005. Tables 2-1 and 2-2 present operating revenue increases for fiscal years 2003 and 2005 by region.

Areas impacted by revenue increases for fiscal years 2003-2005 are presented in Table 3, and ranked as follows:

1. Materials (average of 22.5% of libraries responding)
2. Staffing (average of 16.4% of libraries responding)
3. Electronic access (average of 11.3% of libraries responding)
4. Hours open (average of 5% of libraries responding)

TABLE 2-2. Size of Operating Revenue Increases Experienced by U.S. Public Libraries, by Region, FY 2005

Size of Revenue Increases	Region				
	Midwest	Northeast	South	West	Total
1-2%	13	11	15	7	46
Percent of libraries in region	10.5%	10.3%	10.9%	7.1%	9.8%
3-4%	9	5	14	6	34
Percent of libraries in region	7.3%	4.7%	10.1%	6.1%	7.3%
5-6%	7	9	7	4	27
Percent of libraries in region	5.6%	8.4%	5.1%	4.0%	5.8%
7-8%	6	2	5	2	15
Percent of libraries in region	4.8%	1.9%	3.6%	2.0%	3.2%
9-10%	2	3	0	7	12
Percent of libraries in region	1.6%	2.8%	0.0%	7.1%	2.6%
11% or more	1	9	7	11	28
Percent of libraries in region	0.8%	8.4%	5.1%	11.1%	6.0%

N = 468 (100%)
Chi-square = 31.284, p = .027

TABLE 3. Areas Impacted by Operating Revenue Increases for U.S. Public Libraries, FY 2003-05

Area of Revenue Increase	Fiscal Year		
	FY 2003	FY 2004	FY 2005
Hours	19	22	29
Percent of libraries	4.1%	4.7%	6.2%
Staffing	65	76	89
Percent of libraries	13.9%	16.2%	19.0%
Materials	91	105	120
Percent of libraries	19.4%	22.4%	25.6%
Electronic Access	44	57	58
Percent of libraries	9.4%	12.2%	12.4%

N = 468 (100%)

When considering the comparability of operating revenue increases with other local government agencies and offices, an equal number of libraries sampled reported no increases or the same increase (see Table 4). We begin to see some improvement in fiscal year 2004 in library funding increases as compared with other local government agencies.

Table 5 presents responses regarding anticipated changes in operating budgets for fiscal year 2006 by region. Libraries are cautiously optimistic, with a majority expecting things to remain about the same even into fiscal year 2006.

TABLE 4. Comparability of Operating Revenue Increases Experienced by U.S. Public Libraries with Increases Experienced by Other Local Government Agencies and Offices, FY 2003-05

Comparability	Fiscal Year		
of Revenue Increase	FY 2003	FY 2004	FY 2005
Greater	26	42	39
Percent of libraries	5.6%	9.1%	8.2%
Same	69	75	74
Percent of libraries	14.7%	16.1%	15.8%
Less	22	21	32
Percent of libraries	4.8%	4.4%	6.8%
No increase	65	56	57
Percent of libraries	14.0%	12.0%	12.2%

N = 468 (100%)

TABLE 5. Anticipated Change in FY 2006 Operating Budgets for U.S. Public Libraries, by Region

Anticipated Change	Region				Total
	Midwest	Northeast	South	West	
Improvement in local funding Number	36	40	72	36	184
Percent of libraries	29.0%	37.4%	52.2%	36.4%	39.3%
Same Number	61	56	58	43	218
Percent of libraries	49.2%	52.3%	42.0%	43.4%	46.6%
More cuts Number	20	5	3	12	40
Percent of libraries	16.1%	4.7%	2.2%	12.1%	8.5%

N = 468 (100%)
Chi-square = 31.549, p = .000

Property tax revenue from the housing boom and increased assessed valuation of property was most frequently reported as the source of increased funding for all sizes of communities. The second most frequently cited reason was a funding levy or millage.

Reductions in Funding

There was little variation reported in the fiscal years when looking at responses in the aggregate. Approximately 17% of all public libraries reported mid-year revenue reductions each year studied. Libraries serving populations between 100,000 and 499,999 reported the most significant improvement between fiscal year 2003 and 2005 (19.4%, 12%, and 2.8% respectively). Mid-year funding reductions remained consistent for all fiscal years for public libraries serving populations below 25,000 (approximately 17% of respondents in this category reporting decreases). Table 6-1 present totals for libraries reporting operating revenue reductions, fiscal years 2003-05, and Tables 6-2 to 6-5 present findings by fiscal year and legal service area populations.

There also were differences in funding changes by region, with little relief anticipated for our smallest public libraries in the West and

TABLE 6-1. U.S. Public Libraries That Experienced Operating Revenue Reductions, FY 2003-05

Year	Number	Percent
FY 2003	81	17.2%
FY 2004	83	17.7%
FY 2005	73	15.7%

N = 468 (100%)

TABLE 6-2. U.S. Public Libraries Serving Less Than 25,000 That Experienced Operating Revenue Reductions, FY 2003-05

Year	Number	Percent
FY 2003	33	17.6%
FY 2004	34	18.1%
FY 2005	32	17.0%

N = 188 (100%)

TABLE 6-3. U.S. Public Libraries Serving 25,000-99,999 That Experienced Operating Revenue Reductions, FY 2003-05

Year	Number	Percent
FY 2003	21	14.8%
FY 2004	26	18.3%
FY 2005	19	13.4%

N = 142 (100%)

TABLE 6-4 U.S. Public Libraries Serving 100,000-499,999 That Experienced Operating Revenue Reductions, FY 2003-05

Year	Number	Percent
FY 2003	21	19.4%
FY 2004	13	12.0%
FY 2005	3	2.8%

N = 108 (100%)

TABLE 6-5. U.S. Public Libraries Serving 500,000 or More That Experienced Operating Revenue Reductions, FY 2003-05

Year	Number	Percent
FY 2003	6	20.0%
FY 2004	2	6.7%
FY 2005	2	6.7%

N = 30 (100%)

Midwest–48% experienced reductions in fiscal year 2003, 35.8% in fiscal year 2004, and 34.5% in fiscal year 2005. Nearly 20% of Northeast libraries indicated budget reductions in fiscal year 2004, up from 12% in fiscal year 2003. Tables 6-6 and 6-7 present responses for fiscal years 2003 and 2005. Responses for fiscal year 2004 were not statistically significant.

When correlated with operating revenue reported in the NCES Public Library report for Fiscal Year 2003, libraries with operating budgets under $65,000 were most significantly impacted in each fiscal year studied. The reductions for all respondents clustered in the 1% to 2% and 11% or more ranges, with fairly even distribution in the 3% to 4% to

TABLE 6-6. Operating Revenue Reductions Experienced by U.S. Public Libraries, by Region, FY 2003

Region	Number	Percent of Type
Midwest	35	28.2%
Northeast	13	12.1%
South	13	9.4%
West	20	20.2%
Total	81	17.3%

N = 468 (100%)
Chi-square = 18.895, p = .000

TABLE 6-7. Operating Revenue Reductions Experienced by U.S. Public Libraries, by Region, FY 2005

Region	Number	Percent of Type
Midwest	24	19.4%
Northeast	9	8.4%
South	9	6.5%
West	14	14.1%
Total	56	12.0%

N = 468 (100%)
Chi-square = 17.464, p = .008

8% to 10% categories (see Table 7-1). There appears to be continued reductions in the 1% to 6% ranges for all fiscal years, with some relief in the 7% to 10% range in fiscal years 2004 and 2005. Table 7-2 presents responses by region.

Libraries reported reductions in services fairly consistently regardless of the severity of the reduction. Tables 8-1 to 8-4 present those findings for fiscal years 2003-2005 by population served and region.

Libraries, for the most part, reported the severity of reductions as "not too severe" or "severe" compared with other local government departments and reported their reductions comparable to those experienced by other departments. The interpretation of "not too severe" and "severe" was left to the respondents, recognizing that there could be very different perceptions depending upon the community. Table 9 summarizes responses for fiscal years 2003-2005 by severity of reduction.

TABLE 7-1. Size of Operating Revenue Reductions Experienced by U.S. Public Libraries, FY 2003-05

Size of Revenue Reduction	Fiscal Year		
	FY 2003	FY 2004	FY 2005
1-2% Number	28	28	28
Percent of libraries	6.1%	6.0%	5.9
3-4% Number	11	14	11
Percent of libraries	2.4%	2.9%	2.3%
5-6% Number	13	14	10
Percent of libraries	2.7%	3.0%	2.1%
7-8% Number	2	4	2
Percent of libraries	0.4%	0.8%	0.5%
9-10% Number	10	2	8
Percent of libraries	2.1%	0.4%	1.8%
11% or more Number	19	29	16
Percent of libraries	4.1%	6.2%	3.4%

N = 468 (100%)

TABLE 7-2. Size of Operating Revenue Reductions Experienced by U.S. Public Libraries, by Region, FY 2003

Size of Revenue Reduction	Region				
	Midwest	Northeast	South	West	Total
1-2% Number	19	2	3	10	34
Percent of libraries	15.3%	1.9%	2.2%	10.1%	7.3%
3-4% Number	8	1	2	1	12
Percent of libraries	6.5%	0.9%	1.4%	1.0%	2.6%
5-6% Number	4	3	4	2	13
Percent of libraries	3.2%	2.8%	2.9%	2.0%	2.8%
7-8% Number	4	0	0	1	5
Percent of libraries	3.2%	0.0%	0.0%	1.0%	1.1%
9-10% Number	1	1	1	3	6
Percent of libraries	0.8%	0.9%	0.7%	3.0%	1.3%
11% or more Number	4	6	3	3	16
Percent of libraries	3.2%	5.6%	2.2%	3.0%	3.4%

N = 468 (100%)
Chi-square = 49.760, p = .000
Note: Responses for FY2004 were not statistically significant.

TABLE 8-1. Areas Impacted by Operating Revenue Reductions for U.S. Public Libraries Serving Less Than 25,000, FY 2003-05

Area of Revenue Reduction	Fiscal Year		
	FY 2003	FY 2004	FY 2005
Hours Number	8	10	12
Percent of libraries	4.3%	5.3%	6.4%
Staffing Number	13	15	20
Percent of libraries	6.9%	8.0%	10.6%
Materials Number	27	27	29
Percent of libraries	14.4%	14.4%	15.4%
Electronic Access Number	3	3	6
Percent of libraries	1.6%	1.6%	3.2%

N = 188 (100%)

TABLE 8-2. Areas Impacted by Operating Revenue Reductions for U.S. Public Libraries Serving 25,000-99,999, FY 2003-05

Area of Revenue Reduction	Fiscal Year		
	FY 2003	FY 2004	FY 2005
Hours Number	7	10	6
Percent of libraries	4.9%	7.0%	4.2%
Staffing Number	11	18	12
Percent of libraries	7.7%	12.7%	8.4%
Materials Number	20	29	18
Percent of libraries	14.1%	20.4%	12.7%
Electronic Access Number	5	7	5
Percent of libraries	3.5%	4.9%	3.5%

N = 142 (100%)

TABLE 8-3. Areas Impacted by Operating Revenue Reductions for U.S. Public Libraries Serving 100,000-499,999, FY 2003-05

Area of Revenue Reduction	Fiscal Year		
	FY 2003	FY 2004	FY 2005
Hours Number	9	7	4
Percent of libraries	8.3%	6.5%	3.7%
Staffing Number	15	14	5
Percent of libraries	13.9%	13.0%	4.6%
Materials Number	18	11	5
Percent of libraries	16.7%	10.2%	4.6%
Electronic Access Number	6	3	1
Percent of libraries	5.6%	2.8%	0.9%

N = 108 (100%)

TABLE 8-4. Areas Impacted by Operating Revenue Reductions for U.S. Public Libraries Serving 500,000 or More, FY 2003-05

Area of Revenue Reduction	Fiscal Year		
	FY 2003	FY 2004	FY 2005
Hours Number	1	1	1
Percent of libraries	3.3%	3.3%	3.3%
Staffing Number	4	3	3
Percent of libraries	13.3%	10.0%	10.0%
Materials Number	4	2	3
Percent of libraries	13.3%	6.7%	10.0%
Electronic Access Number	1	1	1
Percent of libraries	3.3%	3.3%	3.3%

N = 30 (100%)

TABLE 9. Severity of Operating Revenue Reductions for U.S. Public Libraries, FY 2003-05

Severity of Revenue Reduction	Fiscal Year		
	FY 2003	FY 2004	FY 2005
Extremely Severe Number	15	15	14
Percent of libraries	3.3%	3.1%	3.0%
Somewhat Severe Number	5	15	14
Percent of libraries	1.1%	3.1%	3.0%
Severe Number	17	20	13
Percent of libraries	3.7%	4.4%	2.8%
Not Too Severe Number	31	37	35
Percent of libraries	6.7%	7.8%	7.4%
Not Severe Number	24	20	17
Percent of libraries	5.2%	4.4%	3.7%

N = 468 (100%)

When asked about the comparability of the reduction, most libraries felt they were not isolated and that reductions were equitable. However, Table 10 shows that reductions were higher for libraries in fiscal years 2003 and 2004, with a 50% improvement in perception reported in fiscal year 2005. The response ranges for reductions were greater, the same, less, or no reduction. Libraries reported "no reduction" when they were level-funded (no reduction, nor increase, in operating revenue). A response of "same" was reported when reductions were equal to other local government agencies or offices.

Libraries more frequently attributed local tax revenue increases or decreases to levies or other tax measures (19.3 % and 15%, respectively). The second most frequent response was budget shortfalls (10.4%), and the third budget surpluses (6.3%). Table 11 presents findings for fiscal years 2003-2005.

The most frequently cited reason for reductions was decisions by local government (city, county or district) to reduce budgets; the second was increased cost in health care and retirement plans; and, the third was

TABLE 10. Comparability of Operating Revenue Reductions Experienced by U.S. Public Libraries with Reductions Experienced by Other Local Government Agencies and Offices, FY 2003-05

| Comparability of | Fiscal Year | | |
Revenue Reduction	FY 2003	FY 2004	FY 2005
Greater	28	30	16
Percent of libraries	5.9%	6.5%	3.5%
Same	29	33	35
Percent of libraries	6.1%	7.1%	7.4%
Less	12	10	14
Percent of libraries	2.5%	2.2%	3.0%
No reduction	43	38	45
Percent of libraries	9.2%	8.1%	9.6%

N = 468 (100%)

TABLE 11. Causes of Operating Revenue Decreases and Increases Experienced by U.S. Public Libraries, FY 2003-05

| Causes of Revenue | Fiscal Year | | |
Decrease/Increase	FY 2003	FY 2004	FY 2005
Levy Increase or Other Tax Measure	95	83	93
Percent of libraries	20.3%	17.8%	19.9%
Levy Decrease or Other Tax Measure	28	38	31
Percent of libraries	5.9%	8.1%	6.7%
Budget Surplus	22	32	35
Percent of libraries	4.6%	6.9%	7.5%
Budget Shortfall	42	57	47
Percent of libraries	9.0%	12.2%	10.1%

N = 468 (100%)

utility costs (fuel and air conditioning, respectively). (See respondents comments section for detail.)

Outlook for Fiscal Year 2006

Anticipating revenue changes for fiscal year 2006, 58.2% of public libraries expected local tax revenue to remain about the same and about 32.4% anticipated some improvement. Approximately 9.4% of libraries anticipated more reductions (see Table 12).

Libraries serving populations over 500,000 reported the most improvement in FY2006, with 63.3% anticipating improvement in operating budgets from local tax revenue. Even libraries serving 25,000 or fewer reported some improvement, with approximately 27% anticipating increases. When looked at regionally, the South and Northeast reported the greatest improvement, with the West and the Midwest reporting slightly less improvement.

What Respondents Told Us

Respondent comments ran the gamut, but some more telling indicators of continued level-funding, continued anticipated reductions, and improved funding came in the following excerpted remarks.

Increases each year were only for staff benefits (retirement and health insurance). All other line items remained the same or decreased.

Our cuts were put in place during the budget process. In 2003 and 2004 fiscal years we lost 2/3rds of our staff FTE and all of our book budget. It was devastating.

TABLE 12. Anticipated Change in FY 2006 Operating Budgets for U.S. Public Libraries

Anticipated Change	Libraries That Experienced Revenue Increases	
	Number	Percent
Improvement in operating budgets from local tax revenue	144	32.4%
Stay about the same as the last three fiscal years	259	58.2%
More reductions than in the past three fiscal years	42	9.4%

N = 445
Note: Excludes blank and "don't know" responses.

The City held a flat budget for 05/06 as it plans for a continued budget shortfall over the next 5 to 6 years.

For the last three years[,] the library has been averaging 5% increase[s] in revenue each year. This is cause[d] mainly by the city revenue starting to pick up and[,] at the same time[,] no changes in the employees' contracts.

Sharply escalating health insurance costs citywide helped cause budget crisis. Another cause was large increases in the amount of local property taxes that the state claimed (money that normally goes to local jurisdictions).

Our funding is primarily through a property tax mill levy. Our area is experiencing high population growth and high building rates, as well as revenue from oil and gas production; thus our revenue is increasing proportionately.

While our budgets have remained stable during the fiscal year, the reductions between the years [have] caused a reduction in services. The budget was reduced almost 4% between 03 and 04 fiscal years and over 6% between the 04 to 05 fiscal years.

We have had normal increases, especially due to rising costs of utilities and insurance. We have not had a decrease in operating expenditures in any of these fiscal years. In fy06, we also received an increase in funding–based on increased cost of utilities.

For the current fiscal year we experienced an 18.5% increase in our budget. This increase was due to a dramatic increase in property values in our county. We were the only department budget increased so dramatically.

Library budgets decreased from FY01/02 to FY02/03 by 3%. Library budgets increased from FY02/03 to FY03/04 by 3%. Library budgets increased from FY03/04 to FY04/05 by 12%.

No materials budget during FY 04 & 05. FY 06 materials budget was returned. We were able to fundraise enough money to buy more than enough materials for the two years!!

Our city used to pay our utilities and phone, and our ins. but now it [is] all in our budget and we hadn't planned on that. The city revenues have been down like $30,000 so I guess it's the trickle down effect and we get to pick up the slack.

Funding has increased each year, but only 5-6% through tax rate increase. Meanwhile, cost of insurance, utilities, and mileage are rising faster than the income.

Due to population growth and resulting construction of housing in our district, and with annexation of property into our district, we have begun to see increased revenue. This is in spite of a property tax cap, which has caused us to lose about $900,000.

In 2003, state wide reassessment that moved from 'true tax value' to 'market value' caused enormous problems for all units of local government and school corporations by delaying the property tax payments. Some areas waited for about 2 years.

In 2003, we were level funded, which was hard to indicate in the question that addressed this. People are having their libraries closed on them, but my town has banded together to keep the library an important fixture.

Funding within FY 03, 04 and 05 (and expected 06) remained unchanged. Between Fy 03, 04 and 05 the library received a nominal increase in funding (roughly 1% to 2%) to cover contracted salary increases. In FY 06, the library has been hit with a 22% budget cut.

Our funding increases are directly related to the requirements for Massachusetts State Aid. The budget has increased during the past three years in direct relation to the required percentage increased dictated by the Commonwealth of Massachusetts.

Currently library is funded 33% from trust income, 42% from municipality, 25% from annual giving and other. We do a LOT of private fund raising!

I think the library has been treated as well as could be hoped for in the city's budget process. We haven't been singled out for cuts and have received our proportionate share of increases. The budget is tough, though. A number of years of small increases.

Funding was not reduced during 2004, but wasn't at the 2003 level originally anticipated. 2005 didn't reach the anticipated 2003 level either. Tax abatements given by the city to attract business are hurting us. IF it works, eventually we'll be ok.

FY 2006 we received a 69% reduction over 2005 in allocation from our Township. No other governmental agency or office experienced ANY reduction at all; only the library.

One of my 2 counties has not raised our money for the last 4 years. The other county gave us an increase this last fiscal year, but we don't know yet for this fiscal year. Katrina hit hard here, and budgets are very very lean right now.

Our funding has remained at the same level for six fiscal years. This year our City voted to put the Library on dedicated millage, enough to maintain the current level of funding (for the seventh year). However, I hope that we will see an increase next year.

While the budget is flat, we are operating on less $ due to increased health insurance, utilities and other inflationary costs. 2004 and 2005 basically stayed the same in terms of budget allotment. However, increased operating costs have required that we change staffing patterns and reduce spending on materials. Our materials budget has been flat or declining since 2001.

Although budgets have increased, salary increases have stagnated. Library's pay scale is below local, county, and state averages. Although there are several public school teachers on Board, there is no attempt to maintain parity with local schoolteacher salaries.

We have been blessed by an increase in oil and gas revenues. Our City government is trying to make across the board increases to all departments. We received, rather uniquely, a pick up truck, as we were one of the last few departments without a vehicle.

Increase in operating revenue can be attributed to higher 1. Property tax collections from increased land values, and 2. Sales tax collections due to increased consumer spending caused by growth in: a. Population, and b. Tourism.

Not reflected in the answers above are despite increases in local funding, the Library has been unable to sustain operations. This has resulted in decreases in staffing and materials. The Library is increasingly reliant upon private funding.

Although we have had a small increase in funding due to an increase in new housing, our mill levy still remains at 5 mills. Initially, the increase did help us to have more hours/staffing.

However the increase no longer allows us to keep up with inflation.

Dependence on one source of income–a portion of the state income tax designated for libraries–left others and us vulnerable when state officials legislated lower distributions. A levy attempt failed in Nov. 2004, and may fail again in Nov. 2005.

The library's fiscal year is based on the calendar year. Total 2005 operating revenue as of September 30th is only 4/10 of 1% more than year-to-date 2004 operating revenue. Library expenditures are increasing faster than library revenue's.

Our city administration has, for decades, left adopted budgets intact through the whole fiscal year (and we're grateful of that!).

Our expenditures 2005-2006 are higher than our anticipated income so we may have to transfer money from a building fund to maintain services.

Our increases ranged from .5% to this year 06 4.6%; we have been very lucky.

The libraries were zeroed out of the County Commission's operating budget beginning fiscal year 1999. We have not received any local funding from the County Commission since then. [Author's note: In a subsequent discussion with the West Virginia State Librarian, it was determined that counties had to absorb regional jail costs beginning in 1999. This resulted in many counties cutting library funding to meet those expenses. As indicated in this comment, funding has yet to be restored.]

SURVEY METHODOLOGY, SAMPLE DESIGN AND SELECTION

The survey was administered between September and November 2005 to a representative random sample of public libraries.[2] The viability of a state-representative sample was explored with nationally recognized library researchers, but such a sample was deemed prohibitive.[3] Instead, a sample was drawn that represents the nation and major ranges of legal service area population.

A random sample of 1,950 public libraries was selected from a universe of 9,211; 468 libraries responded yielding a 24% response rate. The responses were weighted to prevent the distortion of the results by volunteers and low response rate, rather than discarding those extra cases. The survey was completely voluntary. [Note: Public libraries impacted by hurricanes during fall 2005 were removed from the random sample.] The questions were pre-tested in accordance with standard survey research practice.

A traditional direct appeal mailing was sent to directors of libraries chosen for the sample. This mailing included a one-page letter from Keith Michael Fiels, ALA Executive Director requesting participation and providing relevant details, and a one-page summary of the survey questions. The latter facilitated the compilation of data required to complete the survey.

The research team of ALA Office for Research and Statistics staff and RSL Research (http://www.rslresearch.com/index.html) began reviewing incoming responses for reliability and validity in October 2005. Resolution of some questionable responses required direct communication with respondents. Some survey responses were accepted by mail and fax, and were keyed directly into the database by ALA-ORS staff.

In addition to "cleaning" the data based on information learned from follow-up contacts, the data processing stage of this project included merging data in the respondent file with selected identification fields from the FSCS database. Statistical Package for the Social Sciences (SPSS) was used to achieve this matching step.

CONCLUSION

The study was successful in confirming a few anecdotal assumptions:

- Public library operating expenditures have been significantly compromised by the economic downturn in the economy;
- The impact of the downturn resulted in a predominance of level funding for at least three fiscal years for a majority of U.S. public libraries;
- Although a small portion of U.S. public libraries experienced mid-year budget reductions, those that did also experienced year-to-year reductions or flat funding during the period studied;
- Where there were increases, many were directed to specific expenditures (e.g., salaries, utilities, etc.) and did not improve the overall operating budget of the library;
- The historic model of change beginning on the east coast and moving west across the U.S. also was seen in this study; and
- The economic recovery has begun to take hold and libraries have experienced modest budgetary improvements.

Other studies provide additional insight into public library funding from specific expenditure perspectives, and offer more detail on choices libraries made during the period investigated by this study.[4] Looking across various public library operating revenue and expenditure data, and secondary analysis are necessary to fully understand the extent of library revenue fluctuations during the early part of this decade, and to estimate future trends. The ALA hopes to continue this research to support public libraries in their advocacy efforts.

NOTES

1. Legal Basis Code is defined in the National Center for Education Statistics, Public Libraries in the United States: Fiscal Year 2003, ED Tab NCES 2005-363 as "the type of local government structure within which the entity functions. It reflects the state or local law which authorizes the library."

2. 1,950 public libraries were randomly selected from a universe of 9,211; 468 libraries responded yielding a 24% response rate.

3. Because the number of libraries per state varies so greatly, and because many states have relatively few libraries, a state-representative sample would require obtaining survey responses from 7,150 of the nation's 9,212 libraries.

That would have been a sample of 78 percent. A voluntary survey such as this one–even one endorsed by ALA–cannot expect such near-universal cooperation. In about half of the states, a successful sample would have required responses from virtually every library in the state. This fact about state-representative sampling of U.S. public libraries indicates the earlier wisdom of ALA in encouraging the development of the Federal-State Cooperative System (FSCS) for Public Library Data. Under these conditions, one might as well conduct a universe survey as attempt to sample on this intensive a scale.

4. One study in particular is the *Public Libraries and The Internet* series by John Carlo Bertot, Charles R. McClure, et al. <http://www.ii.fsu.edu/plinternet.cfm>.

doi:10.1300/J118v25n01_02

Public Library Public Access Computing and Internet Access: Factors Which Contribute to Quality Services and Resources

John Carlo Bertot
Denise M. Davis

SUMMARY. This article explores a number of variables which can contribute to the quality of public access computing and Internet services that public libraries provide their communities. Through this exploration, the article offers several insights and implications for the development and implementation of high quality public access computing and Internet services which increasingly technology-savvy users expect from service providers. A key focus of the article is determining the extent to which some public libraries can reasonably provide high levels of network-based services given staff, budgetary, and other constraints and challenges. doi:10.1300/J118v25n01_03 *[Article copies available for a fee from The Haworth Document Delivery Service: 1-800-HAWORTH. E-mail address:*

John Carlo Bertot, PhD, is Professor and Associate Director, Information Use Management and Policy Institute, College of Information, Florida State University, 244 Shores Building, Tallahassee, FL 32306-2100 (E-mail: jbertot@fsu.edu).

Denise M. Davis, MLS, is Director, Office of Research and Statistics, American Library Association, 50 East Huron Street, Chicago, IL 60611-2795 (E-mail: dmdavis@ala.org).

The authors would like to thank the Bill & Melinda Gates Foundation for their support of this research.

[Haworth co-indexing entry note]: "Public Library Public Access Computing and Internet Access: Factors Which Contribute to Quality Services and Resources." Bertot, John Carlo, and Denise M. Davis. Co-published simultaneously in *Public Library Quarterly* (The Haworth Press, Inc.) Vol. 25, No. 1/2, 2006, pp. 27-42; and: *Current Practices in Public Libraries* (ed: William Miller, and Rita M. Pellen) The Haworth Press, Inc., 2006, pp. 27-42. Single or multiple copies of this article are available for a fee from The Haworth Document Delivery Service [1-800-HAWORTH, 9:00 a.m. - 5:00 p.m. (EST). E-mail address: docdelivery@haworthpress.com].

Available online at http://plq.haworthpress.com
© 2006 by The Haworth Press, Inc. All rights reserved.
doi:10.1300/J118v25n01_03

<docdelivery@haworthpress.com> Website: <http://www.HaworthPress.com> © 2006 by The Haworth Press, Inc. All rights reserved.]

KEYWORDS. Public access computing, quality Internet access, Internet connectivity

INTRODUCTION

Public access computing and Internet services have increased substantially since 1994.[1] In 1994, only 20.9% of public libraries had an Internet connection, the predominant form of Internet access was through text-based terminals, and only 6.6% of public libraries had direct (leased-line) connections to the Internet.[2] In 2006, nearly all public libraries are connected to the Internet (98.9%), and provide public access services (98.4%). The average number of workstations per library is 10.7, 63.3% have connections speeds of 769 kbps or greater, and 36.7% offer wireless access.[3]

As connectivity and technology infrastructure within public libraries increased, so too did the services that public libraries are able to provide their communities. For example, libraries now offer a host of digital library services via their Websites, engage in interactive services (i.e., digital reference) that extend beyond the walls of the library to near 24/7 coverage, and provide a range of licensed resources such as databases, e-books, downloadable audio books, and many more network-based services and resources.[4] The issue is no longer whether public libraries are connected to the Internet and to what degree they provide public access computing services, but rather, understanding key factors which contribute to the quality of public library Internet connectivity and public access computing services.

This article explores a number of variables which can contribute to the quality of public access computing and Internet services that public libraries provide their communities. Through this exploration, the article offers several insights and implications for the development and implementation of high quality public access computing and Internet services which increasingly technology-savvy users expect from service providers. A key focus of the article is determining the extent to which some public libraries can reasonably provide high levels of network-based services given staff, budgetary, and other constraints and challenges.

METHODOLOGY AND RESEARCH OBJECTIVES

The goal of this research was to:

- Explore a range of issues and factors which contribute to quality public access computing and Internet access services in public libraries;
- Understand which issues and factors enable or impede the ability of public libraries to engage in quality public access computing services and resources;
- Develop a profile of what might constitute vulnerable public libraries in terms of their ability to provide and meet today's network-based service demands; and
- Produce recommendations and areas of additional research to better understand the influence of selected factors on public library public access computing and Internet services given the exploratory nature of this study.

To accomplish these goals, the study created a unique dataset which combined data from three public library datasets:

- The TechAtlas technology inventory dataset which public libraries can access via WebJunction.[5] The TechAtlas tool is a combination of automated data collection about a library's computers (e.g., operating system, memory, and other physical factors) and technology planning tool.
- The 2002 and 2003 public library data made available through the National Center for Education Statistics.[6]
- The 2004 *Public Libraries and the Internet* data collected by Florida State University's Information Institute.[7]

Combining these disparate datasets enabled the researchers to conduct analysis along a number of key library demographic, technology, and budget variables, as described below.

Variables Explored

Through the integration process which occurred in March 2006, the researchers were able to match the data from 701 public library systems across the different datasets. In doing so, the researchers were able to conduct a range of analysis using the following variables:

- Vulnerability, as measured through the characteristics of the library's public access computer operating system and memory (TechAtlas data);[8]
- Population of Legal Service Area, a measure of the population that the library serves (NCES Data);
- Change in "Other" (where information technology items are reported annually) Operating Budget expenditures (NCES Data);
- Full-Time Equivalents (FTEs–staff) (NCES data);
- Information technology training for staff (FSU Public library Internet data);
- E-rate application issues (FSU Public library Internet data); and
- Bandwidth (FSU Public library Internet data).

By looking at these variables simultaneously, it is possible to develop a profile of public library public access computing and Internet infrastructure and selected factors which contribute to the level of connectivity and access which these libraries are able to provide.

Limitations of the Data

The data analysis approach offered in this article has a number of limitations that require mention. In particular, the following factors affect the data presented below and ensuing discussion:

- The dataset used for this research was the result of combining three disparate datasets created for different purposes. While records were matched accurately, the initial purposes of each dataset were divergent, and thus the integration and subsequent analysis are "best fit."
- The data are limited to those records matched. As such, the results are exploratory in nature and would require additional review and consideration for continued study into the future.
- The notion of "vulnerability" with regards to public library public access computing and Internet services is difficult to define and attain. In this study, vulnerability is defined as the ability of public library public access computers to provide access to state-of-the-art Internet services and resources (i.e., streaming media). As discussed in Note 8, vulnerability was measured through certain attributes of library computers such as operating system and memory. There are likely other ways to define and capture the notion of "vulnerability" in terms of public access computing equipment (i.e., age of hardware).

Given these limitations, the study provides indicators of quality public access computing and Internet services that require additional development and study.

DATA ANALYSIS AND FINDINGS

The combined dataset yielded usable data for 701 public libraries. Roughly 66% of the libraries are small, likely rural, and serve populations under 24,999 (see Figure 1). Only 23.4% of High Vulnerable libraries served populations over 25,000, with slightly more in the 50,000-99,999 population served range. Thus, the dataset reflects issues through the lens of smaller public libraries.

As Figure 2 shows, 52% of High Vulnerable libraries have staff Full-time equivalents (FTE) of 3 or less. Nearly half of Moderate and Low Vulnerable libraries have staff FTE of 5 or fewer (46.2% and 52.9%, respectively). Low Vulnerable libraries were somewhat more likely to have more staff FTE 9 +, with 36.7%, followed by 30.7% of Moderate Vulnerable libraries, and 23.5% of High Vulnerable libraries. Overall, 53.2% of the libraries had staffing FTE of 5 or fewer, while 16.3% of libraries had 5-9 staff FTE.

Technology Training for Staff

As Figure 3 shows, the more staff a library has, the more likely a library provides its own training or relies on vendors, other sources, and consortia for training. The fewer staff, the more likely a library was to

FIGURE 1. Vulnerable Libraries by Population Served

Vulnerability	Population Served						
	LT 5,000	5,000-9,999	10,000-24,999	25,000-49,999	50,000-99,999	100,000+	Total
High	36.7%	20.4%	19.4%	7.1%	10.2%	6.1%	100.0%
Moderate	27.8%	13.7%	24.3%	15.4%	10.8%	8.1%	100.0%
Low	26.5%	13.7%	26.5%	11.1%	11.1%	11.1%	100.0%
Unclear	25.0%	25.0%	25.0%	25.0%	–	–	100.0%
Total	28.0% n = 202	14.7% n = 103	23.9% n = 168	13.6% n = 95	10.7% n = 75	8.3% n = 58	100.0%

N = 701

FIGURE 2. Vulnerable Libraries by FTEs

Vulnerability	FTEs						
	0-1	1.1-3.0	3.1-5.0	5.1-7.0	7.1-9.0	9.0+	Total
High	14.3%	37.8%	11.2%	8.2%	5.1%	23.5%	100.0%
Moderate	7.3%	30.5%	15.1%	10.4%	6.0%	30.7%	100.0%
Low	10.3%	25.6%	10.3%	12.0%	5.1%	36.7%	100.0%
Unclear	25.0%	25.0%	25.0%	25.0%	–	–	100.0%
Total	8.7% n = 61	30.8% n = 216	13.7% n = 96	10.6% n = 74	5.7% n = 40	30.5% n = 214	100.0%

N = 701

FIGURE 3. Library Provision of Technology Training for Staff by FTEs

FTEs	Training Providers						
	Library provides training	State library provides training	Library consortium provides training	Vendors provide training	Volunteers provide training	Training provided by other sources	Other source
0-1	21.3%	13.1%	60.7%	14.8%	23.0%	19.7%	31.1%
1.1-3.0	33.8%	11.1%	63.9%	13.9%	10.2%	4.6%	26.4%
3.1-5.0	38.5%	12.5%	69.8%	29.3%	18.8%	11.5%	36.5%
5.1-7.0	37.8%	13.5%	66.2%	27.0%	18.9%	2.7%	35.1%
7.1-9.0	52.5%	10.0%	65.0%	25.0%	27.5%	5.0%	25.0%
9.0+	69.2%	6.5%	57.9%	27.6%	39.3%	6.5%	37.4%
Total	45.6% n = 320	10.3% n = 72	62.9% n = 441	22.3% n = 156	23.3% n = 163	7.3% n = 51	32.4% n = 227

N = 701   Responses will not total to 100% due to the ability to select multiple categories.

rely on the state library and other sources of training. Also, the smaller the size of the staff, the greater the reliance on volunteers for training. Libraries with 3.1 or greater staff were more likely to use a consortium for training, in addition to other training sources. These libraries also were more likely to use vendors for training. An interesting aspect of the data demonstrates that as library staff size increases, so too does the use of volunteers to provide training for staff.

The smaller the population served by the library, the less likely the library was to provide training for staff compared with other populations served ranges (see Figure 4). Libraries benefited fairly equally by

FIGURE 4. Library Provision of Technology Training for Staff by Population of Legal Service Area

Population Served	Training Providers					
	Library provides training	State library provides training	Library consortium provides training	Vendors provide training	Volunteers provide training	Training provided by other sources	Other source
LT 5,000	31.2%	11.4%	68.8%	15.3%	15.8%	9.4%	26.2%
5,000-9,999	44.7%	13.6%	58.3%	24.3%	15.5%	5.8%	31.1%
10,000-24,999	35.7%	10.7%	63.7%	26.2%	19.6%	7.7%	34.5%
25,000-49,999	54.7%	10.5%	64.2%	26.3%	28.4%	4.2%	31.6%
50,000-99,999	73.3%	8.0%	56.0%	17.3%	30.7%	9.3%	34.7%
100,000+	75.9%	1.7%	55.2%	31.0%	55.2%	3.4%	48.3%
Total	45.6% n = 320	10.3% n = 72	62.9% n = 441	22.3% n = 156	23.3% n = 163	7.3% n = 51	32.4% n = 227

N = 701   Responses will not total to 100% due to ability to select multiple categories.

training provided by state library agencies regardless of their populations served range. Libraries serving populations over 5,000 were more likely to get training from a consortium than were those serving fewer than 5,000. The larger the population served, the more likely the library was to get training from vendors, with a 24.5% increase from 50,000-99,999 and 100,000 + . Finally, libraries serving 100,000 + were more likely to get training from other sources (13.6% more likely than the next population range, 50,000-99,999).

Applying for E-Rate

One indicator of the quality of public access computing and Internet access services is bandwidth. By reviewing data regarding E-rate applications and receipt, it is possible to determine some of the challenges, and reasons for those challenges, faced by public libraries.[9] Regardless of number of staff, Figure 5 demonstrates that libraries most frequently responded that staff did not apply (19.9%) or the application process was too complicated (17.1%). The third most common response (12.1%) was that the discount was too low. There was a slight variation in order of response depending upon staff FTE:

- Libraries with 0-3 staff were more likely to report "too complicated" and "did not apply" as the top two responses.
- Libraries with 3-5 staff were more likely to report staff "did not apply" as the most common response, followed by "too complicated"

FIGURE 5. Lack of E-rate Receipt by FTEs

FTEs	E-rate Application Reasons				
	Too complicated	Staff did not apply for it	Discount is too low	Application was denied	CIPA
0-1	13.8%	15.5%	12.1%	5.2%	12.1%
1.1-3.0	15.2%	21.2%	9.6%	3.5%	5.1%
3.1-5.0	11.6%	17.4%	9.3%	8.1%	9.3%
5.1-7.0	25.8%	17.7%	14.5%	4.8%	11.3%
7.1-9.0	21.6%	21.6%	13.5%	2.7%	13.5%
9.0+	18.7%	21.2%	14.6%	4.5%	11.6%
Total	17.1% n = 109	19.9% n = 127	12.1% n = 77	4.7% n = 30	9.4% n = 60

N = 639   Responses will not total to 100% due to ability to select multiple categories and "low discount." This category also was more likely to report that the requirement to filter Internet access through the Children's Internet Protection Act (CIPA) also influenced their decision to apply for e-rate. It may be that the larger libraries (those serving larger populations and having more staff) were more aware of CIPA.

In all likelihood these three factors are interrelated in that low discounts are simply not worth the effort for libraries to apply, particularly given the complexity of the application process.

"Other" Operating Expenditure Change from 2002-2003 and Bandwidth

The percentage of libraries reporting increases in total expenditures was 68%; those libraries reporting decreases were 28.3%. Not surprisingly, "Low Vulnerable" libraries reported the greatest increase in Total Expenditures (73.5%). Increases peaked in the 1-5% and 21% + ranges. The percentage of High Vulnerable libraries reporting increases in Total Expenditures was 70.4%, while 27.5% reported decreases. Sixty-six percent of Moderate Vulnerable libraries reported increases in Total Expenditures, while 29.7% reported decreases. 73.5% of Low Vulnerable libraries reported increases in Total Expenditures, while 23.0% reported decreases. In all categories of vulnerability, libraries reporting decreases in Total Expenditures clustered in the 1-5%, 6-10% or 11-15% ranges in decreasing order from the lowest decrease to the highest.

Regardless of vulnerability level, libraries reported decreases in Total Expenditures in the 1-5% and 6-10% (High Vulnerable, 17.3%; Moderate Vulnerable, 21.6%; and Low Vulnerable, 13.6%). The percentage of libraries reporting decreases in Total Expenditures in the 11-15% range was 12.1%. High Vulnerable libraries were more likely to report decreases in Total Expenditures in the 21 + % range than were libraries in other vulnerability levels.

Figure 6 does not show a clear relationship between bandwidth and changes in "other" operating expenditures. It is possible, however, to make some characterizations. There were no budget increases for libraries with less than 56kbps connectivity. Indeed there were some in this connectivity range that reported decreases in other expenditures. Libraries with no increase in other operating expenditures clustered in 56-128kbps and greater than 1.5mbps (most typically a T1 line) connectivity speeds). In addition, libraries with 769kbps to 1.5mbps connectivity speeds were

FIGURE 6. Bandwidth by Other Public Library Operating Expenditures Category (NCES)*

Change in Other Operating Expenditure	Bandwidth						
	LT 56kbps	56-128kbps	129-256kbps	257-768kbps	769kbps-1.5mbps	GT 1.5mbps	DK
No Data	51.8%	17.6%	14.5%	14.0%	22.3%	9.3%	21.8%
0% (no change)	–	7.7%	23.1%	7.7%	7.7%	23.1%	30.8%
–1% to –5%	2.6%	15.8%	13.2%	10.5%	26.3%	21.1%	10.5%
–6% to –10%	2.1%	12.5%	4.2%	10.4%	33.3%	25.0%	12.5%
–11% to –15%	–	4.0%	16.0%	8.0%	40.0%	16.0%	16.0%
–16% to –20%	7.1%	–	7.1%	7.1%	35.7%	21.4%	21.4%
–20% to –30%	3.0%	5.9%	5.9%	14.7%	14.7%	23.5%	32.4%
–31% to –40%	–	10.3%	12.8%	15.4%	28.2%	15.4%	17.9%
–41% +	–	12.2%	12.2%	7.3%	34.1%	12.2%	22.0%
1% to 5%	–	21.4%	7.1%	10.7%	28.6%	14.3%	17.9%
6% to 10%	–	7.7%	3.8%	15.4%	30.8%	23.1%	19.2%
11% to 15%	–	10.7%	7.1%	7.1%	35.7%	17.9%	21.4%
16% to 20%	–	22.2%	3.7%	7.4%	37.0%	3.7%	25.9%
21% to 30%	–	8.3%	16.7%	5.6%	19.4%	27.85	22.2%
31% to 40%	–	6.3%	18.8%	12.5%	25.0%	12.5%	25.0%
41% +	–	7.8%	12.5%	9.4%	31.3%	9.4%	29.7%
Total	0.8% n = 5	12.7% n = 85	11.6% n = 78	11.2% n = 75	27.2% n = 182	15.1% n = 101	21.5% n = 144

N = 670   Rows total to 100%.
*Changes in public library reported "other operating expense" category during the 2002 and 2003 fiscal years. At the time of analysis, these data were the most current available.

more likely to see an increase in "other" operating expenditures than other libraries.

Libraries with increases of 6-10% and 11-15% in other operating expenditures were more likely to have connectivity speeds of 257kbps-768kbps or higher than libraries with other ranges of other expenditure increases. Libraries with increases of 16-20% or greater in other expenditures were more likely to have connectivity speeds of 769kbps to 1.5mbps or higher. Libraries experiencing reductions in other expenditures, regardless of expenditure reduction range, were equally likely to provide connectivity at speeds of 769kbps to 1.5mbps or higher. This also was the case for libraries experiencing increases in other expenditures in the 16-20% range.

DISCUSSION AND IMPLICATIONS

The above presented data offer a number of insights regarding factors which affect a public library's ability to provide high quality public access computing and Internet services. These factors include the:

- Size of the library. By and large, smaller libraries–most often rural–fall into the higher categories of vulnerability (defined in this article through public access computing hardware and operating system software).
- Number of staff a library has as measured in FTEs. In general, the fewer FTEs the library has, the more likely it is to be vulnerable. Also, the fewer the FTEs a library has, the less likely is it that the library offers its own staff technology training programs. Indeed, the fewer staff a library has, the fewer staff training opportunities will be available to the library and the more the library relies on the state library agencies and others for staff technology training.
- Ability of libraries to apply for, receive, and see the benefit to the E-rate program. Across all categories of FTEs, population of legal service area, vulnerable public libraries indicated issues with the E-rate program that one could characterize as "not worth the effort" due to application denials, low discounts, and a complicated application process.

The impact of a library's budget is less clear. Unfortunately, library technology budgets are not reported in the national annual collection of public library data. Thus, if libraries have a specific technology budget, it is reported in the "other operating expenditures" category. This, however, also can include other non-technology items. The budget data indicate a wide range of results. The one trend that the analysis provided indicates that libraries with greater increases in the "other" expenses tended to have higher bandwidth speeds.

There are a number of implications that the analyzed data suggest regarding the factors which contribute to high quality public access computing and Internet access services and the ability of public libraries to offer quality services. These include:

- Budget increases which go beyond inflationary increases. While the budget data in this study provided a mixed assessment of the impact of the budget on public access computing services, there was a relationship between greater operating budgets and increased bandwidth. But more importantly, the increase had to be beyond a minimal/nominal increase for this to be the case. Said differently, a minimal increase (in the inflation rate range) did not lead to enhanced public access computing and Internet access services.
- Access to technology training for staff impacted on the vulnerability of the library's public access computing and Internet access services. In general, the less access to technology training options for staff the library had, the more vulnerable the library was–that is, the less likely was it that the library had newer public access computers able to provide access to today's demanding network-based services and resources. This may be a factor of having substantial reliance on outside sources (e.g., the state library, volunteers) for training on technology.
- Adequate staffing. A majority of the libraries in this study had five or fewer FTEs; thus the ability of staff to handle the basic operations of the public library, plus the maintenance of public access computing and Internet access services and resources, is challenging. Moreover, it is important to note that FTEs are a composite measure of staff–and in smaller libraries the FTEs are a total in terms of hours worked, but can in fact be, and often are, spread out over several part-time employees. Thus there is a time factor in terms of devotion to information technology issues and solutions.

In short, funds and staffing–both number of staff and their ability to gain access to technology-based training–are the two factors that contribute most significantly to the quality of public access computing and Internet access within public libraries.

RECOMMENDATIONS AND CONCLUSIONS

Given the results of the study, there are a number of recommendations to offer policymakers, practitioners, funders, researchers, and others:

- Provide access to technology training for libraries deemed most vulnerable in terms of their computer hardware. One has to consider how the training is offered to librarians in these libraries, however. In general, these libraries operate with a number of part-time staff who split their time throughout the library's open hours. Thus, it is quite difficult for these individuals to take time off from their library duties to attend training sessions at remote locations. Indeed, it is even difficult for these individuals to attend training within their facilities, if available. Training offerings need to span a range of approaches (e.g., online, computer-based, other) and times to enable attendance. It may also be the case that using substitute librarians, or making other arrangements such as closing the library for a day or more, are necessary to enable attendance or offer time to access training modules.
- Fund adequately public access computing and Internet services and resources. Once public library staff are better educated regarding public access computing and Internet access services, it is essential to enable libraries to upgrade their public access computing and Internet access technology infrastructures over time through a systematic approach that targets libraries in order of vulnerability. These can be through state-aid and other incentives and approaches, such as matched funding to foster community commitment. Up-to-date public access computing and Internet access infrastructure ensures that libraries are able to serve as public access points to e-government and disaster support [Bertot et al., 2006]. Without such infrastructure, public libraries cannot serve this increasingly important function within communities that tend to rely on the public library for access to the Internet.
- Offer e-rate application support. While a number of state libraries and regional consortia do indeed offer a range of assistance to their state's public libraries, others do not. It is particularly essential that libraries defined as vulnerable receive assistance in completing the application forms–even actual completion of the forms–in order for them to participate in the program. While the funds in dollar amount that these libraries could receive might be small, the funds could prove significant in terms of alleviating other budget

constraints. Also, it is likely that vulnerable libraries have very similar situations and e-rate needs; thus there is the ability to create mostly completed application forms for these libraries ahead of time to reduce the application burden.
- Collect and report technology budgets as a separate item. Given the importance of public access computing and Internet access in public libraries, it is important to better understand technology expenditures within public libraries. Policymakers, researchers, practitioners, and others would benefit greatly from the separate reporting of technology expenditures.
- Conduct additional research into library public access computing vulnerability. The use of operating system software and other measures of computing capacity are essentially available proxies for determining the extent to which public library public access computers are adequate to meet the demands of an increasingly interactive and demanding networked environment. Other measures are possible, perhaps even better defined, to enable an accurate determination of public access computing.
- Continue to explore the meaning of quality public access computing and Internet services for public libraries. It is likely that quality is a composite of several variables including funding, staff availability and skills, bandwidth, currency and number of public access workstations, and perhaps others. There is a need to explore the notion of quality in substantially greater detail.
- Conduct research that has as its goal from the onset the exploration of vulnerability, quality public access computing, and the factors which contribute to vulnerability and quality services. The research presented in this article is post-hoc in the sense that the exploration occurred through the integration of three data collection efforts which occurred separately. To fully explore the issues of vulnerability and quality, there is a need to develop a study that has these goals from the onset.

These recommendations offer a beginning approach to enhancing and maintaining public access computing and Internet access services within public libraries.

This study presented issues associated with public library public access computing and Internet access vulnerability and quality. Though exploratory in nature, the study found that the number of staff, staff technology skills, budget, and ability to apply for e-rate funds can contribute to the overall ability of public libraries to maintain, enhance, and upgrade their public access computing and Internet access technology infrastructure. In essence, there appears to be a minimum threshold in terms of staff, staff skills, and budget below which public libraries are unable to provide quality public access computing services. Thus, there exist a set of public libraries which provide minimal, and likely outdated, connectivity and public access computing to their communities. The implications for this can be quite profound, particularly in communities in which the public library is the only public access computing and Internet access point. There is a need to continue to explore, research, and define vulnerability and quality access so as to better understand both the nature and implications of public libraries which face substantial challenges with their public access technology infrastructure.

NOTES

1. Bertot, John Carlo, McClure, Charles R, Jaeger, Paul T., & Ryan, Joe. *Public Libraries and the Internet 2006: Study Results and Findings*. Tallahassee: Information Use Management and Policy Institute, 2006. Last accessed on October 9, 2006 at <http://www.ii.fsu.edu/plinternet_reports.cfm>.

2. McClure, Charles R., Bertot, John Carlo, & Zweizig, Douglas L. *Public Libraries and the Internet: Study Results, Policy Issues, and Recommendations*. Washington, DC: U.S. National Commission on Libraries and Information Science, 1994.

3. Bertot, John Carlo, McClure, Charles R, Jaeger, Paul T., & Ryan, Joe. *Public Libraries and the Internet 2006: Study Results and Findings*.

4. Bertot, John Carlo, & Davis, Denise M. *Planning and Evaluating Library Networked Services and Resources*. Westport: Libraries Unlimited, 2004.

5. More information regarding the TechAtlas tool is available at <http://webjunction.techatlas.org/>.

6. National Center for Education Statistics. *E.D. TAB: Public Libraries in the United States: Fiscal Year 2002*. Washington, DC: U.S. Department of Education, National Center for Education Statistics, 2005. Last accessed on October 12, 2006 at <http://nces.ed.gov/pubs2005/2005356.pdf>. National Center for Education Statistics. *E.D. TAB: Public Libraries in the United States: Fiscal Year 2003*. Washington, DC: U.S. Department of Education, National Center for Education Statistics, 2005. Last accessed on October 12, 2006 at <http://nces.ed.gov/pubs2005/2005363.pdf>.

7. Bertot, John Carlo, McClure, Charles R, & Jaeger, Paul T. *Public Libraries and the Internet 2004: Survey Results and Findings*. Tallahassee: Information Use Management and Policy Institute, 2005. Last accessed on October 9, 2006 at <http://www.ii.fsu.edu/plinternet_reports.cfm>.

8. Vulnerability, as measured through age of hardware, is a proxy measure for the ability of the library's computer hardware and operating system software to meet the demands of today's graphic, video, and streaming demands. The older the hardware and operating system software, the less likely users can access increasingly sophisticated content. The vulnerability variable was divided into four categories–low, medium, high, and unsure. Low vulnerability indicates that with some upgrades (e.g., addition of

memory and the operating system), the library's public access computers could function well. Medium vulnerability indicates that the library's public access computers and their operating system likely need replacement. High vulnerability indicates that the library's public access computer operating systems are out of date (i.e., Windows ME), and the computers cannot be upgraded in order to load the latest Windows operating system software (as of this writing, Windows XP). Unsure indicates that it was unclear whether the library's public access computers could be upgraded or whether they needed outright replacement.

9. E-rate is a program designed to assist public libraries and schools increase their bandwidth through discounts on telecommunications services. More information regarding the e-rate is available on the Schools and Libraries Division of the Universal Service Administrative Company <http://www.universalservice.org/sl/>.

doi:10.1300/J118v25n01_03

Public Library Facility Closure: How Research Can Better Facilitate Proactive Management

Christie M. Koontz
Dean K. Jue

SUMMARY. While there is agreement amongst professionals that the location of a public library facility affects use, there is little research on the impact of closure. Such an investigation is complex and rarely conducted. For the most part–there are simply news stories lamenting closure or impending closures. A recent national study by the authors of this paper offers a methodology for identifying branches which close, and a proposed research agenda to assess the impact of closures. The study provides a base upon which to build additional research on the effects of public library closures on actual and potential users. doi:10.1300/J118v25n01_04 *[Article copies available for a fee from The Haworth Document Delivery Service: 1-800-HAWORTH. E-mail address: <docdelivery@haworthpress.com> Website: <http://www.HaworthPress.com> © 2006 by The Haworth Press, Inc. All rights reserved.]*

Christie M. Koontz, PhD, is Director, GeoLib Program, College of Information, Louis Shores Building, Florida State University, Tallahassee, FL, 32306 USA (E-mail: ckoontz@ci.fsu.edu).

Dean K. Jue, MS, is Director of Technical Assistance, Florida Resources and Environmental Analysis Center, Florida State University, Tallahassee, FL, 32306 USA (E-mail: djue@admin.fsu.edu).

[Haworth co-indexing entry note]: "Public Library Facility Closure: How Research Can Better Facilitate Proactive Management." Koontz, Christie M., and Dean K. Jue. Co-published simultaneously in *Public Library Quarterly* (The Haworth Press, Inc.) Vol. 25, No. 1/2, 2006, pp. 43-56; and: *Current Practices in Public Libraries* (ed: William Miller, and Rita M. Pellen) The Haworth Press, Inc., 2006, pp. 43-56. Single or multiple copies of this article are available for a fee from The Haworth Document Delivery Service [1-800-HAWORTH, 9:00 a.m. - 5:00 p.m. (EST). E-mail address: docdelivery@haworthpress.com].

Available online at http://plq.haworthpress.com
© 2006 by The Haworth Press, Inc. All rights reserved.
doi:10.1300/J118v25n01_04

KEYWORDS. Public library closure, library siting, impact closure of re-siting

INTRODUCTION

While there is agreement in the public library profession that the location of a library facility affects use, there is little research on the impact of closure. Such an investigation is difficult and lengthy and therefore rarely described in the literature. For the most part, there are simply news stories lamenting closure or impending closures.

Because of the lack of research, unanswered questions remain such as, "if the library you use moved to (this location) would you continue to use it?" or "if the library were moved to (another location) would you use the public library service not having used it before?" The answers to such questions in combination with the demographics of the actual and potential users in the library's old and new customer market areas could be critical pieces of information in facility-related plans such as new openings and re-sitings, as well as closures.

Some of the past relevant research offers insight:

- Membership rate declines the farther one lives from the library (Clough, 1965);
- Moving a library from one community to another may sharply increase use by one group and reduce it by another (Jones and King, 1979);
- Some users may have limited range of travel like the elderly, juveniles, less mobile, and less educated (Hayes and Palmer, 1983);
- Circulation gains are larger for new libraries larger in square footage and holdings (Suvak, 1992);
- Increases in use are higher during the second year; increases are *not* related to the size of the building; libraries occupying new headquarters have increased use (Collins & Burgin, 1989);
- The mere presence of a library causes use (i.e., a new building in a place where no library existed before (Lavigne, 1984; Sholam et al., 1990).

This research is indicative of the type of research needed at the local, state, and national level. Currently there is no important national research which provides insight into the effects of closure, or subsequent re-siting of a library to a new location. There may of course be unpublished local research.

Since the late 1980s the federal government through the Federal-State Cooperative System (FSCS), a collaborative among the American Library Association, the Chief Officers of State Library Agencies (COSLA), and the National Center for Education Statistics (NCES) of the US Department of Education, has collected standardized information about public library outlets (an outlet most closely approximates a library branch) throughout the United States.

Although researchers have used the FSCS data sets for various research projects, there has been no systematic longitudinal study using the FSCS data on library outlet closures in the provision of public library services. A recent national study by the authors of this paper (Koontz & Jue, 2005) offers a methodology for identifying branches that close each year, and a proposed research agenda to assess the impact of such closures. The study examined and analyzed closure among public library outlets from 1999 through 2003, providing a base upon which to build additional research efforts on the effects of library outlet closures on actual and potential library users.

METHODOLOGY

The study relied on the public library outlet files (containing both branch and central libraries) which are collected annually by the FSCS. This study used FSCS files from 1999 through calendar year 2003, the last year for which systematically-corrected FSCS data was available.

In the FSCS recordkeeping system, each public library outlet is assigned an FSCSKEY as well as an FSCS Sequence Number. Normally, these values remain the same throughout a public library outlet's existence. Thus, to determine library outlet closures from one year to the next, computer software can help sort and then identify FSCSKEY and FSCS Sequence Number differences from one year to the next. Specifically, library outlets with FSCS numbers that existed in the prior year and not in the current year are usually outlets that closed.

For example, if library outlet TN0022-008 existed in the 1999 FSCS public library outlet file but did not exist in the 2000 FSCS public library outlet file, then that outlet closed in 2000. It is because of the need for two years of FSCS data files to determine one year of library closures that the five years of FSCS data from 1999 through 2003 provide only 4 years of library closures from 1999 through 2002.

Once these potential library outlet closures were identified, manual inspection methods were used to confirm or deny the actual closure for these identified outlets. This cataloging of closed outlets was performed across all years for each state. The results from all states were then used to examine closures across metropolitan status codes as well as by outlet type.

Limitations of the Study Methodology

The FSCS data files represent the only nationally-maintained library outlet information that can be used to track library closures over time. However, there are limitations to using these data sets that should be kept in mind while reading and potentially using the results of this analysis in any other report or study.

First, bookmobiles are explicitly excluded from this entire analysis. Because of their mobility relative to location, it is impossible to meaningful compare bookmobile outlets and their associated statistics with other library outlets with more permanent locations. There are two other broad categories of limitations to using the FSCS data files for studying public library closure. One category arises out of the FSCS codes themselves. The second category arises out of the non-geographic nature of the FSCS data files.

A. Limitations due to FSCS codes. The FSCS codes for a particular library outlet are developed by FSCS to standardize the tracking of state-collected data for public library outlets on a national level. While this may usually coincide with data collection requirements at each individual state level as well, this is not always the case in particular instances. As a result, the FSCS codes are sometimes inadequate for tracking library closures.

For the purposes of this analysis, the unique FSCSKEY and FSCS Sequence Number code assigned to each outlet would ideally correspond to a separate stand-alone facility. While this is usually the case, there were instances in which this did not hold true. An example would be a library outlet that is assigned a unique FSCS code that resides completely within another library outlet with its own (and different) FSCS code. Some library systems do this in order to track statistics for, say, its children or history and genealogy "outlet" relative to the other portions of its outlet. Outlet closures in these instances may not represent true closures but just a consolidation of space and facility tracking. In this case, the closure is more a statistical closure rather than an actual closure from a library user's perspective.

Another kind of statistical anomaly occurs when several single-branch entity outlets apparently became part of a larger system. As a result, the original FSCS code from a prior year may be deleted (i.e., the outlet apparently closed). However, they received a new FSCS code and their library type is changed from being a central library outlet to a branch outlet. Again, this is not a *physical* closure.

For this study, a library outlet was not included in the closed category if the evidence suggested that a library outlet closure was not a true physical closure. Evidence used to make this determination included the continued existence of another public library outlet at the same address as the outlet that was presumed to be closed. However, using such a criterion means that a public library outlet that is replaced by a more modern facility just a block away and assigned a new FSCS code at the same time would be counted as closed. The only way to determine the essential non-closure under this scenario would be to contact on-site librarians directly, a task that was beyond the scope of the original project.

B. Limitations due to non-geographic nature of FSCS data files. In its current form, the FSCS public library outlet files cannot be put into a geographic information system without additional work. An example of such an effort is the work by the GeoLib Program at Florida State University using the FSCS data files to develop an Internet-accessible map that shows the locations of public library outlets relative to local roads, other libraries, and demographic data <*www.geolib.org/PLGDB.cfm*>.

Unless the FSCS public library outlet files are integrated into an analytical geographic environment, it becomes difficult to assess the potential impact of a library closure on its users. Consider the following scenarios:

1. as previously described, a library service (e.g., a specialized law library housed in a public library) no longer keeps track of its library statistics separately so its FSCS code is deleted;
2. a city library and a county library are located two blocks from each other. Under an agreement between the city and the county, the county library closes but city residents can go to the city library for all library services. From a user's perspective, has library service really diminished?
3. a branch library closes but its replacement branch is across a busy street in a culturally different neighborhood. Is the new branch really an adequate replacement for the original branch library from the perspective of a library user who regularly used the original library branch?

It is because of such issues that the initial exploratory research project funded by the ALA cannot definitively determine whether newly-opened library outlets are replacing closed library outlets in all instances or evaluate how user services may be impacted by such closures. To answer such questions would require library surveys and geographic analyses of individual library openings and closings.

RESULTS

The data generated by this study were derived from the FSCS public library data files after removing the bookmobile outlets reported during each year.

There were only 11 states with fewer outlets in calendar year 2003 than in 1999; in all of those instances, the percentage reduction was less than two percent. On a national level, the number of public library outlets grew slightly for each succeeding study year.

Overall Outlet Closure

The largest number of closures was during calendar year 2000. The closure rate for library outlets ranged from 0.6% to 0.7% of existing library outlets across each of the four years used by this study.

There were two states (Hawaii and Montana) and the District of Columbia in which there were no closures of any library outlets during the five-year study period. There were nineteen states that had double-digit library closures over the five years of this study period but only four states (Georgia, Michigan, Missouri, and Pennsylvania) had more than 20 outlet closures.

Library outlet closures are not uniformly distributed across all states over the years. Six states (Arkansas, California, Michigan, Minnesota, Missouri, and Pennsylvania) account for more than half of the public library outlet closures in calendar year 2000. Five of these six states rank in the top 40% of states with the highest total number of public library outlets.

Library Closures and Library Outlet Type

Because the FSCS database tracks outlets by library type (i.e., CE = central library, BR = branch library, BM = books-by-mail, and BS = bookmobiles), it is possible to examine the closure of library outlets by outlet type. This information can shed light on the likely impact of library closures. For instance, the closure of a CE library outlet may eliminate all library services by that library entity within its legal service area whereas the closure of a BR library outlet means that reduced library services may still be available within that library entity's legal service area.

Because of the small numbers of closures within most states, the library type for all library closures within each state was summed for all five years. To keep the analysis of closure by outlet type comparable, the average number of each outlet type over the five-year time span was calculated (not including bookmobiles, of course). See Table 1.

The outlet closures by library type over the five year period show that although book-by-mail outlets constitute a very small percentage of outlet types (about four-hundredths of one percent of outlets), they represent a relatively large number of the closures, over one percent. Further study should be made to understand the impact of this often overlooked channel of distribution. Although central libraries represent over 50% of the library outlets, they represent just over one-third of outlet closures. Library branches, which represent about 45% of all library outlets, constitute almost two-thirds of all the closures. These numbers fit the expected outlet closure pattern, since it is presumed library entities would close library branches before closing the entire library system. Closing a central library is a much more drastic measure than closing a library branch.

Library Closures and Metropolitan Status Codes

The FSCS database also tracks the metropolitan status codes of each library outlet. These codes (CC = central city, NC = non-central city,

TABLE 1. Library Closures by Library Type Over Time Period 1999-2003

	CE	BR	BM	Total
Average No. of Outlet Type over 5-year study period	8,963	7,430	6	16,399
Outlet Type's Percentage of Total (N = 16,399)	54.66%	45.31%	0.04%	100%
Actual Number of Library Type Closure over 5-year period	147	284	7	438
Outlet Type's Percentage of Actual Closures (N = 438)	33.56%	64.84%	1.60%	100%

NO = non-metropolitan area) can be loosely interpreted to be equivalent to urban, suburban, and rural. An examination of library outlet closure relative to this variable will be of interest because it can identify if library outlets in particular stages of urbanization are more prone to closure.

Again, because of the small number of closures within most states, the library metropolitan status code for all library closures within each state was summed for all five years. To keep the analysis of closure by metropolitan status code comparable, the average number of each metropolitan status code over the five-year time span was calculated. Again, bookmobiles were not included in the calculations, along with closed outlets that had missing metropolitan status codes. Thus, the universe of closed library outlets with metropolitan status codes over the five-year time span was only 426 libraries instead of 438. The average number of library outlets within each metropolitan status code over the five-year time span and their associated percentage representation are provided in Table 2.

The pattern of library outlet closures shows that libraries with a NO metropolitan status code were closed at a rate close to their true representation overall (51.41% actual versus 52.07% calculated percentage). In contrast, although outlets with a CC status code represented approximately 16.5% of all library outlets, they represented 24% of the closures. Library outlets with an NC metropolitan status code represent 31% of all the public library outlets but only 24% of the closure. Thus, NC libraries were less likely to be closed than either of their corresponding counterpart libraries with a CC or NO status classification.

Possible Effects of Observed Library Closures

From the list of closed library outlets, it is possible to conjecture the possible effects of library outlet closure on library user services. However, several problems inherent with the FSCS data sets prevented using

TABLE 2. Library Closures by Metropolitan Status Code Over Time Period 1999-2003

	CC	NC	NO	Total
Average No. by Status Code	2,690	5,120	8,483	16,293
Status Code's % of Total	16.51%	31.42%	52.07%	100%
Actual Number of Closures	103	104	219	426
Status Code's % of Closures	24.18%	24.41%	51.41%	100%

the statistics from all 438 closed library outlets in estimating effects of library closures on user services. Specifically:

1. There are few library statistics collected by the FSCS at the branch level (FSCS code BR), so the only definitive library user statistics are collected and maintained at a library entity level (i.e., system-wide).
2. It is impossible to estimate the effects of a branch closure in a library system with several branches since there are no statistics available for the individual branches.
3. Given the above situations, the primary definitive statistics that can be derived from the FSCS data sets are from library entities that closed which have no branches because only then is it certain that the collected statistics can be accurately assigned to the closed outlet.
4. Even in those situations, it is impossible to determine if the closures of the single-outlet library entities represent 100% of library services lost because it is impossible to determine how much, if any, of those library services may have migrated to another library outlet hosted by another library entity that remains open.

Because of these constraints, the only reasonable way to estimate the impact of library closure on user services was to confine the initial analysis only to single-outlet entities that closed from calendar year 2000 to calendar year 2003 and then extrapolate the results. One hundred and seventeen (117) of the 438 library outlet closures during this time period were single-outlet entities, represent 26.7% of the entire universe of outlets that were closed during the study period. The process used to derive the subset of library outlets for this estimate virtually guaranteed that these outlets served areas with smaller populations. Library outlets in more densely-populated areas tend to be multi-branched library systems.

For these 117 closed library outlets, the library statistics from the FSCS public library entity file for the year prior to the entity's closure were used to estimate potential loss of library services. Statistics examined were population size served, number of library visits, adult circulation, and children circulation.

Summing up these four statistics across all 117 library outlets shows that the potential cumulative loss of library services to library users through library outlet closures can be significant. Unless alternative library outlets were available to the almost one million individuals being served by these 117 outlets, almost 3.5 million library visits were not made and over four million items were not circulated. An additional almost 1.5 million items of juvenile circulation were lost as well. If one extrapolates these numbers to the 321 other closed outlets that were not included in deriving these estimates, then a figure approximately four times as large for lost library services to library users would not be unreasonable for the entire universe of 438 libraries closed during the time period of 2000 through 2003. These numbers would be four million library visitors with 14 million library visits, over 16 million adult material items, and 6 million children's material items. These conjectural estimates should be used and conveyed to others only in conjunction with the cautionary notes and constraints noted throughout this paper.

DISCUSSION AND RECOMMENDATIONS

Public library outlets close for a wide variety of reasons. Reduced library funding levels may be the initial impetus for considering the closure of a library outlet. In some instances, factors such as changing demographic trends affecting type and level of library use at a particular outlet as well as the location and physical attractiveness of the facility may affect which specific outlet is selected to be closed.

This initial assessment of library outlet closures provides a picture of library outlet closure over the 2000 through 2003 time period. It shows that outlet closures are not distributed evenly across all states. On an annual basis, approximately 0.75 percent of existing public library outlets are closed. A disproportionate share of those closures are library branches rather than central libraries. Libraries in non-central city areas (i.e., those with an 'NC' metropolitan status code) are less likely to be closed than those in more urbanized or more rural settings. Even if the library outlets serve a small population, the cumulative effects of closures can quickly amount to significant loss in the availability of public library services if alternative library services cannot be found by their library users, or access is diminished further to potential users.

A potentially very interesting area of research is the disproportionately higher level of outlet closure for 'CC' outlets as opposed to 'NC' outlets. This may partially represent the migration of urban populations to more suburban living areas. But how well are the remaining residents of those closed 'CC' outlets being served by other library outlets? Research indicates, if many of the nearby populace are recent immigrants with limited mobility, their library needs may not be met by library facilities one or two miles further away (Koontz 1997, p. 53).

Beyond those statements and the hard numbers of closures during the study period, it is difficult to make firm statements about library closures that can be backed with data based on quality research and thorough investigations. The reasons for this include:

1. because of the short timeframe and exploratory nature of this study, it was not possible to do a detailed historical analysis of the library closures and determine if a new library outlet had been built or was in the planning stages to replace the closed one;
2. the lack of geographic market areas[2] for library outlets (as opposed to the legal service area for library entities) makes it difficult to assess the availability and suitability of alternative sources for library services for library users who may have been using the closed outlet (Koontz, pp. 139-153);
3. the lack of statistical data for individual library outlets when there is more than one outlet controlled by a library entity. The aggregation of library statistical data to the system entity level makes it extremely difficult to gauge the effect of closure of just a single outlet.

The identification and absolute count of the number of closed public library outlets is, of course, only a first step in better understanding the potential impact of library closure in the provision of library services to users. A more complete study on the short and long term impact of library closure would look not only at the impact of the replacement of a closed library facility with a newly-opened one, if any, but also at existing library users of the closed outlet that now do not use library services at all.

A reasonable extension of the above exploratory research would be to simply confirm with the local library entities which library outlets absolutely closed with no replacement outlet and which ones were moved and assigned a different FSCS number. By utilizing geographic information system(GIS)–type software, it would also be possible to review geographic relationships between closed outlets and existing outlets for travel distances as well as to look at demographic and socioeconomic variables around the closed outlet to try to better assess the likely impact of library closures on the surrounding population.

However, the most comprehensive examination of the impact of library closures on library users will need to involve active feedback from the local communities and library entities where the library outlets were closed. Directors of multi-outlet library systems can be interviewed for specific reasons for library closures. These survey results can then be analyzed relative to the GIS analyses to summarize the issues and concerns related to US public library closings.

Even if the identification of which libraries actually closed and the rationale for their closures could be reasonably achieved, there are still other issues which have impact on library closure. The above describes post facto studies. That is, the library outlets are already closed. But, in fact, what is necessary is a better understanding of what factors should be considered *before closure* (Koontz 1997).

The fact that most library systems do not delineate market areas for branches provides little knowledge of the impact of library closures on the populations served. A market area is defined as the geographic area from which primary customers travel to access an organization. While all libraries know the legal *service area (*the ascribed area for which funding is leveraged), few understand their customer market areas. This is critical in understanding usage patterns, and potential customer markets that are thus far untapped. In the public library's case, habit and experience greatly affect how far customers will travel for library services. Desire and convenience vary according to demographics. For example, a child can not travel without transportation to the library, unless the library is within walking distance.

Questions identified by Koontz (1997) that should be considered by library directors for each branch before its actual closure should include:

1. What is the geographic market?
2. What are the characteristics of the population within the market?
3. Are the market characteristics expected to change?
4. Are there higher numbers of juveniles, the elderly, or any ethnic group in close proximity to the library facility?
5. How far is the closest library facility? Is there any topographical or cultural barrier to it?
6. Is any new shopping or other facility planned to be built that may draw more users in?
7. If circulation is low, are other types of use, such as visits or in-library use, recorded that may better measure use?
8. Is the community aware of the services the library provides?
9. Is there outreach or a bookmobile that travels from the library?
10. After a new market analysis is completed, are new services and programs developed and communicated that may better meet the needs of the community?

11. Are the hours of service adequate for the work and leisure lives of the community residents?

CONCLUSION

To date there is little research on library closure, and the subsequent impact on the populations the library served. This lack of evidence is due largely to a lack of identification of library market areas across the country. This precludes comparative data, as well as developing long-term proactive data that can help a library manager facing unexpected and undesired closures. The opportunity to explore this topic at this time will provide valuable knowledge for public library managers who are competing for public funds in their communities. While many closures go unnoticed because a new facility is being built, there is no knowledge or understanding of who never uses a library again, and what economic, social, cultural, or educational impact that has on the whole of the community served.

NOTES

1. The initial phase of this research was funded by the American Library Association Office of Research and Statistics in Spring 2005.
2. A geographic market area is the estimated geographic area in which the library's actual and potential customers live.

REFERENCES

Clough, E. A. (1965). Where do readers live? *Research in Librarianship, 1*, 164-169.
Collins, M. H. & Burgin, R. (1989). The effects of a new main library on circulation and other selected performance indicators. *North Carolina Libraries, 47*, 90-97.
Jones, A. & King, M. B. (1979). The effect of re-siting a library. *Journal of Librarianship, 11*, 215-231.
Hayes, R. & Palmer, E. S. (1983). The effects of distance upon the use of libraries: Case studies based on a survey of users of the Los Angeles Public Library Central Library and branches. *Library Research, 5*, 67-100.
Koontz, C. (1997). *Library Facility Siting and Location Handbook.* Westport, CT: Greenwood Press.
Koontz, C. & Jue, D. (2005). *FSCS library outlet closures from 1999 through 2003: An initial assessment.* Unpublished report for the American Library Association Office of Research, Chicago, IL.

Lavigge, N. (1984). A library in the metro-station. *Public Library Quarterly, 5*, 47-57.
Shoham, S., Hershkovitz, S., & Metzer, D. (1990). Distribution of libraries in urban space and its effect on their use: The case of Tel Aviv. *Library & Information Science Research, 12*, 167-181.
Suvak, D. (1992). Opening day: what to expect in a new library. *Wilson Library Bulletin, 57*, 140.

doi:10.1300/J118v25n01_04

Public Libraries and Human Rights

Kathleen de la Pena McCook
Katharine J. Phenix

SUMMARY. Public librarians derive the philosophical and ethical principles that guide our practice from transcendent ideals which are also embodied in the Universal Declaration of Human Rights. This article reviews the foundation of the U.S. public library and key documents that have characterized its development. Recent violations of human rights in U.S. libraries include closure; exclusion of the homeless; refusal to purchase Spanish-language materials; ordinances against gay pride display; and filtering. The importance of the public librarian's commitment to human rights as the ethical basis for library service is defined and discussed. doi:10.1300/J118v25n01_05 *[Article copies available for a fee from The Haworth Document Delivery Service: 1-800-HAWORTH. E-mail address: <docdelivery@haworthpress.com> Website: <http://www.HaworthPress.com> © 2006 by The Haworth Press, Inc. All rights reserved.]*

KEYWORDS. Universal Declaration of Human Rights, Library Bill of Rights, human rights, public librarians, public libraries, American Library Association

---

Kathleen de la Peña McCook is Distinguished University Professor at the University of South Florida, School of Library and Information Science. She is the author of *Introduction to Public Librarianship* (Neal-Schuman, 2004) (E-mail: kmccook@tampabay.rr.com).

Katharine J. Phenix is Adult Services Librarian at Rangeview Library District near Denver, Colorado (E-mail: phenix@rangeviewld.org).

[Haworth co-indexing entry note]: "Public Libraries and Human Rights." McCook, Kathleen de la Pena, and Katharine J. Phenix. Co-published simultaneously in *Public Library Quarterly* (The Haworth Press, Inc.) Vol. 25, No. 1/2, 2006, pp. 57-73; and: *Current Practices in Public Libraries* (ed: William Miller, and Rita M. Pellen) The Haworth Press, Inc., 2006, pp. 57-73. Single or multiple copies of this article are available for a fee from The Haworth Document Delivery Service [1-800-HAWORTH, 9:00 a.m. - 5:00 p.m. (EST). E-mail address: docdelivery@haworthpress.com].

Available online at http://plq.haworthpress.com
© 2006 by The Haworth Press, Inc. All rights reserved.
doi:10.1300/J118v25n01_05

INTRODUCTION

> If this nation is to be wise as well as strong, if we are to achieve our destiny, then we need more new ideas for more wise men reading more good books in more public libraries. These libraries should be open to all except the censor. We must know all the facts and hear all the alternatives and listen to all the criticisms. Let us welcome controversial books and controversial authors. For the Bill of Rights is the guardian of our security as well as our liberty. (Kennedy, 1960)

> The American Library Association is unswerving in its commitment to human rights and intellectual freedom; the two are inseparably linked and inextricably entwined. (American Library Association. Office for Intellectual Freedom [ALA OIF] 2002, p. 194)

Public libraries provide the resources for the still voice within each person to be nurtured and to grow. Public libraries provide a public space for discussion of issues important to the common good. These opportunities occur because public librarians in the United States have developed philosophies of collection development, outreach, and community building that are expansive and inclusive. Yet external attacks on public libraries–efforts to censor books, efforts to tear down displays, efforts to close meeting rooms–continue unabated in the twenty-first century. Public librarians within the American Library Association and Public Library Association join together with other organizations dedicated to freedom of expression such as the American Civil Liberties Union, the American Medical Association, the Center for Democracy and Technology, the American Historical Association, the AAUP, Project Gutenberg and many others to ensure that First Amendment rights are safeguarded. Coalitions among people and organizations that embrace democracy are critical during this period of governmental repression (Center for Constitutional Rights, 2006). In these times, libraries and librarians are facing scrutiny from the USA PATRIOT ACT, curtailment from CIPA (Children's Internet Protection Act) and censorship from DOPA (Deleting Online Predators Act), and we confront extinction from budget cutting and closings. For example, the Environmental Protection Agency headquarters library was not funded and was closed on October 1, 2006 (Environmental News Service, 2006). Faced with these external erosions of our primary mission, we should use the codes and standards we have already adopted and unite our work with that of national and international human rights efforts.

This essay considers the worldview that public librarians have formed vis-à-vis service in the context of human rights. The authors recognize that librarianship has not frequently used the language of human rights to characterize service modes. We assert that the philosophical framework offered by the ideals of human rights is a framework that is incorporated in ALA policies and documents. Many writers have already historically underscored the connection between education, democracy, and public libraries, including ALA's *Core Values Statement*:

> A democracy presupposes an informed citizenry. The First Amendment mandates the right of all persons to free expression, and the corollary right to receive the constitutionally protected expression of others. The publicly supported library provides free and equal access to information for all people of the community the library serves.

Inscribed on the right side of the Madison Building of the Library of Congress are the words: "What spectacle can be more edifying or more seasonable, than that of liberty and learning, each leaning on the other for their mutual and surest support" and then, on the left side: "Knowledge will forever govern ignorance: and a people who mean to be their own governours, must arm themselves with the power which knowledge gives" (Library of Congress).

In the 19th century the idea of universal education as promoted by Horace Mann framed the development of public institutions. In his Twelfth Annual Report as Secretary of the Massachusetts State Board of Education (1848) Mann stated:

> Now surely nothing but universal education can counterwork this tendency to the domination of capital and the servility of labor. If one class possesses all the wealth and the education, while the residue of society is ignorant and poor, it matters not by what name the relation between them may be called: the latter, in fact and in truth, will be the servile dependents and subjects of the former. But, if education be equally diffused, it will draw property after it by the strongest of all attractions; for such a thing never did happen, and never can happen, as that an intelligent and practical body of men should be permanently poor. Property and labor in different classes are essentially antagonistic; but property and labor in the same class are essentially fraternal. (Mann, para. 7)

In the 1850s the founders of public libraries imbued with the thoughtfulness of educational philosophers like Mann emphasized that citizens' access to reading materials would extend the education process and cultivate the democratic process (McCook, 2004, p. 16). Today the American Library Association calls this lifelong learning and includes it in the core values, mission statement, and policy manuals:

> ALA promotes the creation, maintenance, and enhancement of a learning society, encouraging its members to work with educators, government officials, and organizations in coalitions to initiate and support comprehensive efforts to ensure that school, public, academic, and special libraries in every community cooperate to provide lifelong learning services to all. (ALA, *Core Values Statement*, para. 6, 2006)

This commitment to lifelong learning is also reiterated in ALA's "Libraries: An American Value" (Policy 53.8): "We celebrate and preserve our democratic society by making available the widest possible range of viewpoints, opinions and ideas, so that all individuals have the opportunity to become lifelong learners–informed, literate, educated, and culturally enriched" (ALA *Policy Manual* 2005-2006 p. 51 and *Intellectual Freedom Manual* (2002) pp. 228-231).

This aspect of library services is listed again in "12 Ways Libraries are Good for the County" (2000):

> Libraries inform citizens. Democracy vests supreme power in the people. Libraries make democracy work by providing access to information so that citizens can make the decisions necessary to govern themselves. The public library is the only institution in American society whose purpose is to guard against the tyrannies of ignorance and conformity, and its existence indicates the extent to which a democratic society values knowledge, truth, justice, books, and culture.

The very idea that people should tax themselves for the support of the public library–an institution that activates human capabilities, diminishes the divisions between people of different classes, and provides for access to information–is an indicator of a society's commitment to fundamental human rights. The concept of the library as an important component in the public sphere has been explored at length by Buschman:

> Librarianship has historically extended the democratic public sphere within its walls: the flawed democratic bases on which librarianship was founded have been revised, extended, and made more inclusive; the essential purpose of public enlightenment was reasonably well-supported by tax and tuition dollars for over 120 years; the

Library Bill of Rights has been extended over the years; there have been conscious attempts to reach out to the poor, the disabled, and to better represent the historically underrepresented on our shelves and screens (2003, pp. 48-49).

CONNECTING PUBLIC LIBRARY SERVICE TO HUMAN RIGHTS

From 1852-1966 the scope of public library services in the United States had been set forth in the founding documents of public librarianship: Boston Public Library (1852); *A National Plan for Public Library Service* (Joeckel and Winslow, 1948); and national standards for public library service in 1933, 1943, 1956, 1966 (McCook, 2004, pp. 88-91). Concurrent with the release of the 1966 Standards librarians pondered the results of the 1963 report, *Access to Public Libraries*, which reported on the lack of service to poor people and people of color. After 1966 public librarians came to the conclusion that the United States public library was not doing an adequate job serving all people (McCook, 91) and the Public Library Association (PLA) launched a Goals Feasibility Study resulting in the 1972 report *A Strategy for Public Library Change* (Martin). The focus on community-based planning shifted the profession's discourse to the idea of local planning models (Lynch, 1981). The PLA decided that national standards were no longer feasible and collaborated with Ernest R. De Prospo on a study to measure the effectiveness of public libraries which was reported in *Performance Measures for Public Libraries* (1974). Ultimately the PLA Planning Process was developed resulting in the 1987 *Planning and Role Setting for Public Libraries* by McClure (1987), which identified eight roles for public libraries: (1) community activities center; (2) community information center; (3) formal education support center; (4) independent learning center; (5) popular materials library; (6) preschoolers door to learning; (7) reference library; and 8) research center. The shift from standards to a planning process has been analyzed by Pungitore (1993) in *Innovation and the Library*.

The 1987 *Planning and Role Setting* manual, while idealistic in its description of roles, failed to provide a philosophical or intellectual rationale for their selection. The reason for this omission was in part because the field had rejected a 1979 project titled, *The Public Library Mission Statement and its Imperatives for Service* (PLA, Goals, Guidelines and Standards Committee). The *Public Library Mission Statement* was ambitious and idealistic. It identified actions public libraries could take to move the nation toward total egalitarianism (McCook 2004, p. 93). In a special report published in the 1987 *Bowker Annual* Kenneth E. Dowlin wrote "... the ability of librarians to strive for, defend, and increase access to information will not only have an impact on the profession but on the communities librarians serve. A committed, trained, and caring profession is required to safeguard existing access to information and to ensure access in the years ahead." In hindsight the profession's rejection of the *Public Library Mission Statement* can also be viewed as a withdrawal from a transcendent and over-arching approach and replacement with an acceptance of practical local actions with an emphasis on measurement.

The 1980s were the Reagan years–a time when those in power promoted a conservative agenda that caused government to take an ideological turn to the right in the oversight of public institutions. For an analysis that demonstrates how even well-intended career administrators have traded a commitment to equal opportunity for bureaucratic expertise consisting of neutral instrumentalities (control, measurement, efficiency) see Michael W. Apple's *Educating the "Right" Way* (2006, pp. 104-108). In public libraries this was manifested in the output measures movement. Additionally, the United States moved away from cultural development with a global viewpoint by withdrawing from UNESCO and the nation drifted away from the world cultural stage. In spite of a profession-wide commitment to education and documents to confirm and spur movement in this direction (such as the Faure report, 1972), public library philosophy seems to have moved toward the Baltimore County model during the 1990s (Baltimore, 1992).

In 1998 after internal study the PLA issued a revised manual for the Planning Process titled *Planning for Results: A Public Library Transformation Process* (Himmel and Wilson) and another revision in 2001, *The New Planning for Results: A Streamlined Process* (Nelson). This model suggested thirteen library "responses" to community needs: (1) basic literacy; (2) business and career information; (3) commons; (4) community referral; (5) consumer information; (6) cultural awareness; (7) current topics and titles; (8) formal learning support; (9) general information; (10) government information; (11) information literacy; (12) lifelong learning; and (13) local history and genealogy.

Like the eight roles determined in 1987, the thirteen responses identified in 1998 and 2001 are presented without substantive connection to values or principles. While we would all acknowledge that the thirteen responses are meritorious and appropriate, the transformation process is presented with little connection to enduring values.

Writing of the tension between the Towson Theory of measurable results to show governing and budgeting authorities and the broader vision of the founders of the Boston Public Library John N. Berry III (2006) has observed:

> What I regret and worry about is that public libraries have rarely delivered on that honorable mission set out in 1852. Public libraries have never really provided enough of the information on current issues to inform citizens fully, nor have they, alas, ever aggressively pushed that information to those citizens, or told them they need to attend to it. Public libraries have never "induced" people to learn in-depth about the questions on our public agenda, in the word the Boston trustees used. In contrast to its great success at "building a better Borders," the public library, in its greatest failure, has neglected to inform democracy, to convince citizens to use its resources to become more knowledgeable in order to decide public issues. It is the problem that keeps me awake at night.

Thinkers like Joan Durrance in her 1984 classic, *Armed for Action*, recognized the need for public libraries to support citizen action groups with a high level of information support. Durrance also noted that the Public Library Mission Statement encouraged focus on users rather than institutions (p. 174).

So, in the absence of standards, how have public librarians determined the mission, roles and responses, goals and objectives that guide the services provided? While there is little documentation as to underlying philosophies in these various guidelines and manuals, we know that the profession has drawn from a variety of traditions of justice as ancient as the Code of Hammurabi (1780 BC) right on up to the *Universal Declaration of Human Rights* (1948) and subsequent treaties (Ishay 2004).[1]

We believe the *Universal Declaration of Human Rights* (UDHR) to be "rooted in an attractive moral vision of human beings as equal and autonomous agents living in states that treat each citizen with equal concern and respect" as characterized by Donnelly (2003, p. 38). Thus the *Universal Declaration of Human Rights* can provide public librarians with a widely understood international document that iterates and consolidates values that should guide the development of services.

Reviewing the articles of the UDHR (1948) we find values that librarians use. The 30 Articles in the UDHR fall into six or more families of rights, as described in the *Stanford Encyclopedia of Philosophy*.

These families include security rights (provide a safe environment), due process rights (no excessive punishment), liberty rights (freedom of expression, assembly, association), political rights (governance), equality rights (non-discrimination), and social, or welfare rights (education, information). Group rights have been added in subsequent treaties protecting ethnic groups and state sovereignty.

The articles of the *Universal Declaration of Human Rights* provide a way to think about public library service. We suggest that these articles inform a philosophy of library practice. There are many contemporary examples of the families of rights that public librarians enforce, provide, and protect.

THE UNIVERSAL DECLARATION OF HUMAN RIGHTS AND THE AMERICAN LIBRARY ASSOCIATION

> As we carry on with our duties as public service librarians, we should keep in mind our history of human rights advocacy, and note the work we do today as a continuation of the commitment to the contributions of our programs, collections and services towards keeping an open society, a public space where democracy lives. (Phenix and McCook, 2005)

The American Library Association is on record as a supporter of human rights. The *Library Bill of Rights* (LBR) was adopted in its current form by Council on June 18th, 1948. It is ALA Policy 53.1 of the ALA *Policy Manual*.

In 1961 the *Library Bill of Rights* was amended to include civil rights to ensure library rights are not denied because of race, religion, national origin, or political views. In 1980 and again in 1996, ALA reaffirmed these rights to persons of all ages. The final section on access in the LBR states: "A person's right to use a library should not be denied or abridged because of origin, age, background, or views."

In 1971 ALA OIF announced its intention to identify and collect Interpretations of the Library Bill of Rights. The Interpretations, in many cases, refer to ALA Policy 53: Intellectual Freedom. Political, social and technological history is reflected in the progression of these statements. For example, the 1951 statement against labeling arose during the McCarthy era to discourage labeling materials as subversive. It was revised in 1990 to address concerns regarding audiovisual rating guides (53.1.7). Contemporary pressures to limit intellectual freedom and human rights are reflected in statements about infringement of access through electronic filtering (53.1.16), invasion of privacy, which requires a distinction from confidentiality, and recognition of economic barriers (53.1.14).

Foremost among these is the *Universal Right to Freedom of Expression*, endorsed by Council on January 16, 1991 and quoted at the beginning of this essay:

> The American Library Association endorses this principle, which is also set forth in the Universal Declaration of Human Rights, adopted by the United Nations General Assembly. The Preamble of this document states that "... recognition of the inherent dignity and of the equal and inalienable rights of all members of the human family is the foundation of freedom, justice, and peace in the world ... and ... the advent of a world in which human beings shall enjoy freedom of speech and belief and freedom from fear and want has been proclaimed as the highest aspiration of the common people.

Public librarians have many supporting materials in their repertory as they endeavor to promote the principles of human rights in practice. The Resolution on IFLA, Human Rights, and Freedom of Expression, passed by ALA Council on July 2nd, 1997, highlights UDHR Article 19 and ALA's endorsement of it which states, quite simply: "Article 19. Everyone has the right to freedom of opinion and expression; this right includes freedom to hold opinions without interference and to seek, receive and impart information and ideas through any media and regardless of frontiers." (UDHR)

The ALA Policy Manual provides us with ALA Mission Statement (Policy 1.1), Code of Ethics, which was adopted in 1939, revised several times, in ALA Policy 40.2 and currently under review; Freedom to Read (Policy 53.3) and Freedom to View (53.2), Libraries, An American Value (53.8), and the Core Values Statement. ALA also addresses minority concerns in Policy 60.1-60.6. These address the human and information rights of cultural minorities, persons with disabilities, and prejudices and stereotypes. Furthermore, the Service to Poor People (Policy 61) states most strongly "the urgent need to respond to the increasing number of poor children, adults, and families in America. These people are affected by a combination of limitations, including illiteracy, illness, social isolation, homelessness, hunger, and discrimination, which hamper the effectiveness of traditional library services."

RECENT EXAMPLES OF THREATS TO HUMAN RIGHTS IN US PUBLIC LIBRARIES

The Universal Right to Freedom of Expression continues "There is no good censorship. Any effort to restrict free expression and the free flow of information aids the oppressor. Fighting oppression with censorship is self-defeating" (ALA. OIF. Interpretations). In spite of all we have discussed above, human rights have a fragile home in libraries and they are increasingly under attack. Consider that "all human beings are born free and equal in dignity and rights" (UDHR Article 1), and that "everyone is entitled to all the rights and freedoms set forth" (UDHR Article 2), that they have "without any discrimination equal protection of the law" (UDHR Article 7) and "freedom of thought, conscience and religion" (UDHR Article 18) and of course, finally the right to "receive and impart information and ideas through any media . . . " (UDHR Article 19), and then observe library service to the poor, homeless, immigrant and gay populations. Take note of the increase in challenges to information access, through the closing of EPA libraries and unending challenges to books. Human rights violations in libraries happen all the time throughout the nation.

Library Service to Gay, Lesbian, BiSexual and Transgendered People

In May 2005 the House of Representatives approved a resolution asking Oklahoma libraries to "confine homosexually themed books and other age-inappropriate material to areas exclusively for adult access and distribution." The lawmakers further threatened to deny state funding to libraries that don't comply (Oder, 2006). In 2003 a citizens' group in Montgomery County (outside Houston, TX) listed 119 books–most with gay content–it would like to see moved from their current location into an adult section (Oder, 2004).

More recently, the Hillsborough County Public Library (Oder, 2005) removed a display for Gay Pride Month due to the "current political climate" (Alexander 2005, Varian, 2005). In spite of community comment and protest the ban remains in effect and gay and lesbian people have been denied the right to celebrate Gay Pride Month using county resources.

Poor and Homeless People

Human dignity, human rights and libraries intersect on other levels when citizens are denied library service because of their economic status. Recently, lack of equitable library services to homeless individuals and families has surfaced in Valparaiso, Indiana (Library bans homeless kids from checking out books) where the board of the Porter County Public Library temporarily limited lending privileges to homeless people, and in Worcester, Massachusetts, where a class action lawsuit was filed in July and won in September by three homeless patrons (Hammel, Reis). The Hunger, Homelessness and Poverty Task Force of the Social Responsibilities Round Table (SRRT) of the American Library Association has reported on odor policies and civility campaigns that lead to the criminalization of poor people (Are public libraries criminalizing poor people?).

Gehner has tied treatment of poor and homeless people to literacy and the lack of attention to the needs of the poor by librarians: "Despite the well-established, life-long advantages that literacy and reading offer to individuals and society as a whole, we fail as a profession and as a nation, to deliver adequate resources to those who would benefit from them the most" (p. 117).

In contradiction to ALA Policy 61, Library Services to the Poor and the Library Bill of Rights which promotes, among other things, "the removal of all barriers to library and information services, particularly fees and overdue charges" (ALA Policy Manual) the profession fails to live up to its ideals and those of human rights advocates in these circumstances. Overdue fines are another barrier public libraries may wish to reconsider in the light of economic hardships.

Spanish-Speaking People and Immigration

In Denver, the Denver Public Library was challenged by contemporary Know-Nothings who do not support Spanish language library branches and/or Spanish language materials, focusing their protests on the genre of "fotonovelas." On August 8, 2005, the Coalition for A Closer Look (including the Colorado Minuteman Project, Sovereignty Colorado, and Colorado Alliance for Immigration Reform) held a protest at the Denver Public Library. A letter was hand-delivered to the library demanding head librarian Rick Ashton's resignation (Colorado Alliance for Immigration Reform).

A year later, Gwinett County Public Library, outside Atlanta, Georgia, faced losing their director and cutting their Spanish language materials budget because of resident complaints. "We can't supply pleasure reading material for all language groups, so we're not going to go down that road," said Lloyd Breck, chairman of the Gwinnett County Public Library Board (Grisham en espanol?).

Access to Information and Filtering

Contemporary civil rights challenges at the federal level which affect libraries are CIPA (Children's Internet Protection Act) which requires libraries to install filters on their internet computers) and DOPA (Deleting Online Predators Act H.R. 5319, 2006), which was aimed at "social networking" tools such as MySpace.com and Facebook.com. These legislative initiatives that seek to limit access to information (and to free association) through internet channels ripple beyond the intended protections to deny access to many educational resources (Carvin).

These actions reflect the authoritarian populism described by Apple (2006, p. 46). Librarians, committed to an open information environment must struggle to work creatively with conservative community members to balance those members' desire for control of information with the rest of the community's desire for open access.

CONCLUSION

The challenges facing public libraries are emblematic of the struggle in the United States to maintain civil, social, and even environmental freedoms guaranteed by laws in an era when conservative forces have gathered to suppress dissent about governmental actions. In "Librarians at the Gates" Joseph Huff-Hannon describes the courageous stand librarians are taking by defending access to controversial books, staving off budget cuts, providing a commons, and protecting the freedom of inquiry (2006).

It is up to the individual librarian to what degree she or he will defend the principles of human rights. In some cases a library's administrators may permit human rights violations but front-line librarians can make brave stands in defense. Durrani and Smallwood assert that the myth of the "neutral" librarian needs to be exploded and that it is the librarian's social responsibility to ensure that people get correct information (2006, pp. 6-7). Thus, for example, when a librarian recognizes that the U.S. government has provided disinformation on topics such as the environment, reasons for going to war, or scientific reports, it is imperative that this be corrected. Frank Rich's book on government disinformation (2006) provides numerous examples of disinformation since 2000. It is clearly within the public librarian's scope of responsibility to identify disinformation and to provide the alternate and correct facts.

Finally, public librarians, in the quest to practice library service as a profession committed to human rights, should consider what human beings require to become content, enlightened and fulfilled. The codes and promises we make to ourselves and our patrons are the same bulwarks enlightened nations use to protect their citizens. Librarians in the United States should embrace the United Nations Educational, Scientific and Cultural Organization (UNESCO) Public Library Manifesto:

> Freedom, prosperity and the development of society and individuals are fundamental human values. They will only be attained through the ability of well-informed citizens to exercise their democratic rights and to play an active role in society. Constructive participation and the development of democracy depend on satisfactory education as well as on free and unlimited access to knowledge, thought, culture and information.
>
> The public library, the local gateway to knowledge, provides a basic condition for lifelong learning, independent decision-making and cultural development of the individual and social groups.
>
> This Manifesto proclaims UNESCO's belief in the public library as a living force for education, culture and information, and as an essential agent for the fostering of peace and spiritual welfare through the minds of men and women.
>
> UNESCO therefore encourages national and local governments to support and actively engage in the development of public libraries. (UNESCO)

Public libraries and human rights are inextricably bound. We can use the sublime language of international experts to lift us up and support our efforts to standardize and improve libraries and library service. By internalizing the idealism of human rights and looking to the global manifesto of the realization of a librarian's commitment to these ideals public librarians enter the 21st century with a clear agenda, with the goal to amplify that still voice.

NOTE

1. Some of the writings and documents that form the modern conception of human rights include: the Vedas, the Bible, the Qur'an, Analects of Confucius, Magna Carta (1215), Milton's *Areopagitica* (1643), Locke's *Letter Concerning Tolerance and Second Treatise of Civil Government* (1690), Jean-Jacques Rousseau's *Social Contract* (1761), Thomas Paine's *The Rights of Man* (1791-92), the Declaration of Independence (1976), Abigail Adams, "Remember the Ladies" (1776), U.S. Bill of Rights (1791), French Declaration of the Rights of Man and of the Citizen (1789), Mary Wollstonecraft's *A Vindication of the Rights of Women* (1792), Kant's *Perpetual Peace* (1797), Britain Outlaws Slave Trade (1807), Robert Owen's *New View of Society* (1817), Susan B. Anthony and Elizabeth Cady Stanton, "Declaration of Sentiments at Seneca Falls," (1848), *Civil Disobedience* by Henry David Thoreau (1849), John Stuart Mill, *On Liberty* (1859), Amsterdam Resolution Against Colonialism (1904), Mahatma Gandhi's *Passive Resistance* (1909), Declaration of the Rights of Toiling and Exploited Peoples (1918), International Labor Organization Charter, (1919), International Convention for the Suppression of the Traffic in Women and Children (1921), Declaration of the Rights of Children (1924), League of Nations Convention to Suppress the Slave Trade and Slavery (1926), Franklin Delano Roosevelt, "Four Freedoms" (1941), UNESCO Public Library Manifesto (1994).

REFERENCES

"12 Ways Libraries Are Good for the Country." American Library Association. 2000. Retrieved August 29, 2006, from <http://www.ala.org/ala/alonline/selectedarticles/12wayslibraries.htm>.

Access to public libraries. (1963). Chicago: American Library Association.

Alexander, Linda. 2005. Gay display controversy: A threat to intellectual freedom. *Florida Libraries, 48*(Fall), 26-27.

American Library Association. (1995). Code of Ethics. Retrieved July 10, 2006 from <http://www.ala.org/ala/oif/statementspols/codeofethics/codeethics.htm>.

American Library Association. (2004). Core values statement. Retrieved June 5, 2006, from <http://www.ala.org/ala/oif/statementspols/corevaluesstatement/corevalues.htm>.

American Library Association. *Policy Manual*. Retrieved June 5, from <http://www.ala.org/ala/ourassociation/governingdocs/policymanual/intellectual.htm>.

American Library Association. International Relations Office. (1997). Resolution on IFLA, Human Rights and Freedom of Expression. Retrieved July 10, 2006, from <http://www.ala.org/ala/iro/awardsactivities/resolutionifla.htm>.

American Library Association. (2002). Office for Intellectual Freedom. *Intellectual freedom manual*. (5th ed.) Chicago. American Library Association.

American Library Association. Office for Intellectual Freedom. (1999). "Libraries: An American Value." Retrieved August 26, 2006, from <http://www.ala.org/ala/oif/statementspols/americanvalue/librariesamerican.htm>.

American Library Association. Office for Intellectual Freedom (1991). Universal Right to Free Expression. Retrieved August 29, 2006, from <http://www.ala.org/ala/oif/statementspols/statementsif/interpretations/universalright.htm>.

American Library Association. Social Responsibilities Roundtable. Hunger, Homelessness & Poverty Task Force. (2006). More on library fees and fines. Retrieved September 27, 2006, from <http://hhptf.org/article/330/more-on-library-fees-and-fines>.

Apple, M.W. (2006). *Educating the "right" way: Markets, standards, God and inequality* (2nd ed.). New York: Routledge.

Are public libraries criminalizing poor people? A report from the ALA's Hunger, Homelessness, and Poverty Task Force. (2005). *Public Libraries, 44*(3), 175.

Baltimore County Public Library's Blue Ribbon Committee. 1992. *Give 'em what they want! Managing the public's library*. Chicago: American Library Association.

Berry, J.N., III. (2006). "More Missions Are Better." *Library Journal, 131*(12), 10.

Boston Public Library. (1852) Report of the Trustees of the Public Library to the City of Boston, 1852 (reproduced in McCook 2004), pp. 28-41.

Buschman, J.E. (2003). *Dismantling the public sphere: Situating and sustaining librarianship in the age of the new public philosophy*. Westport: Libraries Unlimited.

Carvin, A. (2006). *DPOA Dies on the Vine.learning.now*. PBS Teachers (December). Retrieved April 13, 2007. <http://www.pbs.org/teachers/learning.now/2006/12/dopa_dies_on_the_vine>.

Center for Constitutional Rights (ongoing). The Center for Constitutional Rights (CCR) is a non-profit legal and educational organization dedicated to protecting and advancing the rights guaranteed by the U.S. Constitution and the Universal Declaration of Human Rights. Retrieved August 25, 2006, from <http://www.ccr-ny.org/v2/home.asp>.

Colorado Alliance for Immigration Reform. Spanish language Denver Public Libraries at taxpayer expense. Retrieved July 20, 2006, from <http://www.cairco.org/library/library.html>.

De Prospo, E.R. (1973). *Performance measures for public libraries*. Chicago: American Library Association.

Delors, J. (1996). *Learning the treasure within: Report to UNESCO of the International Commission on Education for the Twenty-First Century*. Paris. UNESCO.

Donnelly, J. (2003). *Universal human rights in theory and practice*. (2nd ed.). Ithaca, NY: Cornell University Press.

Dowlin, Kenneth E. (1987). "Access to information: A human right?" In *The Bowker annual of library and book trade information*. New York, R.R. Bowker, pp. 64-68.

Duranni, S. and Smallwood, E. (2006). The professional is political: Redefining the Social Role of Public Libraries. *Progressive Librarian, 27*(Summer), 3-22.

Durrance, Joan C. (1984). *Armed for action: library response to citizen information needs*. New York. Neal-Schuman.

Environmental News Service. (2006). EPA closing headquarters library. Retrieved September 27, 2006, from <http://www.ens-newswire.com/ens/sep2006/2006-09-22-09.asp>.

Environmental Protection Agency. EPA Library Network Workgroup (2005). EPA library network: Challenges for fiscal year 2007 and beyond. Retrieved September 27, 2006, from <http://www.peer.org/docs/epa/06_9_2_library_network.pdf>.

Faure, E. (1972). *Learning to be: The world of education today and tomorrow*. Paris. UNESCO.

Gehner, J. (2005). Poverty, poor people and our priorities. *Reference and User Services Quarterly*. 45 (Winter), 117.

Goldhor, H. (Ed.). (1997). Buildings, books, and bytes: Perspectives on the Benton report on libraries in the digital age. *Library Trends, 46*(1).

Grisham en espanol? Suburban Atlanta says no! (2006). *Access North Georgia.com*. Retrieved September 23, 2006, from <http://www.accessnorthga.com/news/ap_newfullstory.asp?ID=76733>.

Hammel, L. (2006, July 7). Library sued over borrowing limits: Homeless patrons limited to 2 items. *Worcester Telegram & Gazette News*. Retrieved July 23, 2006 from <http://www.telegram.com/apps/pbcs.dll/article?AID=/20060707/NEWS/607070715/1116/NEWSREWIN>.

Himmel, E. and Wilson, W.J. (1998). *Planning for results: A public library transformation process*. Chicago: American Library Association.

Huff-Hannon, J. (August 22, 2006). Librarians at the gates. *The Nation*. Retrieved August 22, 2006, from <http://www.thenation.com/doc/20060828/librarians>.

Ishay, M.R. (2004). *The history of human rights from ancient times to the globalization era*. Berkeley, CA: University of California Press.

Joeckel, C.B. and Winslow, A. (1948). *A national plan for public library service*. Chicago: American Library Association.

Kennedy, J. F. (1960). *Saturday Review*, October 29, 42-44. Also *Wilson Library Bulletin* (1969) 44, cover.

Leckie, G. (2004). Three perspectives on libraries as public space. *Feliciter, 50*(6), 233-236.

Library bans homeless kids from checking out books. (June 31, 2006). *Suntimes.com*. Retrieved July 23, 2006, from <http://www.suntimes.com/output/news/cst-nws-lib21.html>.

Library of Congress. On these walls: inscriptions and quotations on the buildings of the Library of Congress. Madison to W.T. Barry, August 4, 1822. Retrieved March 15, 2006, from <http://www.loc.gov/loc/walls/madison.html>.

Lynch, M.J. (1981). The Public Library Association and public library planning, *Journal of Library Administration, 2*(Summer), 29-41.

McClure, C.R. (1987). *Planning and role setting for public libraries*. Chicago: American Library Association.

McCook, Kathleen de la Pena. (2004). *Introduction to public librarianship*. New York: Neal Schuman.

McCook, Kathleen de la Pena. (2001). Poverty, democracy and public libraries. In N. Kranich (Ed.), *Libraries & democracy: The cornerstones of liberty* (pp. 28-46). Chicago: American Library Association.

Mann, Horace. (1848). (Twelfth Annual Report of Horace Mann as Secretary of Massachusetts State Board of Education). Retrieved August 28, 2006, from <http://www.tncrimlaw.com/civil_bible/horace_mann.htm>.

Martin, A.B. (1972). *A strategy for public library change*. Chicago: American Library Association.

Nelson, S. (2001). *The new planning for results: A streamlined process*. Chicago: American Library Association.
Nickel, James. Human rights. *The Stanford Encyclopedia of Philosophy* (Fall 2006 ed.). Edward N. Zalta (ed.). forthcoming URL = <http://plato.stanford.edu/archives/fall2006/entries/rights-human/>.
No mas: library nixes Spanish fiction: Decision by suburban Atlanta County angers Hispanics. (June 22, 2006). *CBSnews.com*. Retrieved July 23, 2006, from <http://www.cbsnews.com/stories/2006/06/22/national/main1745183.shtml>.
Oder, N. (2005). Florida county bans gay pride. *Library Journal, 130*(13),16-17.
Oder, N. (2004). More book challenges in TX. *Library Journal, 129*(14), 20-22.
Oder, N. (2006). Oklahoma targets gay books. *Library Journal, 131*(7), 20.
Phenix, K.J. and de la Peña McCook, K. (2005). Human rights and librarians. *Reference and User Services Quarterly, 45*(1), 23-26.
Poynder, R. (2004). Fiddling while Rome burns. *Information Today, 21*(1), 1 Retrieved July 10, 2006, from <http://dspace.dial.pipex.com/town/parade/df04/fiddling_while_rome_burns.htm>.
Public Agenda (2006). *Long overdue: A fresh look at public and leadership attitudes about libraries in the 21st century*. Americans for Libraries Council; Bill and Melinda Gates Foundation. [Electronic version]. From <http://www.publicagenda.org/research/research_reports_details.cfm?list=99>.
Public Library Association (1979). Goals, Guidelines and Standards Committee. *The public library mission statement and its imperatives for service*. Chicago: American Library Association.
Pungitore, V.L. (1993). *Innovation and the library: The adoption of new ideas in public libraries*. Westport, CT: Greenwood.
Reis, Jacqueline. (September 14, 2006). Library changes borrowing policy for homeless. *Worcester Telegram and Gazette*. Retrieved September 22, 2006, from <http://www.telegram.com/apps/pbcs.dll/article?AID=/20060914/NEWS/609140769&SearchID=73257651082380>.
Rich, Frank. (2006). *The greatest story ever sold: The decline and fall of truth from 9/11 to Katrina*. NY: Penguin.
Robbins, L.S. (1999). *The dismissal of Miss Ruth Brown: Civil rights, censorship and the American library*. Norman, OK: University of Oklahoma Press.
Smith, B.H. (2000). To filter or not to filter: The role of the public library in determining internet access. *Communication Law & Policy, 5*(3), 385-422.
United Nations. General Assembly. Universal Declaration of Human Rights. 1948. Retrieved September 17, 2006 from <http://www.un.org/Overview/rights.html>.
United Nations Educational, Scientific, and Cultural Organization. Public library manifesto. Retrieved June 24, 2005, from <http://www.unesco.org/webworld/libraries/manifestos/libraman.html>.
Varian, Bill. (June 9, 2005). Library no place for gay pride display, Storms says. *St. Petersburg Times*. Retrieved June 9, 2006, from <http://www.sptimes.com/2005/06/09/Hillsborough/Library_no_place_for_.shtml>.

doi:10.1300/J118v25n01_05

Open for Business: The NYPL Science, Industry, and Business Library Takes Stock

Kristin McDonough
Madeleine Cohen

SUMMARY. The NYPL Science, Industry and Business Library (SIBL) opened in 1996 with a primary mission to support local small business development. In the intervening ten years, changes in the information environment, including the mass adoption of the Internet, have led the library to customize its information and instructional services for small businesses with limited time to spend in the library. A dedicated small business Website serves off-site users. SIBL has adopted a range of marketing strategies including the use of its customers and partners in the non-profit and government sectors to market itself more effectively. doi:10.1300/J118v25n01_06 *[Article copies available for a fee from The Haworth Document Delivery Service: 1-800-HAWORTH. E-mail address: <docdelivery@haworthpress.com> Website: <http://www.HaworthPress.com> © 2006 by The Haworth Press, Inc. All rights reserved.]*

Kristin McDonough, MLS, MS, is Robert and Joyce Menschel Director, The New York Public Library, Science, Industry and Business Library, 188 Madison Avenue @ 34th Street, New York, NY 10016-4314 (E-mail: kmcdonough@nypl.org).

Madeleine Cohen, MLS, MA, is Assistant Director for Electronic Resources, The New York Public Library, Science, Industry and Business Library, 188 Madison Avenue @ 34th Street, New York, NY 10016-4314 (E-mail: mcohen@nypl.org).

[Haworth co-indexing entry note]: "Open for Business:The NYPL Science, Industry, and Business Library Takes Stock." McDonough, Kristin and Madeleine Cohen. Co-published simultaneously in *Public Library Quarterly* (The Haworth Press, Inc.) Vol. 25, No. 1/2, 2006, pp. 75-90; and: *Current Practices in Public Libraries* (ed: William Miller, and Rita M. Pellen) The Haworth Press, Inc., 2006, pp. 75-90. Single or multiple copies of this article are available for a fee from The Haworth Document Delivery Service [1-800-HAWORTH, 9:00 a.m. - 5:00 p.m. (EST). E-mail address: docdelivery@haworthpress.com].

Available online at http://plq.haworthpress.com
© 2006 by The Haworth Press, Inc. All rights reserved.
doi:10.1300/J118v25n01_06

KEYWORDS. Library services to small business, entrepreneurs, customization of library services, public libraries–marketing and promotion, targeted services

NYPL TAKES ON A NEW MISSION

New York City is the acknowledged hub of global financial services, and home to numerous Fortune 500 companies, Big 4 accounting behemoths, top advertising agencies, and white-glove law firms. It may come as a surprise, then, that figures from the latest *Reference USA* database of U.S. companies confirm a startling reality: firms with fewer than 100 employees account for more than 95% of the labor force in the Big Apple. Whether you follow the city's definition of small business as "fewer than 100 employees" or adopt the federal (SBA) definition ("fewer than 500 employees"), small business is the primary employer in the New York metropolitan area.

Given this reality, support for local small businesses became mission number one when The New York Public Library integrated the collections and staff of two of its Research Libraries divisions–Science/Technology and Economics/Public Affairs–with the circulating materials and librarians from its bustling Mid-Manhattan Central Library. The resulting creation became the Science Industry and Business Library (SIBL) whose name reflects the Library's focus on business, science, and technical literature that is applied by industry.

2006 marks the l0th anniversary of SIBL, the most ambitious capital project undertaken by NYPL since it broke ground for its iconic "library with the lions" at 42nd Street and Fifth Avenue. 2006 is also the start of ALA's Small Business @ Your Library campaign, which had nation-wide media coverage about public library resources and services to local businesses. This is the time, then, to see what SIBL offers to the small business community in the NYC metro area.

This merging of a branch and research library yields a comprehensive 1.4 million volume consultation-only research collection extended by a 50,000 item circulating library. More than 170 databases are licensed for on-site use only, while a smaller core of business databases is available to users at home. A robust, hands-on training curriculum developed by librarians bolsters an ongoing series of practical after-work seminars and workshops by business experts. A small business Website features links to business support groups, forms and permits, business plans, a metro area calendar of training and networking events, moderated forums and how-to videos. Add SIBL's on-site business counseling by volunteers from the Service Corps of Retired Executives and assistance from full time city employees who staff a Business Solutions Center in the library and you have all the elements of one-stop shopping for the small business community.

Many of these resources and services were not in the original plan for SIBL. Our increasingly market-oriented perspective is not the result of formal training or intentional initiatives such as a funded marketing campaign or an external consultant's report. Instead, our library managers and staff became more customer-focused and saw the need to develop new services and new products for our users as we have listened to, and learned from, those whom we serve: the aspiring entrepreneurs, business owners, business assistance groups, and expert practitioners in the metro-area small business community.

DEVELOPING NEW STRATEGIES

It wasn't always so. When we opened SIBL, many librarians believed that our superb collections constituted what in marketing parlance is a "*unique selling proposition*" that would brook little serious competition. We had the respected NYPL brand. No other information source offered our wealth of trade and technical literature–from industry magazines and journals, proceedings, and directories to product catalogs, technical manuals, equipment specs, and standards. Only here could people find free, and, under one roof, authoritative and current information on key NYC industries and the latest thinking on operations and personnel management, financing, and marketing. No other publicly accessible venue offered the comprehensive provision of city, state, federal, and international commercial regulations that came with our GPO, USPTO, UN, and EU depository status. However, we soon learned that having this goldmine wasn't enough.

In spite of daily attendance figures hovering close to 2,000 and lines snaking out the door, we were not achieving our desired *market penetration* into the small business community we were mandated to serve. Our outreach efforts confirmed that too many aspiring entrepreneurs didn't know about us, and those who did often reported that they did not have the time to find what they needed at SIBL. The majority of users at the public access workstations were surfing the Web, playing games, and reading email. A project to analyze use of stack materials in 1998 yielded the sobering conclusion that the highest use of this consultation-only material was by academics and students, not by the unaffiliated solo business owner or consultant. An intercept survey conducted several years later confirmed what we had started to suspect–that many of the regulars whom our opening announcement implored not to "Push, run, or shove as you enter SIBL" were entering for Web access. But unfortunately, those running businesses had less expendable time to compete with internet users for access to library resources. They told us that getting the information and services from SIBL simply cost them too much.

As librarians, we may have incorrectly assumed that we have a *competitive advantage* in serving all types of consumers because we do not charge fees for our resources and services. But small business users who place a high value on their time were particularly deterred by the costs in time and effort, once on-site, to access a computer, figure out how the library works, learn to use the catalog, or find an answer using a library database. We had to act.

MORE CONVENIENT CUSTOMER SERVICE

And act we did! First, Access Service staff reduced delivery time for closed stack materials. Next we took a tip from the browsing collection of our entry level branch facility and eased the retrieval of the most heavily used of our trade magazines. Close but no cigar. Our users really started to take notice when we launched "Call Ahead," in which they could phone or email requests in advance to have material waiting for them when they arrived. Another convenient new service appealed to time-pressured users: Our reference consultations by appointment designate librarians to do background research in advance of a 30-minute personalized session on optimal search strategies and resources for a business project.

The most important change took place in our Rohatyn Electronic Information Center (EIC) where users were often unable to get to the library's high end subscription databases without waiting for hours. We undertook a major reconfiguration of the EIC, and used a proxy server to dedicate more than half of the computers for database access only. The result of this reorganization was immediate access to these key resources without competition from the more casual, though avid, internet users. We require no reservations and place no time limits on the use of the database-dedicated computers. This solution, we realized in hindsight, created an *enhanced level of access for a preferred customer.*

   Streamlining access to this premium content is only part of our approach. Our *promotion* of this bounty of online information includes welcome menus with an A-Z of resources by title and a classified list of resources by broad categories. Printed versions of these lists, widely available at service desks throughout the facility, lead researchers to choices which include *Advertising Redbooks, Emerging Markets, e-Marketer, Tablebase, Business Source Premier*, and several online directories, from *Reference USA* to *Hoovers, Mergent Online*, and *Duns (D&B)* products. We added more specialized market research databases such as *Market Research Monitor*; *Market Research.com Academic, World Consumer Lifestyles* and investment and financial databases including *Investext, Galante's Directory of Venture Capital* and *S&P NetAdvantage.* We complemented these resources with niche products such as *Sports Business Research, Textile Technology Index, Food Science &Technology Abstracts, and Women's Wear Daily* online. For access to emerging technologies, SIBL subscribed to *Compendex, INSPEC, and IEEE* Explore. These e-resources can be accessed simultaneously at 45 workstations, while some databases, such as *Bloomberg* and *Factiva*, are accessible on stand-alone terminals because of license restrictions on simultaneous users.

   The Internet was fast becoming ubiquitous, an easy alternative to using the library for quick facts and ready reference. Faced with increasing competition for information *market share*, SIBL resorted to an ad-hoc marketing mix. For those unfamiliar with the "marketing process" this passage from Philip Kotler's *Principles of Marketing* is illuminating:

> Target customers stand in the center. The company identifies the total market, divides it into smaller segments, selects the most promising segments, and focuses on serving, and satisfying these segments. It designs a marketing mix made up of factors under its control–product, price, place, and promotion. To find the best marketing mix and put it into action, the company engages in marketing analysis, planning, implementation and control. Through these activities, the company watches and adapts to the marketing environment. (Kotler and Armstrong, 44)

We realized that serving the small business segment of our user population requires a mix of strategies. We have had to ask ourselves, why would even the *"preferred customer"* be willing to spend time at SIBL when the NYPL Branch Libraries offer remote access to a core of business databases? We knew that we had to heighten the *perceived added value* of the high end resources available only on-site.

ADDING VALUE

Staff makes the real difference. We've discovered that even busy New Yorkers will opt for on-site over remote because of our extraordinary *customer service*. At both our information and reference desks and out on the floor of the EIC, approachable staff direct people to the most relevant resources and give hands-on demonstrations. The staff working with small business owners and aspiring entrepreneurs ask questions about their businesses, products, and services, to form an idea of what they are trying to find and why. Small businesses are always on the lookout for new customers and clients, so business owners, when prompted, will seize the opportunity to deliver a *30-second elevator pitch* and promote their products or services. The professional library staff, ten years ago, might have thought this probing intrusive. Now most have found that there are real differences between questioning an individual about personal reading, and helping small business owners identify the information so crucial to their business needs. To assist users, a cadre of library technical assistants continually roves in the EIC, dispensing point-of-use help in the mechanics of printing, downloading, and exporting data.

Like Fred Hassan, CEO of Schering-Plough, interviewed by Stewart and Champion in a recent *Harvard Business Review*, who ranks an empowered sales force as *the* key factor in corporate success, the library's sales force, its front line staff, excel in a form of *personal selling*. They share innovative, advanced database searching techniques that justify a researcher's investment of time at SIBL. SIBL staff pride themselves on their expertise in exploiting the full functionality of databases for business solutions, such as:

- Using *Thomas Register* to identify manufacturers and to find their catalogs to ballpark equipment costs for the Capital Expenses section on a business plan,
- Demonstrating *Emerging Markets* as a source of market and company information for developing countries and as a handy same-day window into late breaking business or general news in the vernacular languages of these countries,

- Creating a list of potential subcontractors who head women- and minority-owned businesses for government contracts using *D&B Million Dollar Directory Total US,*
- Generating business-to-business (B2B) contact and mailing lists in *Reference USA* and using the data summary feature to compile market research for a business plan,
- Using *D&B International Million Dollar Directory* to find the top clothing manufacturers worldwide, ranking them by sales.

In addition to ad hoc demonstrations in one-to-one, point of use instruction, formal classes have proven to be a particularly effective and scaleable approach to making SIBL indispensable to the business community. SIBL emphasized its teaching role from the day we opened, with a high level instruction manager coordinating the efforts of more than 20 librarian "trainers." Hands-on classroom based instruction, as described by Thornton, was a major programmatic shift for the Research Libraries. Pre-SIBL, the Research Libraries had limited its teaching function to personalized exchanges with individual researchers. With SIBL and its four state-of- the-art electronic training labs came the mandate to orient the general public to information technology. In the late '90s, the Internet was a new phenomenon. We saw our role as gateway for the eager and curious public to the World Wide Web. But a few years later, when the NYPL Branch Libraries debuted its massive "Click on" at the Library program with hundreds of Web-searching and software applications classes, SIBL seized the opportunity to rethink our teaching mission. The result has been a program for a *niche audience* for our more specialized databases. In many cases we alone offer them to the public in the metro area.

We exploited the tried and true practice of *listening to the customer*. Over the decade, we had accommodated close to 65,000 students in our training programs, all of whom completed evaluations. These written assessments rated the instructor and content but also asked for input about topics and skills of most interest. This continuous customer input has helped to shape the fluid curriculum of classes that SIBL offers to walk-ins. See Figure 1 for current small business class offerings in 2006.

In the early days of SIBL's then-unique training program, instructional materials were necessarily generic, since librarians accommodated a lab full of people without common interests or needs. Several years ago, with the business world riding the crest of *service customization and personalization,* SIBL started to offer instructional sessions tailored

FIGURE 1. SIBL Business Classes

Advertising Research for Business. Presents a synergistic approach to doing an advertising plan for your small business: from doing background market research to choosing the right information sources and finally designing an effective advertising plan

Apparel & Textiles: Finding Industry & Technology Resources. Learn how to locate apparel and textile companies and manufacturers, fabric/fiber producers and finishers testing, measurement standards, market research, trends, industry surveys, tradeshows and associations.

Companies & Contacts: Creating Customized Lists. Create your own mailing lists customized by any variety of criteria. (location, zip code, sales, industry, SIC or NAICs code) and download to disk or USB flash drive.

Digital Photography Resources for Professionals. Find information resources photographers can draw on to learn about and keep up to date with this fast-changing field.

Finding Company & Industry Information for Career Transition. Learn strategies for finding industry news and forecasts, and company information that will prepare for a career transition.

Getting Started in Export Research. Locate a wealth of export information resources and services available at SIBL.

Introduction to Patents. Find patents and learn basic steps in conducting a patent search at SIBL.

Introduction to Trademarks. Locate trademarks and learn basic steps for conducting a trademark search at SIBL.

Market Research Information Sources. Locate the print and electronic resources for doing market research data at SIBL.

Small Business Information Network. Discover the resources available at SIBL and on the Web for small business development.

to the more specific needs of business owners. Many attendees are clients of service providers such as the Workshop in Business Opportunities and the Industrial Technology Assistance Corporation. Entrepreneurs are shown how to retrieve valuable market research reports and industry profiles, data from which can be plugged right into a business plan and stored on a disk for re-use in a marketing piece. Someone seeking to manufacture wooden desks can identify competitors, source suppliers of drawer fixtures, or find a distributor to the schools.

Not surprisingly, local colleges, business schools, and technical institutes with entrepreneurship tracks became fans of SIBL's classes which we gear to the specific assignments in their fashion or product design and merchandising programs. Rhode Island School of Design (RISDI), which sponsors its Idea to Product Boot Camp in NYC, features an information specialist from SIBL among the experts who advise its alumni on ways to develop, trademark, patent and market their product.

PARTNERING

SIBL's professional staff are real information handling pros, but the majority do not have long term business experience. SIBL's strategic move has been to create an hospitable and attractive environment where users seasoned with business expertise and experience come together to share knowledge. The staff at SIBL surrounds itself with women and men who are successful at commercial enterprises. These owners, consultants, and practitioners use our facilities and services, and in return they counsel or offer workshops and seminars on-site at SIBL at no charge to us. While serving our end users, these partners also enrich and deepen the SIBL staff's knowledge base about real world business situations. SIBL's reciprocal relationships with SCORE, New York City's Small Business Services Department, (SBS), and our public program presenters are mutually beneficial to all parties.

Our relationship with the Service Corps of Retired Executives (SCORE) spans the decade of SIBL's being open for business. The deal is a simple one. We provide this SBA affiliate with an attractive and well equipped venue in convenient mid-town Manhattan. SCORE gives SIBL 35 hours per week of one-on-one counseling to both start-ups and expanding businesses. SCORE counselors refer clients to our library resources and services. When they lease our facilities at very competitive prices for the low-cost seminars which they run for the public, SIBL sends staff to these sessions for free. With their established reputation for helping those with a dream to write a winning business plan and secure low interest loans, SCORE brings people into the library. In 2003, SIBL was invited to keynote a symposium on "Business Assisting Services in Libraries" in Tokyo, hosted by the Research Institute for the Economy Trade and Industry (RIETI). We suggested that SCORE also be featured to introduce the concept of voluntarism by experienced executives. SCORE's New York regional director was included in the program, and three years later we continue to refer interested parties to each other's presentations on the RIETI Website.

SIBL has also become a NYC Business Solutions Center (BSC) location, staffed by a New York City Department of Small Business Services (SBS) employee. Its office is opposite SCORE's in a prominent location near the main reference desk. This started as a straight business deal, with the SBS renting our conference facilities for a day-long planning retreat. Now it's a partnership. Impressed by the library's location, resources, and service ethos, they wanted a presence in the midst of our business start-up activities. Rather than duplicate the SBA services offered by SCORE, the Business Solutions Center deals with city permits, licenses, and regulations, and gives very targeted advice in areas such as employee training, retail site location, recycling, environmental issues, and workforce development.

Both of these organizations provide an invaluable promotional role by making the library a destination for business users. Once here, their clients are referred to library information resources and service as well as to each other.

SIBL also started to partner with business experts who are solo practitioners and entrepreneurs offering targeted consulting services in accounting, financial planning, legal services, advertising, marketing, and Web design. SIBL's program of after-work seminars, comprised of a series of small business, finance and investment, and technology programs, is based totally on their donated services. These business presenters provide us with onsite workshops and seminars in return for SIBL's providing them with *visibility and a venue,* or in the 4P's marketing paradigm, *the promotion* and *placement* of their *product.* And the *price*–from both perspectives–is right. Figure 2 shows a list of recent small business programs.

Each of these hundred or more presenters invariably becomes an unpaid promoter of the library's resources and services. Some have plugged us in the local media; others testified on our behalf at government budget hearings or nominated our small business team members for the Librarian Awards sponsored by *The New York Times.* Some of the most fervent of these champions are entrepreneurs whose businesses have been launched at SIBL. Sean Sabol is one example. Sabol designed a motorcycle detailing kit, doing all of his product, marketing, and financing research at SIBL. His success story was described in a recent profile in *The New York Times,* in which Sabol credits the library resources and the SIBL staff who helped him. When he keynoted a special networking breakfast for 60 entrepreneurs, he described and demonstrated the databases he used to create mailing lists of companies with "A" credit ratings to work with as potential distributors of his product. This kind of invaluable *product endorsement,* it's gratifying to note, is becoming more routine at the library.

Like a small business, the library relies on its customers for their feedback and for promotion. Library users who make a practice of

FIGURE 2. Small Business Programs at SIBL January-June 2006

- Accounting and Bookkeeping Essentials*
- Advertising Planning for Your Business
- Business Basics @ SIBL
- Business Monitor–Online for Your Business Needs
- Business Planning That Gets Funding
- Credit Management and Credit Repair for Entrepreneurs*
- Discover Your Marketing Genius Now . . .
- Fashion 101–How to Start Your Own Fashion Line in Today's Market*
- Free Money for Your Business
- How to Start and Operate a Home Based Business
- Import & Export Compliance 101
- Introduction to World Trade: Essentials of International Business
- Investor Education Seminar
- IRS Small Business Tax Workshop
- Latino Boom! What Every Business Needs to Know About the Hispanic Market
- Listening: The Key to Effective Selling
- Obtaining Import/Export Financing
- Pricing Strategies for Freelancers and Consultants
- Project Management and the Small Business Owner
- Real Estate: From Bricks to Clicks
- Record Keeping and Financial Statement Basics for Small Business Owners
- Self-Promotion On-Line and Off
- Trademarks: To Brand or Not To Brand
- What You Need to Know About Patents
- Writing for Trade Magazines and Trade Websites

***Available as a smallbiz.nypl.org How-To Video**

business networking and exchanging information in their professional lives have become valuable partners by promoting SIBL through positive word-of-mouth. Some bring in their colleagues to work together on a project. One free-lance business consultant regularly makes SIBL a destination for his clients, to demonstrate information databases which he can put to work for their business needs. At SIBL, we use our staff, our partners, and our customers, to help us improve and assess our products, resources, and service offerings.

Perhaps our track record with these strategic alliances or partnerships–formal and informal, institutional and individual–inspired the

British Library to work closely with SIBL for three years on planning for its newly opened Business and Intellectual Property Centre (BIPC). Colleagues from the British Library wished to exploit its incredibly rich collections and resources for business innovation and commercial enterprise. Currently they are seeking funding from the London Development Authority for a SCORE-type counseling service on their premises, on the SIBL pattern.

What has been described to this point requires our end users to come to SIBL. For too many in the small business arena, this is an unaffordable luxury. We made a big breakthrough in serving this user population several years ago when we launched a new *distribution channel*, a Website dedicated to the small business community.

SERVING USERS WHEREVER THEY ARE

"I need money to start my business, can you help me? I need a business plan–do you have samples for a day care center?" Librarians deluged with similar questions will understand why a dedicated small business Website offering 24/7 access to information and referrals to assistance agencies and experts was SIBL's next step to take us before the metro-area small business community. The result, smallbiz.nypl.org, is SIBL's virtual NYC Small Business Resource Center, with over 130 sample business plans for downloading day or night with a NYPL borrower's card. A Business Owners Manual provides a great window on the NYC regulatory environment, with links to government agency Websites for permits and licenses. An electronic rolodex, the Services Directory, brings together over 200 public and private, locally based programs, from a myriad of funding sources. This confusing alphabet soup of low- or no-cost assistance options is clarified in our fully searchable database so that someone seeking a business loan is led to listings for 100 programs or agencies for "Financing Your Business."

Confirmation that our smallbiz site was perceived as *adding value* came in 2002. The New York City Council sought permission to publish a print version of our Web directory, "*The Resource Guide to Small Business Development in the Five Boroughs*." Two years later the federal government added its endorsement when the Department of Commerce awarded SIBL a Technology Opportunities Program (TOP) grant to enhance the smallbiz Website and create a virtual small business community.

TOP funded a metro area calendar of training and networking events; a dozen how-to videos and podcasts; and moderated discussion forums. Some of the best seminar programs offered onsite at the library are videotaped and compressed for viewing on the Website. The most popular among these are "Retail Essentials: How to Open and Run a Retail Store," presented by Mercedes Gonzalez, a dynamic and knowledgeable buyer, consultant and teacher at trade shows. The workshop is chock full of practical advice and tips, as is Chuck Hunt's "Tips for Opening and Running a Restaurant." These how-to programs, viewable any time and any place through an Internet connection, are excellent resources for anyone going into the retail or restaurant industry. SIBL's partner groups and other organizations now have the option of promoting their business training and networking events on our calendar and can offer some of their best programming for possible inclusion on the Website. Program presenters from these groups, e.g., the New York Restaurant Association or the Better Business Bureau, also moderate smallbiz online forums, another valuable vehicle for promoting their service. Use of the smallbiz Website is reflected in the Figure 3, and is a strong indicator of market acceptance.

However, we need to promote the site to small businesses and start-up companies which aren't currently library users. Finding these potential customers requires that our Website be easily discoverable by search engines and offer "value-added" content. Our small business team works closely with the library's Web office, and SIBL is now looking for potential new partners for content, and sponsors and grants for additional funding support.

PROACTIVE APPROACHES

Given the pace of change, it might be foolish to try to predict what the next ten years may bring for SIBL and other libraries. Librarians can't overestimate Google's influence, since its dominance in the search area is leading many information providers to redesign their structured databases to function more like Google, and library catalog vendors are following suit.

The Internet is rapidly evolving as a mass distribution channel changing the ways that people obtain and exchange information. Social networking possibilities of the Web are beginning to infiltrate the business, professional, and education realms, and Websites including MySpace and Flickr permit everyone to publish and connect. Businesses now use

FIGURE 3. Smallbiz Website Summary Statistics, January-June 2006

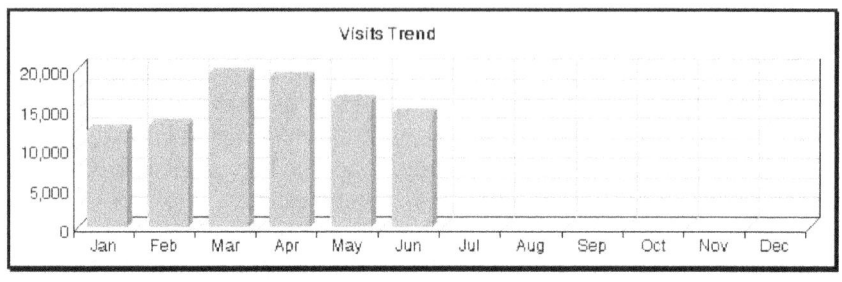

Visit Summary	
Visits	94,436
Average per Day	521
Average Visit Length	00:09:54
Median Visit Length	00:02:18
International Visits	4.63%
Visits of Unknown Origin	8.72%
Visits from Your Country: United States (US)	86.64%
Page View Summary	
Page Views	259,119
Average per Day	1,431
Average Page Views per Visit	2.74
Visitor Summary	
Unique Visitors	50,249
Visitors Who Visited Once	40,019
Visitors Who Visited More Than Once	10,230
Average Visits per Visitor	1.88

"*customer relationship management*" (CRM) software systems to gather in-depth information from their customers. We at SIBL have been particularly interested in how a company like Hewlett Packard relies on customer feedback to shift from a pure sales approach to a customer relationship focus. HP sees that its success in being perceived as a trusted partner is dependent upon a continuing relationship with its customers. Other IT and service companies have created online customer "communities" where users provide feedback on new designs, discuss or answer questions, and give technical advice, relieving the company of some of its support role. At Amazon.com, the customer gets personal recommendations and also product reviews and ratings supplied by Amazon customers.

We find these models compelling and feel that libraries could explore expanded customer feedback within our own library systems. In spite of being early adopters of the Internet, libraries have been slow to incorporate customer participation into library technology or to give library users more control over their user-library experience, aware that using even aggregated information about library customers could violate their confidentiality.

As the public increasingly has more choices, many will abandon libraries unless libraries can demonstrate good reasons not to do so. Philip Kotler notes in his marketing text, "effective positioning begins with actually *differentiating* the company's marketing offer so that it gives consumers more value than they are offered by the competition (46)." Roy Tennant, in *Library Journal*, echoes the results of the extensive 2005 OCLC study of perceptions of libraries when he observes that many people are not aware of what modern libraries have to offer, and think of the library brand as a book repository. Tennant contends libraries must rethink our services to align with the needs and expectations of current users and then find ways to spread the word about our improved services to a much broader constituency.

SIBL agrees. Our experience has shown us, in fact, that satisfied users *do* "spread the word." The venerable public library tradition of open access for all has not meant a one size fits all approach at SIBL. As SIBL began to customize our offerings to a targeted constituency it has been these users and partners in the small business community who have been our most effective marketers. And as we continue to do what every good public library does–develop customer-centric service and responsive policies–we engage in marketing–as defined by the American Marketing Association in its *Dictionary of Marketing Terms*–"the process of planning and executing the conception, pricing, promotion, and distribution of ideas, goods, and services to create exchanges that satisfy individual and organizational goals."

REFERENCES

Bulik, Beth Snyder. "HP leverages deep customer insight with opt-in-e-mail newsletter," *B to B*, 91, 4, (April 3, 2006): 59-60.

Kotler, Philip and Gary Armstrong. *Principles of Marketing*. 8th ed.; Upper Saddle River, New Jersey: Prentice Hall, 1998.

Perceptions of Libraries and Information Resources. OCLC Online Computer Center, Inc. Dublin, Ohio: OCLC Online Computer Center, Inc., 2005. <www.oclc.org/reports/2005perceptions.htm>.

*ReferenceUSA. info*USA. <http://www.referenceusa.com> accessed September 2006.

Stewart, Thomas and David Champion. "Leading Change From the Top Line." *Harvard Business Review* 84, no. 7/8 (July/August 2006): 90-97.
Technology Opportunity Program Grant <http://ntiaotiant2.ntia.doc.gov/top/details.cfm?oeam=366003002>.
Tennant, Roy. "The Library Brand." *Library Journal* 131, no. 1 (2006): 38-38.
Thornton, Ann. "Teaching the Library at SIBL." *Computers in Libraries* 19.2 (February 1999): 50-52.

doi:10.1300/J118v25n01_06

Effect of Multiculturalism and Automation on Public Library Collection Development and Technical Services

Phyllis Sue Alpert

SUMMARY. The Internet, as well as the proliferation of online resources available for purchase, has significantly changed collection management from selection to acquisitions to cataloging and processing. The nature of this work has become much more complex as our communities have become more culturally, ethnically, and linguistically diverse, as the number of information delivery mechanisms has increased, and as library consumers' expectations for speed of receipt of information have accelerated. doi:10.1300/J118v25n01_07 *[Article copies available for a fee from The Haworth Document Delivery Service: 1-800-HAWORTH. E-mail address: <docdelivery@haworthpress.com> Website: <http://www.HaworthPress.com> © 2006 by The Haworth Press, Inc. All rights reserved.]*

KEYWORDS. Acquisitions, collection development, collection management, formats, integrated library systems, outsourcing, technical services

---

Phyllis Sue Alpert is the Assistant Director in charge of Main Library, Collection Development, Automated and Technical Services at Miami-Dade Public Library System in Miami-Dade County, Florida, Miami Dade Public Library System, 101 West Flagler Street, Miami, FL 33130 (E-mail: alpertp@mdpls.org).

[Haworth co-indexing entry note]: "Effect of Multiculturalism and Automation on Public Library Collection Development and Technical Services." Alpert, Phyllis Sue. Co-published simultaneously in *Public Library Quarterly* (The Haworth Press, Inc.) Vol. 25, No. 1/2, 2006, pp. 91-104; and: *Current Practices in Public Libraries* (ed: William Miller, and Rita M. Pellen) The Haworth Press, Inc., 2006, pp. 91-104. Single or multiple copies of this article are available for a fee from The Haworth Document Delivery Service [1-800-HAWORTH, 9:00 a.m. - 5:00 p.m. (EST). E-mail address: docdelivery@haworthpress.com].

Available online at http://plq.haworthpress.com
© 2006 by The Haworth Press, Inc. All rights reserved.
doi:10.1300/J118v25n01_07

INTRODUCTION

Public libraries strive to meet the diverse needs of their community members. Mission statements frequently speak of providing "resources," "materials," or "collections" to meet the "educational," "cultural," "recreational," "informational" or "professional" needs of residents. These desires are ever changing and growing as our communities become more diverse. Today's collection management librarian must be concerned with building collections to satisfy multicultural, multiethnic, and multilingual users and must also concern him/herself with providing the materials and information in record speed. Waiting two weeks to acquire an item through Interlibrary Loan (ILL) just isn't good enough for most library users these days.

Formats for inclusion in collections continue to grow, evolving from the traditional books and magazines through the audiobooks and videos/CDs stage to a conglomerate of formats including online databases, e-books, downloadable audio, and e-videos. Some parts of collection development and technical services are much more complex and require skills, such as vendor negotiation, that have not always been taught in library schools. Yet other aspects, such as acquiring multicultural materials and items in languages other than English, are actually becoming easier to manage. Major publishers and book/material vendors have begun to realize that there is money to be made by providing these materials and are working with public libraries to address these issues. This article explores the various aspects of Collection Development and Technical Services and the technological and other changes that have taken place in recent years that have made the process much more complex in some ways yet easier to manage in other ways.

FORMATS AND BUDGET ALLOCATION

The first challenge in public library collection development is deciding how to allocate the materials budget. As the number of formats multiplies, this task becomes ever more challenging and numerous questions arise. When is the right time to add or drop a format? Now that many people in the community have DVD players, do we still need VHS? Does the community have a large enough saturation of MP3 devices to merit investing heavily in downloadables? Should the library purchase and circulate the devices? The answers vary community by community, but the constant is that this multiplicity of formats is stretching the budget thinner and thinner. Clearly it is essential for librarians today to understand the needs and wants of their neighborhoods. Careful and detailed community assessment is more important than ever in order to appropriately distribute resources for collection development.

The newer formats such as e-books, downloadable audio, and e-videos are becoming a critical part of the public library collection in order to meet the growing urgency for materials. In a world where e-mail and faxing have replaced traditional mail, consumers expect immediate accessibility to whatever they need. Library users are no exception, and these newer formats, which require no physical processing, enable the library to meet this demand. A further advantage of these newer formats is that, at those libraries with remote access, these items provide information when the library is closed. Public libraries have truly become 24/7 operations.

GROWING AND CHANGING COMMUNITY NEEDS

The U.S. Census Bureau reports 11.7 percent of the population of the United States as being foreign-born, with 53.3 percent coming from Latin America, 25.0 percent from Asia, 13.7 percent from Europe, and the remaining 8.0 percent from other regions. The foreign born population is spread throughout the country, with 11.3 percent living in the Midwest, 22.2 percent in the Northeast, 29.2 in the South and 37.3 percent in the West. Therefore, public libraries in all areas of this nation, not just in border communities, need to serve culturally and ethnically diverse populations.

The Library System at which I am employed, Miami-Dade Public Library System, has a great deal of knowledge and expertise in providing services to and building collections for an extremely diverse community. The Library System is located in Florida in Miami-Dade County, home to one of the largest immigrant populations in the United States. Over 50 percent of the population was born in a foreign country, and 68 percent of those five years old and older speak a language other than English in the home. The Library collects in 30 different languages, with heavy emphasis on fiction and nonfiction in Spanish, French, Creole, German, Italian, Portuguese, Polish, Russian, Chinese, and Yiddish.

Experience has shown that a comprehensive collection that will serve both new and well-acclimated immigrants must have items such as:

- language instruction materials in book, video, CD, and online formats;

- high interest/low vocabulary materials for adults who are just learning English;
- materials dealing with the immigration and naturalization process;
- sources on resume writing, interviewing, and obtaining employment;
- materials that support family literacy, such as bilingual books and audiobook combination sets which enable parents and children to read together;
- materials, such as folktales, folk music, and works by well-known authors, that support the preservation and sharing of various cultures;
- both original writings and translations of English items in the native languages of residents;
- magazines and newspapers from the countries of origin.

CHALLENGES OF PURCHASING FOREIGN LANGUAGE MATERIALS

There are many challenges to collection development in languages other than English. Not the least of these is the ability of staff to select and catalog materials in a language with which they are not familiar. Miami-Dade is very fortunate to have a diversified staff who speak and read a variety of languages, but this is not the case throughout the country despite the fact that library users are requesting these non-English materials.

At the Public Library Association Conference in Boston in March 2006, OCLC convened a meeting of representatives from several large public library systems to begin some discussion of the issues involved with identifying, obtaining, and processing non-English language materials and to possibly develop some collaborative efforts to improve the processes for everyone. The group identified the following concerns:

- inability to acquire new releases if you do not order immediately because of low press runs;
- lack of cataloging-in-publication (CIP) information;
- growing need for non-book materials in other languages;
- extreme difficulty in acquiring materials in African, Haitian Creole, Eastern European, and Northern and Southern Indian languages;
- need for descriptions in English so that librarians who need to select materials and/or assist patrons in finding materials in languages other than English can do so even when they are not familiar with the language.

The first step in the collaborative efforts will be to establish a platform, such as a listserv or registry, where libraries can share information regarding the languages in which they collect, those in which they have expertise, and those in which they need help, and the vendors/distributors from whom they purchase each language. It is hoped that this sharing of information might lead to a system for outsourcing acquisition and cataloging of particular languages to members of the group who have experience and competence in those languages. Since this service is rarely available from vendors, the sharing of foreign language cataloging is a particularly welcomed endeavor. As the project moves forward, the group intends to involve publishers and distributors in the discussions.

A second collaborative effort currently underway is a project by Kent State University School of Library and Information Science to translate Library of Congress Subject Headings (LCSH) into Spanish in order to provide better access for Hispanic library users. Several large libraries, including Miami-Dade Public Library System, have agreed to participate by providing bibliographic records containing English and Spanish subject headings. Although in the early stages, the project has been endorsed by the Library of Congress, which has offered its support. Both of these projects should make the process of acquiring and cataloging non-English language materials easier.

For those libraries just beginning to collect in Spanish, the ability to purchase and process Spanish language materials is actually becoming easier. The major English language vendors are now realizing that there are profits to be made selling Spanish language materials. Thus, Baker and Taylor acquired the foreign-language company *Libros Sin Fronteras* in 2004, and Brodart acquired *Books on Wings* the same year. Both companies now offer cataloging and processing on the Spanish language materials they provide.

Until recently, the materials available from the large vendors did not necessarily provide the depth and breadth needed by many institutions. The titles available were geared more for startup collections than as additions to well established collections.

Finding vendors who are willing and able to catalog/process materials in other languages is extremely difficult. Smaller, more focused vendors who are able to provide a wider variety of foreign language materials (see Appendix) do not usually offer cataloging/processing services.

SELECTION: CENTRALIZED/DECENTRALIZED VS. THE BEST OF BOTH WORLDS

The trend in public libraries nationwide is toward centralizing the decision making regarding what materials will be ordered. The days when branch staff visited a "New Book Room" at the central facility to personally select those materials most appropriate for their users are long gone. Rarely does today's branch staff pore over the latest issues of *Library Journal*, *Kirkus*, *Booklist*, *Publishers Weekly*, or *Public Library Quarterly* in search of the best books or materials to add to the collection. Instead a small group of "centralized selectors" make the decision for everyone with input from branch staff relegated to providing a "community profile," making an occasional suggestion for purchase, and sometimes having a small budget for replacements.

The benefits stated for this system of selecting materials are:

- to allow public service staff to have more time to assist the public
- to speed up the ordering process.

However, proponents of this method do not often speak about what has been lost by this move to centralize all selection. They do not mention that we have minimal input from those with the greatest knowledge of what materials a community wants in its library collection–the local branch librarians. They do not mention that, as our community's needs become more diverse, we have limited the number of selectors and, therefore, the possibility of wider and more diverse collection decisions. They do not mention that most public librarians continue to view collection development as a major and important part of the role of librarians and are extremely dissatisfied with the removal of this function from their job descriptions.

There is a better way–why not have the "best of both worlds"? By outsourcing aspects of collection development such as the creation of selection lists (not the actual selection) and the processing, cataloging and linking of materials, as well as by using centralized oversight of the lists, selection, and the acquisition process, public libraries can accomplish the positives of centralized selection and ordering without the negatives. Decentralized selection, with centralized oversight, provides just the right balance to produce a far better systemwide collection than a centrally ordered collection.

OUTSOURCING TECHNICAL SERVICES

Outsourcing refers to using vendors to accomplish a portion of an organization's business that has traditionally been done in-house. Over the last decade or more, many public libraries have outsourced various aspects of technical services such as the development of selection lists and the cataloging, processing, and linking of materials.

One area in which the major English language book vendors excel is the development of selection lists. The collection development staff of vendors have far better and quicker access to information on forthcoming and recently published materials, as well as to older materials, than do most libraries. The vendors are quite willing, sometimes at no charge but often for a cost, to produce selection lists tailored to the specific needs of a particular institution based on a profile developed by the library. The profile can ensure inclusion of titles reviewed in particular journals and specify subject areas and/or publishers to be included. This can be a major time saver, freeing library staff from poring over review journals, publishers' catalogs, and online sources. Although vendor Websites such as Brodart's "bibz.com," Baker and Taylor's "TitleSource3," and Ingram's "iPage" have significantly reduced the time necessary for library staff to produce selection lists, having vendors create tailor-made lists for an institution and place them in "carts" on the Website is far more efficient.

With the addition of just one library staff person to oversee the vendor lists, adding patron/staff recommendations to the list and rejecting items on the list that may be too esoteric for public library users, these lists can actually be far more comprehensive and better adapted to the institution than those created by library staff. The development of selection lists should be the first area that a library considers for outsourcing as the benefits most definitely outweigh the negatives, if there are any.

Outsourcing the actual selection of the materials is a far more controversial concept. Many librarians, including this author, continue to believe that selection remains an "essential" or "core" task of librarianship that should not be outsourced.

What about outsourcing cataloging, processing, and linking? Why are public libraries moving in the direction of outsourcing these areas? The stated answer is usually to increase the speed of getting materials to the public and decrease costs. In reality, however, the reason may be very different; in many cases it is actually to increase public service staffing. In a session at a recent American Library Association Annual Conference, three Directors of major urban library systems agreed that the most difficult item to get past their city/county governing bodies, regardless of the ability to cover costs within the existing budgets, is the addition of staff. Many locations have moved or are moving to outsourcing aspects of technical services in order to move behind-the-scenes positions out into public service.

Miami-Dade Public Library System has been using vendor cataloging for eight years and vendor processing for much longer. This has enabled the library to significantly reduce the number of technical service positions and move positions, as vacancies occurred, to public service. A Department that once had over 50 positions now functions very effectively with only 22 and the Administrator who manages Technical Services has also assumed responsibility for patron and staff training systemwide.

A decade ago, as libraries began demanding cataloging and processing services, the major English language book vendors were eager to take on these value-added services at a relatively low price in order to attract and/or keep business. As time goes by, the prices are creeping up and those carefully constructed cost/benefit analyses that some institutions produced several years ago might provide very different results regarding costs if conducted today.

Nevertheless, the gain in public service staff and the time saved, from ordering to placing on the shelf, especially if vendors ship the shelf-ready materials directly to the branches, may well make outsourcing worthwhile despite the costs.

VENDOR NEGOTIATIONS FOR CATALOGING/PROCESSING

Today's Collection Management Librarian will face vendor negotiations in two additional areas beyond the traditional discount from list price. These are:

1. cataloging, processing, linking, and drop-shipping of materials directly to branches;
2. purchase/lease of online products including databases, downloadable products, and e-books.

The first area is relatively straightforward and easy to negotiate. Most libraries have a clear understanding of their specifications for cataloging and processing. Those who are doing this work in-house tend to have very specific requirements; however, these may or may not be clearly documented. Libraries that do not have a written "Collection

Cataloging and Processing Manual" that lists all of the specific nuances for their institution need to develop one before initiating vendor cataloging/processing.

All the details of the technical services procedures should be rethought before negotiating with the vendors. Each of the small steps of the process will cost money. Are these steps really needed to assist the public in accessing library materials, or are they being done because "we've always done it that way?" For example, would it suffice to place the library property stamp in two places instead of three? One instead of two?

Once the specifications are clearly written, they can be presented to several vendors through whatever formal or informal bidding procedures the organization uses. Since all vendors are bidding on the exact same procedures, from a cost perspective it is easy to make comparisons between vendors. Those whose prices are way too high or way too low should obviously be avoided, especially by those libraries that do not use contracts or have very short contract terms. One needs to be careful of vendors who lowball in order to obtain your business but then cannot produce the expected quality or need to raise prices at their next opportunity.

Miami-Dade Public Library System deliberately spreads out the ordering to numerous book/material vendors. Having procedures and pricing in place with many different vendors provides libraries a much higher competitive advantage. Once the vendors are responsible for the cataloging and processing, most libraries tend to reduce the number of technical service staff on their table of organization. This makes it extremely difficult to reverse course should a particular vendor be unable to deliver the quality expected, the fill-rate needed, and the timeliness of delivery, or should the vendor demand an unrealistic rate increase at the end of a contract. The ability to easily switch business from one vendor to another is a major benefit to the library.

A testing period with every new vendor is absolutely essential. It takes a while to "train" the vendor staff to catalog and process to the library's specifications. Within a few weeks, the process should begin to run smoothly; however, library staff will probably notice very quickly each time a vendor changes cataloging/processing staff. Glitches will be inevitable until the library "trains" the new vendor staff; this is just the same as when working with new library staff.

Over the last decade or more, the large library systems have pushed all of the major English language vendors, as well as many smaller vendors, to offer these value-added services. While ten years ago, it may have been cost-prohibitive for smaller libraries to avail themselves of these services, now that these vendors have their own well-defined cataloging/processing divisions it is more likely that even smaller libraries can obtain these services at a reasonable cost, although this cost may higher than if the library were to catalog/process on its own.

The price for vendor cataloging/processing of non-print media–CDs, DVDs, audiobooks, etc.–is significantly higher than that for books and may be an area libraries may prefer to continue handling in-house.

Clearly vendor cataloging/processing allows for a reduction in technical services staff but certainly not the elimination of the department. In-house catalogers and processors will be needed to handle those items the library doesn't wish to, or cannot, outsource and will also be needed to oversee the outsourced cataloging and processing.

VENDOR NEGOTIATIONS FOR ONLINE PRODUCTS

Negotiating for either purchase or lease of online products is far trickier and much less clear-cut than negotiating for cataloging/processing. The major problem is that no two products are identical and no two library systems are equal in population, library cardholders, and other factors that vendors claim they use to establish a price. Thus it is almost impossible to make comparisons between vendors' prices. Several years ago, the State Library in Florida compiled a survey of databases purchased by libraries within the state and the prices paid for these databases. Because of the disparity in size of libraries in the state and because different libraries had different agreements with the vendors, such as unlimited access versus simultaneous users, the survey turned out to be less useful than originally intended. As a consumer, it is very difficult to determine what a fair price is for any particular database. Librarians should be pushing vendors of online products to develop more realistic pricing mechanisms that enable customers to evaluate fairly the worth of the products.

The more the vendor wants his/her product in your library, the more leverage you have in negotiating. Large library systems have a tremendous edge because vendors are eager to claim them as customers. Especially if a library is not required to follow formal bid procedures to acquire electronic products, the Collection Management Librarian needs to use the words "No thank you." Repeatedly telling the vendor that the product is very good, but the cost is excessive usually brings significant price reductions.

As pointed out by Carolyn Coco (see bibliography), "negotiating is a full-time occupation for the vendor and only an occasional event for the librarian." Librarians need to build up their bargaining skills and need to be more assertive when negotiating with vendors.

ACQUISITIONS MODULES OF ILS SYSTEMS

The electronic age has brought a major tool to the collection management process–the acquisitions module of the Integrated Library System (ILS). Miami-Dade Public Library System uses the SirsiDynix Horizon system. The other major automation vendors all have a similar module. Surprisingly, few public libraries use this section of their ILS to its fullest potential. This module allows for:

- creating selections lists or uploading lists from book/material vendors;
- transmitting orders electronically to vendors;
- receiving confirmation notices for orders;
- tracking receipt of materials;
- uploading MARC records;
- claiming items which have not been received;
- managing budgets.

Complete use of this module is not only a major time saver but also allows for systematic control of all aspects of the budget. This budget control is the major advantage of fully using the ILS module over ordering directly from the vendor Websites. The hierarchical arrangement used by the acquisition modules of most ILS systems allows the library to break down the budget to very specific categories so that it can be tracked to the branch level, the format level, or both. Although the original set-up is time consuming, once established, it can be carried over year to year. At any given time, the Collection Management Librarian is only a few keystrokes away from knowing what the budget is, how much is encumbered, how much is actually spent, and the remaining balance for any given format at any given location. This is valuable information regardless of whether one has centralized or decentralized selection.

For those libraries that are having materials drop-shipped to the branches, reports can be run from the ILS system which will enable staff to know that the materials have arrived and the invoices can be paid.

In the early days of drop-shipping to the branches, Miami-Dade had branch staff send packing slips to Technical Services where staff matched the slips to the invoices. As the amount of drop-shipping increased, this process became totally unmanageable and it was soon replaced with the ILS report method, which has worked well.

Miami-Dade has developed a checks and balances system for materials invoices. A separate database with the total of each individual invoice is balanced against the more detailed accounting from the acquisitions module which is based on ideas encumbered, received, and paid. This enables the library to easily correct the inevitable human errors that happen when handling up to one thousand invoices a month.

Another advantage of using the acquisitions module for ordering is that the items are automatically entered into the catalog, allowing patrons to place requests for materials as soon as they have been ordered.

CONCLUSION

It is clear that technology has changed the way the Collection Management Librarian does business. The process is significantly more complex than even a decade ago. However, the tools available have in many ways made the process more efficient and have enabled public libraries to keep pace with the changing needs of customers.

REFERENCES

Caron, S. (2004, May 15). Transitioning to DVD: Years of planning made for a smooth format change at Toronto Public Library. *Library Journal, 129*, S4-S5.

Coco, C. (1999, Winter). Working with library vendors: trouble-free negotiations. *LLA Bulletin, 61*, 163-71. Retrieved June 14, 2006, from H.W. Wilson *Library Literature & Information Science* database.

Dodge, C. (2005, July-August). Knowledge for sale: Are America's public libraries on the verge of losing their way? *Utne Reader, 130*, 72-77. Retrieved June 21, 2006, from SIRS Knowledge Source database (SIRS Researcher).

Fialkoff, F. (2005, July 1). Balancing act: We're way beyond "give 'em what they want." (editorial). *Library Journal, 130*, 8.

Fischer, R. & Lugg, R. (2005, July 1). The acquisitions tool belt: Ruth Fischer and Rick Lugg make sense of vendor systems. (Acquisitions' Next Wave) (Product/Service Evaluation). *Library Journal, 130*, S2-S3.

Guenther, K. (2000, June). Making smart licensing decisions. *Computers in Libraries. 20*, 58-60.

Hoffert, B. (2004, February 15). Facing down the crunch. *Library Journal. 129*, 38-40.

Jacobsen, T. (2006, March 15). Spending spree. *Library Journal, 131*, 30-33.
Kim, A. (2005, May 15). The future is now. *Library Journal, 131*, 60-63.
Knight Foundation. (n.d.) *Key Aspects of the Foreign-Born Population in Miami-Dade County, Florida.* National Venture Fund's Immigrant Integration Initiative. Retrieved May 10, 2006, from <http://www.knightfdn.org/ventures/immigrants/pdf/immigration-stats_2005_national.pdf>.
LaGuardia, C. (2004, September 1). Latino literature online (e-views and reviews). *Library Journal, 129*, 32-33.
Lugg, R. & Fischer R. (2005, July). Acquisitions' next step. *Library Journal,130*, pp. 30-32.
Marquis, S. K. (2003, March-April). Collections and services for the Spanish-speaking: Issues and resources. *Public Libraries. 42*, 106-112.
Mid-Hudson Public Library System. (2005, September). *Sample Mission Statements.* Retrieved May 3, 2006, from <http://midhudson.org/department/member_information/missions.htm>.
Pawlik, D. (2000, March 31). *The Art of the Deal: Negotiating with Vendors.* Paper presented at the PLA National Conference, Charlotte, North Carolina.
Sullivan, K. (2004, June 15). Beyond cookie-cutter selection: Two years into centralized selection at Phoenix PL, the collection is more varied than ever. *Library Journal, 129*, 44-46.
U.S. Census Bureau. State & County QuickFacts. (2006, June 8). *Miami-Dade County QuickFacts from the U.S.Census Bureau.* Retrieved May 10, 2006, from <http://quickfacts.census.gov/qfd/states/12/12086.html>.
U.S. Census Bureau (2004, August). *The Foreign-born Population in the United States: 2003.* Retrieved May 10, 2006, from <http://www.census.gov/prod/2004pubs/p20-551.pdf>.

doi:10.1300/J118v25n01_07

APPENDIX

FOREIGN LANGUAGE VENDORS

Downtown Book Center
247 S. E. 1 Street
Miami, Florida 33131
Contact: Rachel Roque (owner)
P: 305-377-9941
F: 305-371-5926
E: rax101@bellsouth.net
Materials: Spanish books, audiobooks, language instruction

Brazilian Books
10001 N. W. 50 Street, #102A
Sunrise, Florida 33351
Contact: Jose Xavier Soares (owner)
P: 954-742-8299
F: 954-741-9544
W: brazilianbooks.com
Materials: Brazilian books

Educa Vision
Educational Materials Publishing Group
7550 N. W. 47 Avenue
Coconut Creek, Florida 33073
Contact: Fequiere Vilsaint, Publisher
P: 954-725-0701
F: 954-427-6739
E: educa@aol.com
W: http://www.educavision.com
Materials: French and Creole titles

Spanish Multimedia
311 S. Pine Street, #102
Madera, California 93637
P: 800-249-2133
F: 559-674-3650
W: http://www.spanishmultimedia.com
Materials: Videos and audiobooks in foreign languages

Miami China City
41 N. W. 167 Street
North Miami Beach, Florida 33169
P: 305-655-9698
F: 305-655-9666
W: http://www.miamichinacity.com
Materials: Chinese titles

Pierre Books
18185 Biscayne Blvd.
Aventura, Florida 33160
P: 305-792-0766
F: 305-792-0613
W: http://www.pierrebooks.com
Materials: French titles

Russian Publishing House Ltd.
19 West 34 Street, Ste. 1125
New York, New York 10001
P: 212-967-1050
F: 212-967-2280
Materials: Russian titles

Swimming Upstream

Linda J. Mielke
Paula M. Singer
Gail L. Griffith

SUMMARY. "Swimming upstream" suggests a leadership model in our era of chaos and complexity that replaces the traditional hierarchical command and control way of leading in libraries. It requires the leadership actions of connection, contributions, and collaboration to build trust, success, and a healthy library system. doi:10.1300/J118v25n01_08 *[Article copies available for a fee from The Haworth Document Delivery Service: 1-800-HAWORTH. E-mail address: <docdelivery@haworthpress.com> Website: <http://www.HaworthPress.com> © 2006 by The Haworth Press, Inc. All rights reserved.]*

Linda J. Mielke, BA Business Administration, MSLS Wayne State University Library Science (Distinguished Alumna 1996), is CEO, Indianapolis Marion County Public Library, 2450 North Meridian Street Indianapolis, IN 46206 (E-mail: lmielke@imcpl.org).

Paula M. Singer, PhD, BS Cornell University, Industrial and Labor Relations, MA Johns Hopkins University, Administrative Sciences, MA Fielding Graduate University, Organization Development, PhD Fielding Graduate University, Human and Organization Systems, is Principal Consultant, The Singer Group, Inc., 12915 Dover Road, Reisterstown, MD 21136 (E-mail, & Website: pmsinger@singergrp.com, & www.singergrp.com).

Gail L. Griffith, BA Otterbein College, Sociology, MLS University of Maryland, MS Johns Hopkins University, Applied Behavioral Science, Organization Development, is Deputy Director, Carroll County Public Library, 115 Airport Drive, Westminster, MD 21157 (E-mail: gailg@carr.org).

[Haworth co-indexing entry note]: "Swimming Upstream." Mielke, Linda J., Paula M. Singer, and Gail L. Griffith. Co-published simultaneously in *Public Library Quarterly* (The Haworth Press, Inc.) Vol. 25, No. 1/2, 2006, pp. 105-116; and: *Current Practices in Public Libraries* (ed: William Miller, and Rita M. Pellen) The Haworth Press, Inc., 2006, pp. 105-116. Single or multiple copies of this article are available for a fee from The Haworth Document Delivery Service [1-800-HAWORTH, 9:00 a.m. - 5:00 p.m. (EST). E-mail address: docdelivery@haworthpress.com].

Available online at http://plq.haworthpress.com
© 2006 by The Haworth Press, Inc. All rights reserved.
doi:10.1300/J118v25n01_08

KEYWORDS. Leadership, change management, leader role, complex change

INTRODUCTION

"Swimming upstream" suggests a leadership model in our era of chaos and complexity that replaces the traditional hierarchical way of leading in libraries. It requires the leadership actions of connection, contributions, and collaboration to build trust, success and a healthy library system. This article:

- Discusses traditional and current change theories and practices, focusing on our current environment of constant change, and a letting go of the status quo
- Provides two examples in public libraries that required taking the leadership role in times of major change and stress
- Provides a model for leadership based on connection, collaboration and contribution
- Offers suggestions for leading in a world of chaos and complexity.

Woodrow Wilson said, "If you want to make enemies, try to change something."

But if you don't listen to customers, you will lose them. If you ignore staff, they will leave . . . or unionize. If you don't actively welcome children and youth, they will grow up believing you are irrelevant. If you do not hear your community, your hours will be cut, materials budget cut, staff cut, and reputation threatened. If you do not hear your funders and local Council or Authority, they will fund another project, a park, a tractor. If you don't respond to your Board, they will not respond to you. They might not hear you at all. They might ask you to leave. If you don't change, you will wither and die. If you do change, you will make enemies . . . and even on a good day, you may feel you are swimming upstream.

For many of us, our youth and careers were marked by stability. Change was inevitable, but was followed by periods of stability and constancy. One of the earliest change models, promulgated by Kurt Lewin, called for *stability, change, stability*: a freezing of the situation, followed by *a* change, which in turn was followed by a refreezing of the situation, or a new normal (Lewin). We no longer have that period of stability. There is no refreeze; there is only the "permanent whitewater" of constant change (Vaill). It is less important today to learn something new–a new skill, technology or technique–than it is to learn how to learn, as change continues to be constant.

Change is coming at us with increasing frequency, from many directions, locations, places, and levels of urgency. And not one at a time; in multiplicities. You've lived with it in the past ten years or so . . . possibly without taking a breath. You've gone to a customer-centered staffing, service, and materials model, indeed from "books" to "materials." You are networked, have partnerships, and operate 24/7. While not leaving bricks and mortar, you've added clicks, teams, technologies, talent management, and staff competencies. The library is more flexible and adaptable, less hierarchical and linear. You are sharing control and realize you can't do it alone. Your future success, indeed your survival, depends on your ability to adapt. This is a time to look at ourselves and make conscious choices, which of course is not easy in an age of permanent whitewater. There is little time for reflection when the rapids are coming at you with increasing force, speed, and duration. One can only learn how to adapt, to trust the process and to trust people. In fact, the biggest challenge for leaders is often more personal: "Senior executives were good at championing change but poor at changing themselves" (Hout and Carter).

WHY CHANGE? THE HARD FACTS

> Change is more likely to come not because the leader sees the light, but rather because she feels the heat.

Sometimes leaders choose to make changes in their organizations so they can stay on the cutting edge. More often, and more painfully, changes come about because of problems or circumstances that may be beyond the leader's control. Demographic, technological, leadership, political, and budget changes can all lead to new models and new ways of looking at and being a leader. It's not easy. It's often painful.

NEW LEADERSHIP, NEW MODEL: THE INDIANAPOLIS-MARION COUNTY PUBLIC LIBRARY STORY

We are moving the model at IMCPL toward self-service, more popular collection, centralized telephone reference, and 24/7 Web access. We are making the change because of customer demands and because the old staff-intensive model is no longer affordable. Patrons are responding to the new model by demanding more and more, and it has worked. In 2006, circulation increased 20% and door count 5%. They are happy with our changes.

Budget savings are necessary to plan for opening a newly-transformed Central Library without additional money. *Utilities alone at Central will cost us $2,000,000 a year.*

There is never enough time. Beginning a new job is difficult under the best of circumstances, but during the first few months as CEO of IMCPL I faced unwelcome changes that came at an alarmingly fast pace. I discovered that a special audit was being conducted on library finances; the Central Library building project was halted because of major construction problems; the State Legislature passed a bill taking budget authority away from the Library Board and giving it to the City/County Council; and the Council cut our operating budget $1,500,000 with the promise of more cuts based on cost overruns associated with the Central Library project. There was barely enough time to introduce myself to staff before making cuts and streamlining operations. No time to make alliances, no time to reflect on IMCPL culture, no time to educate the Board. It was a challenging time, indeed, to be a leader.

My first staff forums were held to explain that we were broke and to share a plan of how we were going to meet the payroll under our reduced circumstances. I explained "happy" things, such as capping pay ranges, redlining most positions, eliminating longevity and overtime pay, eliminating health care for future retirees, instituting a moratorium on hiring, replacing full-time people with part-time employees, outsourcing, centralizing book and material selection, floating the collection to eliminate agency ownership of materials (thereby reducing processing and transit time), eliminating outreach service to senior citizens, and transferring a literacy program (and staff) to a private non-profit. This was not the vision I expected to share, yet I believed each step was necessary to restore the library's financial health.

In addition, half of the book and materials budget was funded through bonds that were expiring. I, therefore, needed to find an additional $3,000,000 to bring the materials budget back up to $6,000,000, or 18% of the total budget. *The IMCPL Library Board feels now is the time to live within our means.*

Other libraries which either ignored or resisted the need for change have begun feeling the consequences. As an example, the Buffalo and Erie County Public Library System chose not to change ten years ago after a consultant predicted disastrous financial problems. Not adapting to this news resulted in the closure of over ten branch libraries and deteriorating service to taxpayers.

"Living within our means," the Board's mantra, has implications not only for the library's patrons, but also for staff. The public, as I indicated, is happy with more books and materials on our shelves and longer open hours. But staff ... well that is another story! The most difficult change for staff involved centralizing collection development and emphasizing more popular material. You can probably hear the comments:

> Management is dumbing-down the collection;
>
> There is a lack of specialized materials since Central subject specialists no longer have primary selection responsibility, and
>
> Weeding out older books to make way for newer books is ruining the library.

Soothing staff fears about the collection continues. Initial comments and concerns from patrons about perceived changes, motivated by a few vociferous staff, have now lessened as the staff realizes that patrons *are* indeed being served. Also, patrons are reminded that our collection extends beyond IMCPL through ILL. If you need to make severe changes to long established practices, remember that not all staff will be onboard with changes, ever. A few of ours want to form an employee union.

Staff is also not happy about their decreased earning potential. However, philosophical changes, such as centralizing collection development, are more troublesome to staff than wanting more money–which is typical for library workers.

Management staff has also had to cope with many fewer full-time staff and many more part-time and hourly employees. Turnover is greater and more training is necessary, which does change the corporate culture. Where full-time staff people tend to stay, part-timers move on at will. Full-time staff become worried that they are endangered, causing resentment and fear. Until our budget situation stabilizes, staff will be justified in their resentment and fear. We are looking at outsourcing processing and cataloging; introducing self-service for DVDs, thus reducing the need for circulation staff; and working on how many master's-degreed reference librarians are needed based on dwindling reference transaction figures.

Staff who will thrive under these circumstances are comfortable with change and see that patrons are being served well. But even the most flexible staff members can be confused and feel threatened by the number of changes and the speed at which they are occurring. If it is difficult for the leader to navigate in permanent whitewater, it is equally–or perhaps more–difficult for the rest of the staff. After all, most of us not only value what the library does, we believe that we do our jobs well. Questioning and changing the status quo brings confusion, anger, and grief at the loss of those things that are familiar, and that we value.

LEADERSHIP IN AN AGE OF CHAOS AND COMPLEXITY

Faced with such serious and complex issues, it's evident that the model of management and leadership we learned, that of command and control, is not going to survive in an era of complexity. As can be seen in Figures 1 and 2, command and control characteristics, values and leadership behavior are very different than the characteristics, values and

FIGURE 1. Values and Leadership Actions Under Traditional Command and Control Organizational Models

CHARACTERISTICS	SYSTEM VALUES	LEADERSHIP ACTIONS
Hierarchical, top-down structure Control as organizing force Predictive Organization as machine	Efficiency Expertness Replication Standardization	Commanding Controlling Delegating and/or communicating downward

Used with permission. Christi A. Olson and Paula M. Singer, *Winning with Library Leadership: Enhancing Services Through Connection, Contribution, & Collaboration* (Chicago: American Library Association. 2004).

FIGURE 2. Values and Leadership Actions Under Chaos and Complexity Organizational Models

CHARACTERISTICS	SYSTEM VALUES	LEADERSHIP ACTIONS
Flat, networked structure Change as organizing force Flexible, adaptive Organization as living system	Relationships Effectiveness Openness Local solutions Information sharing	Connecting Contributing Collaborating

Used with permission. Christi A. Olson and Paula M. Singer, *Winning with Library Leadership: Enhancing Services Through Connection, Contribution, & Collaboration* (Chicago: American Library Association. 2004).

leadership behavior demanded of us in today's era of complexity and change (Wheatley).

One primary characteristic of a complex system is its flat, networked structure. More emphasis is placed on peer relations and informal networks of information sharing. For example, a circulation assistant can email the IT Director to get information, provide customer feedback, or request services, making it more likely that customers can be served at the first point of contact. Complex organizations expect change and, therefore, they organize around it, quickly responding to emerging events or trends. This is in contrast to command and control, where change is viewed as disruptive and where the library–especially the library director– tries to control events. Leaders who want to make their libraries more adaptable will find ways to encourage staff to communicate up, across, and down the organization as needed.

The leader's goal needs to shift from trying to control change that is often out of our immediate or direct control, to *being opportunistic and responding* to change that makes library programs and services adaptable within our communities for our constituents. Examples of adaptability abound. We now have coffee bars that serve as a central hub for social and intellectual connections. The Web or internet has extended our reach to more and different users. We are open 24/7. The library goes to hospitals, schools, day care, nursing homes, and community centers. Libraries are very much alive and integral to the communities we serve. Our libraries are living systems.

In order to maintain their adaptability and take advantage of key changes in the environment, libraries need to encourage people to create and maintain many informal relationships. Libraries need to be highly networked, both internally among staff and employees, and externally with customers, constituents, partners, public officials, and other stakeholders. Building and sustaining relationships is critical because it is a primary way the library can find out "what's going on" in order to monitor activity and change. Complex organizations tend to be very open because they rely on critical information networks to get work done. Information sharing among members of the library becomes a top priority, allowing people to respond positively to events and decisions that impact the organization. Mutual trust among staff is critical in order to create and sustain healthy relations that contribute to openness and information exchange. For example, it is possible to create a budget through an open process. Rather than begin the conversation with a few people in the room, an open process encourages input from all departments. Budget allocations and tradeoffs can be set by the larger group or team if key priorities and strategic initiatives are communicated and shared by team members and the executive staff. Project budgets can be shared among team members and tradeoff decisions made in the same way. A staff used to working in this way can more easily collaborate to deal with more serious issues when they arise.

We need to emphasize *effectiveness over efficiency*. Effectiveness means that people consider solutions that serve the stated needs of your partners and constituents as a first priority. What is effective may not necessarily be efficient and vice versa. In many instances, project designs and outcomes can and should be both effective and efficient. Beginning a discussion of the effectiveness of current practices is a good way to quickly identify the values–and sacred cows–in any library. In some libraries, considering how to use MLS staff most *effectively* to meet customer needs will spark a spirited discussion about how many MLS staff are needed and what tasks it takes an MLS to perform *effectively*. In some libraries, having a staff of MLS-prepared catalogers was once considered an *effective* practice; now, most public libraries consider that to be neither effective nor efficient.

In complex organizations, local solutions are favored over replication and standardization across the system. For example, the same new Young Adult program that is being implemented in a San Francisco Bay Area suburb will not necessarily work the same way in Phoenix or a suburb in the greater Baltimore area or even in San Francisco's center city or Chinatown. In addition, centralized collection development works best when particular needs of local branch libraries can be accommodated. A good rule of thumb is that 70% to 80% of a process can be replicated across different branches, but the remaining 20% to 30% needs to be modified to meet local needs.

CONNECTION, CONTRIBUTION, AND COLLABORATION

Leadership actions that make chaos and complex systems work are *connection, contribution and collaboration*. Leaders working out of this framework focus their energies on connecting. *Connecting* is a critical leadership skill because connections support and make possible the relational structure that fosters information sharing and keeps the system open and working. These leaders create and sustain connections both internally among employees and externally with the community, city or county government, and other relevant stakeholders. Leaders also re-form and even change connections based on the library's goals and strategies, priority projects and political processes and key players, including appointed and elected officials. Leaders take actions that are situational; they take advantage of change to move and leverage the organization so that it is always positioned for growth and success. *They make sure the library always has a place at the table.*

The work of leaders involves *contribution,* the second action, consisting of linking to and making explicit each employee's specific work or job and tying it to the success of the library's goals and strategies. In other words, each employee needs to be able to see how she or he makes an impact in the overall success of a project or the everyday running of the library. We view our people resources in terms of job functions and, therefore, make assumptions about what employees can and can not do based on their formal role. Yet people have multiple talents and gifts that are sometimes underutilized at work because they are not encouraged or allowed to work outside of their specific job duties. Identifying contribution as a key leadership focus enables people to form new and different relationships and share information across departments. It encourages creativity and often inspires excitement among employees because more of their talents are being utilized. It breaks down boundaries and fosters networking within the library and between the library and its stakeholders and partner organizations. In other words, it helps to keep the system healthy and strong.

Collaboration is the third reinforcing action. Collaboration refers to the way we do our primary work. It is used when problems or situations are viewed as complex, new, unfamiliar and challenging. Collaborating on projects, programs, budgets, and strategic plans creates a sense of shared understanding and interdependency among staff members. It also results in effective and creative solutions because more people are involved at the outset. Collaboration brings in more diverse perspectives and talents. Collaboration can also be slow and messy because team members have to work out differences and be willing to make tradeoffs on behalf of the good of the whole team, rather than one individual's needs. Leaders need to encourage collaboration because of the value it brings in implementing new programs and services and solving big and complex problems. If library leaders are not engaging their employees and stakeholders in the work of connection, contribution, and collaboration, the library will find it difficult to respond effectively and quickly enough to changes in the environment.

OUR "BOTH/AND" WORLD

These two approaches–command and control, and chaos and complexity–are both present and active in our daily behaviors and actions. The reality is that we live and work in what we call a "both/and" world. At times our teams and libraries reflect the characteristics of command and control; at other times they are highly responsive and adaptable to change. There is a natural and necessary tension between these two influences and ways of leading. Library leaders need to be able to navigate so that libraries can maximize the benefits of each approach. Too much of either is not healthy and can result in underperforming projects and target shortfalls. If a leader, team, or organization is overbalanced toward command and control, then people will experience the organization as rigid and bureaucratic (lots of rules and policies that tend to delay decision-making or prevent people from getting the real work done), stifling (lack of initiative and creativity because people are afraid to take risks for fear of retribution), and out of date with current management and leadership practices. On the other hand, if a library is too chaotic and reacts to all change, then people will experience it as too disruptive (not enough stability or consistency), slow moving in terms of decision-making (usually characterized by an over reliance on consensus), and a diffusion of vision or focus (deploying scarce resources on multiple or too many opportunities and initiatives).

TRYING TO GET IT RIGHT

Unfortunately, there is no perfect environment, no laboratory where a leader can apply the principles of Connecting, Contributing, and Collaborating and guarantee a good outcome. In most real-life situations, one or more of these things can happen:

- Communication goes awry. It's easy to assume that people hear what is said, or understand what it means to them–when in fact, most of us need to hear it more than once and need time to absorb it. The situation may be so urgent, or so rapidly-evolving, that there is not enough time to share information widely. If the news media are interested, staff and even Board may be learning about unfolding events through a reporter. Without full, frequent, and frank communication, it is hard for a leader to establish and maintain trust.

- A new leader who "inherits" a crisis may not have enough time to establish trust, or even a good working relationship with staff and Board before he or she has to act. As a result, staff may not perceive a need to change, may not see clear direction, or may disagree with the direction because the leader has not had time to establish credibility.
- Board members may disagree with each other or with elected officials, and the leader can be caught in the crossfire.
- When quick action is required, solutions are sometimes designed without enough staff involvement–or without having the right people involved.
- Leaders and senior managers have often had longer to think about the changes that will need to occur, may forget that other staff members need some time to absorb the information, and become impatient with the normal process of change and transition (Bridges).

When the change is out of the leader's control, and when staff experience fear, they often express that fear by having unreasonable expectations of the leader. In truth, no leaders can guarantee safety and security. The best they can do is to try to get it right, usually with less than sufficient information.

WHEN IT WORKS

When a leader is able to navigate the "permanent whitewater" successfully, the transformational impact on the organization may be felt for years to come. Consider the story of the Carroll County (MD) Public Library, a county system threatened with a 14% budget cut in the late '90s because of a downturn in the state's economy. In this case, the leader was also Linda Mielke. Her strategy was to flatten the organization in order to avoid layoffs while maintaining service to customers. A number of the short-term strategies were very unpopular with staff, and some of the longer-term changes were controversial as well. For example, the library chose to eliminate registration for storytime programs in order to save staff time and allow more people to attend the programs. This decision was made in order to increase both efficiency and effectiveness, and triggered a series of conversations about what constituted a *quality* program experience. The bottom-line result was that program attendance increased and more library customers were served. But the real transformation occurred because the library moved to cross-functional teamwork–a decision by senior leaders to change themselves and share their power. Teamwork took several years to become fully institutionalized, but it has allowed staff at all levels to *contribute* their skills, *collaborate* with each other, and *connect* with each other and the community to create results they care about.

CONCLUSION

There are no guarantees that leaders can guide their libraries safely through the many challenges sure to come. Even the most astute leaders may find themselves unable to finish the job for reasons beyond their control. In some situations, leaders must look at themselves from the beginning as change agents whose job is temporary. But even without guarantees, it is possible to prepare for the unknown. The most effective preparation is to concentrate on the quality of relationships and engage staff in meaningful work together. Working together in this way, leaders and staff make it more likely that their libraries can not only survive turmoil, but grow and thrive. And for many leaders, helping their libraries transform means being willing to transform their skills, their leadership styles, and themselves.

REFERENCES

William Bridges, *Managing Transitions: Making the Most of Change* (Cambridge, MA: Perseus Publishing, 2003).
Thomas M. Hout and John C. Carter, "Getting It Done: New Roles for Senior Executives," *Harvard Business Review* 73 (1995): 133-146.
Kurt Lewin, *Resolving Social Conflicts.* (Washington, DC: American Psychological Association, 1997).
Christi A. Olson and Paula M. Singer, *Winning with Library Leadership: Enhancing Services Through Connection, Contribution, & Collaboration* (Chicago: American Library Association, 2004).
Peter Vaill, *Managing as a Performing Art: New Ideas for a World of Chaotic Change* (San Francisco: Jossey-Bass, 1991).
Margaret Wheatley, *Leadership and the New Science: Discovering Order in a Chaotic World,* 3rd ed. (San Francisco: Berrett-Koehler Publishers, 2006).

doi:10.1300/J118v25n01_08

Marketing and Advocacy: Collaboration in Principle and Practice

James A. Nelson

SUMMARY. There is renewed interest in building and sustaining support for public libraries in this country. This paper looks at the concepts of marketing and advocacy as integral components for building this sustainability and uses two related initiatives in the State of Kentucky to illustrate, in practice, how these concepts differ and how they need to work together for long term success. In short, "selling" libraries in itself won't get the job done; nor will just building a public advocacy infrastructure. Taken together, however, both can advance the case for libraries and build the support needed for sustainability. doi:10.1300/J118v25n01_09 *[Article copies available for a fee from The Haworth Document Delivery Service: 1-800-HAWORTH. E-mail address: <docdelivery@haworthpress.com> Website: <http://www.HaworthPress.com> © 2006 by The Haworth Press, Inc. All rights reserved.]*

KEWORDS. Marketing, advocacy, sustainability, public libraries, state library agencies, state library associations, Institute for Museums and Library Services, federal library programs, legislature, public library caucus, libraries build communities, legislative committee state budget

---

James A. Nelson, MSLS, is State Librarian and Commissioner of the Kentucky Department for Libraries and Archives, 300 Coffee Tree Road, Frankfort, KY 40501 (E-mail: jimmpnelson@adelphia.net).

[Haworth co-indexing entry note]: "Marketing and Advocacy: Collaboration in Principle and Practice." Nelson, James A. Co-published simultaneously in *Public Library Quarterly* (The Haworth Press, Inc.) Vol. 25, No. 1/2, 2006, pp. 117-135; and: *Current Practices in Public Libraries* (ed: William Miller, and Rita M. Pellen) The Haworth Press, Inc., 2006, pp. 117-135. Single or multiple copies of this article are available for a fee from The Haworth Document Delivery Service [1-800-HAWORTH, 9:00 a.m. - 5:00 p.m. (EST). E-mail address: docdelivery@haworthpress.com].

Available online at http://plq.haworthpress.com
© 2006 by The Haworth Press, Inc. All rights reserved.
doi:10.1300/J118v25n01_09

INTRODUCTION

Public libraries have consistently been engaged in various strategies to garner and sustain support for their services over the many years they have been around. One thing everyone one seems to have come to understand is that it's not enough to simply state, "libraries are good and essential services for people in our community" and expect everyone to "get it." Another issue which seems to be clear is that to garner sustaining support requires both good marketing and effective advocacy efforts, working in tandem, feeding off each other to get the job done.

A recent benchmark public opinion survey done by Public Agenda, a survey research firm founded in 1975 by social scientist and author Daniel Yankelovich and former US Secretary of State Cyrus Vance, found the need for better marketing and advocacy by public libraries to be an important issue for building successful community support for libraries. This survey was paid for by The Americans for Libraries Council and the Bill and Melinda Gates Foundation as part of their long term efforts to help develop self-sustaining public library services in this country. The report from this survey is called *Long Overdue: A Fresh look at Public and Leadership Attitudes about Libraries in the 21st Century*, and there are several issues mentioned in the report which are quite revealing about what public libraries should do to advance their missions and services into the next century.

Long Overdue does say that people generally understand libraries to be good and essential services. In fact they found that "by a significant margin, well-run libraries are at the very top of the list of services that people believe their own local communities do a good job of providing; ranking them ahead of parks, public education, health care and well-maintained streets."[1] All the positive reactions the survey team found would make one believe that libraries are secure in having good community support and sustainability; however, when community leaders were polled, the results indicate that "Public Libraries' lack of marketing, impassive advocacy and isolation from the community were also cited as shortcomings in library performance."[2]

There is no question that libraries must be intimately involved in their community and focus their services and resources on key community problems, but effective marketing and advocacy are important to make sure people understand that there are indeed partners for progress in the communities they serve. One group which was specifically asked for their attitudes about libraries is referred to in the report as "Community Soldiers"–not elected officials, but civically engaged individuals who can sway public opinion and influence outcomes on various issues because of who they are (vote in every election, volunteer a great deal, belong to civic clubs and/or donate money to charitable causes). They tend to be library users and view libraries as essential services, but "the people whom local politicians are most likely to listen to are also the most likely to be unaware of possible threats to the funding of library services."[3] This finding obviously speaks to the need to inform, in a meaningful, community oriented way, these important library supporters.

Sometimes we blur the issues of marketing and advocacy, blend them, or confuse them altogether and that is a problem for making the kind of impact our libraries will need to be better appreciated and to sustain the kind of support required for quality library services. The report even finds that "library education needs to change so the librarians are better trained to be advocates and leaders of institutional growth and change."[4]

This paper will attempt to clarify the relationships between marketing and advocacy while linking the essential impact potential of both. This will be done through a description of marketing and advocacy efforts being implemented in Kentucky by two statewide organizations with shared missions–the Kentucky Public Library Association and the Kentucky Department for Libraries and Archives. In doing this, it should become apparent that blending the principles of both marketing and advocacy through collaboration between these two statewide organizations offers one model for practice that could help ensure the sustainability of public libraries in a very competitive public agenda.

After a brief discussion of general marketing and advocacy principles, we can look more specifically at how the two statewide organizations with shared missions were able to put these principles into practice to help advance public library support and sustainability for the people of Kentucky.

Marketing and Advocacy Principles

Just for the sake of context, it makes sense to look at how those in the business of marketing and advocacy approach their work. First, the American Marketing Association defines marketing as "an organizational function and a set of processes for creating, communicating, and delivering value to customers and for managing customer relationships in ways that benefit the organization and its stakeholders."[5] While this is obviously the authoritative definition, set by a national organization which represents marketing interests, a quick trip to Wikipedia not only uses this definition, but adds, "Marketing is the ongoing process of moving people closer to making a decision to purchase, use, follow . . . or conform to someone else's products, services or values. Simply, if it doesn't facilitate a 'sale' then it's not marketing."[6] Given these definitions, the essential elements here seem to be effectively communicating with an organization's customers so they will make decisions favorable to the organization and its stakeholders, be they stockholders or other individuals or organizations who will benefit from the marketing efforts.

In looking for similar assistance on understanding the general principles underlying advocacy efforts, it seemed that one good authoritative source would be to look at an organization which helps nonprofits do just this–NP Action, an online resource developed by OMB Watch to provide a "constantly updated mix of information and tools, drawn from the expertise of organizations and seasoned advocates across a wide range of advocacy activities and policy disciplines in order to encourage greater participation by nonprofits in the policy arena." This organization is important because it helps nonprofits understand what they can and cannot do within the constraints of other public policy. They have been long engaged in helping organizations like libraries compete in the challenging environment of public policy at the federal level, but their advice offers good direction at the state and local level as well.

NP Action says that "'advocacy' encompasses any activity that a person or organization undertakes to influence policies. There is great latitude in this definition, and some people consider advocacy to be all activities that are not specifically lobbying, such as public demonstrations, or the filing of friend of the court briefs."[7] They go on to say that

> Lobbying is one important form of advocacy and public policy participation that involves attempts to influence specific legislation. Lobbying by public charities, 501 (c)(3) organizations, is protected by the constitution. The Internal Revenue Code regulates charities, foundations and other nonprofits lobbying activities and expenditures. It is important for all nonprofits to understand the legal opportunities for them to lobby and influence legislation that affects their mission. Why? Because lobbying can bring about policy changes that improve people's lives.[8]

In the most general of terms, marketing is selling and advocacy is lobbying by implication, so let's look at two Kentucky library organizations with shared missions and their efforts to put these principles into practice.

Marketing in Practice

While marketing and advocacy efforts have been going on in Kentucky for some time, both gained momentum and focus in the last several years. One issue driving the plan for improving marketing skills in our public libraries was the general concern that our profession frequently looks inward in "selling libraries"–library marketing campaigns tend to reflect what we see and think about libraries, not what community leaders and the general public see and think, or need to think about libraries. To help address this issue, KDLA, as part of its federal program funded by the Institute for Museums and Library Services, began its KDLA@yourlibrary initiative to help lay a foundation for library marketing which would be based on strong citizen input.

This initiative was designed by the communications office and Field Services Division (public library development division) at KDLA. An RFP was published to hire a consultant to help with designing and implementation the KDLA@yourlibrary project and implementation began in 2001. The fundamental purpose of this ongoing project has been to develop a cadre of savvy public library staff and trustees who can help articulate the importance of public libraries in Kentucky and their need for community support.

During the summer and fall of 2001, KDLA held five Citizens' Forums throughout the Commonwealth: in Paducah, Bowling Green, Pikeville, Georgetown, and Somerset. These meetings brought together about 150 movers and shakers from these and surrounding communities, who were targeted by local and regional librarians, along with suggestions from trustees. This was an intentional effort to reach out to the citizen stakeholders and community leadership, not just the library community, to help provide a foundation to plan marketing efforts.

At each forum, participants were asked six critical questions: "What is it that the public library does that is of value to the community?"; "What does the library do better than anyone else in town?"; "If you were to change anything about the public library, what would it be?"; "What is the greatest threat to the public library?"; "What is your greatest fear about the future of public libraries?"; and, "If the public library were meeting all of your community needs, what would it look like in five years–considering programs, services, facilities?"[9]

Second, at each Forum, participants were asked to tell their own stories: to give a brief account of "What my public library means to me." This also provided valuable and sometimes moving anecdotal material.

With this information as a base, and with the assistance and approval of the Kentucky State Advisory Council on Libraries, the planning team crafted an enduring statement of "Values" which expresses the importance of libraries to the Commonwealth of Kentucky. Based upon that statement of values, the team also created a "Case for Support," which will be edited from time to time, as factual information evolves. These two documents will be useful to Kentucky's library community in both awareness and advocacy efforts.

The "case for support" which emerged was "Public Libraries are the center of our communities. They demonstrate democracy, neighborliness, community pride and provide access to technology and lifelong learning for all citizens in Kentucky."[10] While the statement is brief and succinct, intentionally so to be of more interest to community leaders and the general public, each component was developed in a "Values" section, which was edited and approved by the State Advisory Council on Libraries. These values came out as follows:

Democracy

Public libraries provide equal opportunities for everyone. They represent the essence of democracy and diversity, providing services to all citizens, regardless of age, socio-economic position, or race. Through services and programs, public libraries build equity in their communities–providing forums for expressing all points of view, along with equal access to information and programs.

Lifelong learning

Public libraries help patrons build a brighter future, through library research materials and on-line learning. Librarians are trained experts in finding information wherever it exists, on the Web, or from more traditional sources. Public libraries are also places of entertainment for all ages. Patrons seek the public library to provide many "first" experiences such as parent-child story hours, access to computers, on-line job searches, inquiries to state government, voting information, and research. For many, early experiences with public libraries are the source of their love of learning and reading.

Neighborliness

In communities across Kentucky, the public library serves as the family-friendly cultural and community center. Libraries build communities, providing a focal point through classes, services, activities, and a place for the community to come together. People are welcomed equally when they walk through the door. Public libraries are unique in this aspect: providing access to nearly anything in print or on the Internet as well as personal service and assistance.

Technology

Libraries are on the forefront of the new information age. They provide equal access to the information highway, opening doors to knowledge in a world where information is power. The public library provides your neighborhood access to state government, job searches, developing resumes, globe-trotting, doing homework. It's the local "how to" resource, complete with trained professionals to help navigate the information.

Pride

Public libraries reflect our local pride. They are integral to economic development as a factor in attracting businesses to communities. They provide tourist attractions to citizens researching genealogy, as well as offering special collections and exhibits. Public libraries are repositories of local history, culture and shared knowledge. As community centers, they are a hub of activities, building respect for cultural, intellectual and racial diversity.[11]

Given this set of fundamental values, the planning team initiated a Public Awareness Institute to help train library staff and trustees in the techniques and methods for better communicating the value of libraries to Kentucky communities and they set about designing the training program itself. This program begins with an open application process where local libraries apply to become part of a year long process which includes periodic training sessions around the state designed to assist them in actually planning a local marketing project for their libraries. The project planning team selects participants based on these applications, and the groups are relatively small, in the teens, to give more individual attention to the projects being planned and implemented.

The Institute itself consists of four sessions, each 1½ days in length, at a state park. Each session features a specialist who can assist participants in better understanding the elements of marketing their libraries and the format helps build a sense of teamwork so they have colleagues to learn and get support from. The final session of the institute is designed to allow participants to present their marketing programs to the group and get collegial feedback from other participants. Over time, as more and more individuals go through this process, a body of knowledge on successful (and not successful) marketing strategies and programs will be developed to create a critical mass of library messages and strategies which can raise awareness of the value and importance of public library services in the Commonwealth.

The projects done this year reflect the varied nature of how each county approached its own particular needs for local promotion and marketing–promoting the library as "the Answer Place" in Madison County; creating new logo/marketing materials in Taylor County; inaugurating a library newsletter in Hancock County; developing new procedures/policies regarding staff relations in Nelson County; putting in place new ideas for community outreach in Rowan County; starting a friends group in Boyd County; Expanding technology and bookmobile outreach in Fleming County; creating a library cultural series with the local college in Laurel County; development of a community health-related program in Meade County; "The Smartest Card" billboards and ad campaign in Scott County; Website development in Pike, Calloway, and Crittenden Counties: and, new logo and community activities in Mercer County. All of these projects were deemed to be of the most importance and value by the local library, so the participants in the Institute were all motivated to attend all sessions and complete their projects.

Advocacy in Practice

The Kentucky Library Association (KLA) has long had some form of legislative effort, including a committee whose mission has been to build political support for library issues. As with many professional association committees, the leadership represented various types of libraries and individuals from various positions in those libraries. The terms of members and leadership followed the typical limited appointments and this situation hampers the kind of steady and ongoing leadership which allows for meaningful patterns of influence to develop. The fact is, in our profession only public libraries and state library agencies have direct access to the political infrastructure and that was missing in the KLA efforts. In the early 1990s, the Public Library Section of KLA decided that it needed to form its own legislative committee and proceeded to do so. As part of this committee structure, KDLA was invited to be a non-voting member of the committee to help unify state association and state agency policy. This actually fit an earlier effort by the two parent organizations in the early '80s.

In these earlier years, KLA and KDLA reached out to each other to unify the statewide influence of the two organizations. What resulted was to make the State Librarian a permanent non-voting member of the KLA Board of Directors and the KLA president a permanent non-voting member of the State Advisory Council on Libraries. Once the Public Library Section formed its legislative committee, it included the State Librarian along with the directors of the two library divisions at KDLA and the individual who manages communications for the department. As it has evolved, this arrangement works well since the KDLA members of the legislative committee don't vote (in fact, most business is done by consensus and there are seldom votes taken), but the communication is tight and there is a very real and ongoing coordination between the two organizations.

The KLA Public Library Section followed the pattern of forming its own association while remaining a unit of KLA and became the Kentucky Public Library Association, KPLA. Now the legislative committee is officially the KPLA Legislative Committee and its leadership has been consistent for several years. The other main action this group has done–the KPLA members, not KDLA–is to hire a legislative agent who works in their interests with legislators.

While it might appear that this evolving relationship between KDLA and the public library community is exclusive to that community of interest, it actually isn't–Kentucky has a remarkably close and collaborative library community of all types. In fact, there are few political issues affecting other types of libraries that don't also impact public libraries and it's also true that most library customers are ultimately impacted by the health and welfare of their local public libraries. With their natural connection with community leadership–the "Community Soldiers"–public libraries have considerable potential to impact many issues which all types of libraries are struggling with.

Over the years, the KPLA Legislative Committee has had several campaigns and activities to influence state library issues, but the most impressive have occurred over the last two legislative sessions and these reflect the growing maturity and sophistication of their political influence. In the 2004 session, the KPLA Legislative Committee launched a major bookmobile campaign to use this legacy Kentucky program (we have traditionally had the largest bookmobile fleet in the country and it's an extremely popular service in Kentucky) to gain visibility for public libraries and to garner support for the library legislative agenda. This also happened to be the year of our 50th anniversary of the state bookmobile program and several local and regional events were planned to follow the legislative session.

Kentucky has 107 outreach vehicles on the road–84 traditional bookmobiles, two cybermobiles (wireless with satellite dishes on them), and 21 outreach vehicles. In 2004, these vehicles spent over 100,000 hours on the road and served almost 500,000 customers with 1.7 million materials circulated, so it's big business for our state. The KPLA Legislative Committee planned a two-phase campaign to highlight public library needs: a "Public Library and Bookmobile Day" in Frankfort and a second phase which would consist of grassroots celebrations of the Golden Anniversary of Kentucky's statewide bookmobile program. Judith Gibbons, director of the KDLA Field Services Division, wrote an article for *Marketing Library Services* about this ambitious initiative, a significantly visible example of library advocacy in 2004.[12] With 70 bookmobiles circling the capital during the legislative session, Kentucky's public libraries demonstrated their presence in a meaningful way.

For the 2006 legislative session, the KPLA legislative committee planned a campaigned based on the theme that "Libraries Build Communities," the same theme that ALA took to New Orleans this year. Going into the session, the KDLA budget and the "ask" for the KPLA legislative advocacy mirrored each other. The same description of need and program request was made in the budget overview which KDLA submitted and the handout the KPLA Legislative Committee took to Frankfort during the session. Their message was highlighted by having the theme printed in black on yellow construction hats which the advocates wore and presented to their members in the legislature.

The following document is what was handed to Representatives and Senators in the Kentucky General Assembly to articulate the needs of public libraries in Kentucky and what kind of appropriation would address those needs.

LIBRARIES BUILD COMMUNITIES

Over 2 million Kentuckians are registered at their local public library. These include teachers, students, parents, children, grandparents, faith communities, government workers–people from all walks of life. Our libraries are trying to serve this large and geographically diverse population, but local resources are stretched to the maximum.

Only 4% of local library budgets come from the state while public schools receive 50.5% state support and our public postsecondary institutions receive 50%. In order to address the needs of library users across the state, it's critical that we have a greater investment from the Commonwealth. This investment should come in the following ways:

PUBLIC LIBRARY FACILITIES CONSTRUCTION FUND, KRS 171.027–*creating a sense of place and a place to meet, learn and relax*

Kentucky's public library facilities are 539,718 sq ft short of minimum standard and 78 of the existing buildings are over 20 years old. As major institutions for bringing communities together, libraries need more and better space to address an information driven economy and a bewildering array of educational, cultural and social challenges facing us. It would take nearly 95 million dollars just to address the minimum square foot standards shortfall. Using local government bonding capacity, we could accomplish 25% of this unmet need in the biennium with $1 million in 2007 and an additional $1 million in 2008.

PUBLIC LIBRARY IMPROVEMENT AND EQUALIZATION FUND, KRS 171.201–*building resources and services for learning, earning and nurturing families"*

This program was established to assure quality and equity in contemporary library and information services to improve early childhood development; support lifelong learning opportunities; enhance economic development; enrich cultural resource opportunities for all Kentuckians; and, expand adult education and adult literacy programs. Although the statute became law in 2000, it has never been funded. We seek $6 million annually to help local libraries provide the services listed above; as stated in KRS 171.201(4).

LIBRARY SCIENCE SCHOLARSHIP FUND, KRS 171.303–*educating professional staff for 21st century information services*

Kentucky ranks 45th in the number of librarians with master's degree education. Nationally it is estimated that over 46% of librarians will retire by 2008. Clearly we need to be recruiting and educating new professional librarians for our state. To accomplish this, we are requesting a modest beginning of 10 scholarships in 2007 and 20 in 2008 at $5,000 each in order to help Kentucky meet its growing need for a new and diverse professional library workforce. We need $50,000 in 2007 and $100,000 in 2008 to get this critical program started.

MOBILE AND VIRTUAL ACCESS–*serving the information and knowledge needs of a geographically diverse population*

Kentucky is still primarily a rural state and our people are spread over a broad geographic region. We need to restore funds used to continue our historic bookmobile program as well as the grants we give for access to resources in the Kentucky Virtual Library. We need $275.000 annually to help overcome the problems of an aging bookmobile fleet. Of our 101 bookmobiles on the road today, six are over 17 years old and another 29 are between 10 and 16 years old. KYVL serves all Kentuckians, but it is a critical resource for teachers and students in our P-16 education programs. We need $111,100 annually to restore funding cut from that program.

Libraries: the forgotten partner in strengthening families, improving lifelong learning and fostering economic well being. Library Legislative Day February 8, 2006

Compare this Legislative Committee information to the KDLA Budget Overview component dealing with just the agencies' public library request for appropriations. The purpose here was to make sure those who were reviewing the budget request would see essentially the same information from the KPLA document–another example of how collaboration can work at a variety of levels.

KENTUCKY DEPARTMENT FOR LIBRARIES AND ARCHIVES

"Serving Kentucky's Need to Know"
2006–2008 Budget Overview

The Kentucky Department for Libraries and Archives (KDLA) is an agency within the Education Cabinet whose mission is "to support and promote equitable access to quality library services and information resources, and to ensure that adequate documentation of governmental programs is created, maintained, and available for public use." This mission guides the department in developing programs and services to help improve living, learning, and working in Kentucky. In order to fulfill this commitment, the department's budget request emphasizes the following identified needs.

Equitable Access to Quality Library Services and Information Resources

Over 2 million Kentuckians are registered at their local public library. These include teachers, students, parents, children, grandparents, community groups, government workers–people from all walks of life. Libraries are trying to serve this large and geographically diverse population, but local resources are stretched to the maximum. Only 4% of local library budgets is provided by the state, while public schools receive 50.5% state support and public postsecondary institutions receive 50%. To address the needs of library users across the state, it's critical that we have a greater investment from Commonwealth Government. This investment should come in the following ways:

Public Library Services Improvement and Equalization Fund, *KRS 171.201–building resources and services for learning, earning, and nurturing families*

> This program was established to assure quality and equity in contemporary library and information services to improve early childhood development; support lifelong learning opportunities; enhance economic development; enrich cultural resource opportunities for all Kentuckians; and expand adult education and adult literacy programs. Although the statute became law in 2000, it has never been funded. The department is requesting $6 million annually to help local libraries provide the services listed above, as stated in KRS 171.201(4).

Public Library Facilities Construction Fund, *KRS 171.02–creating a sense of community and a place to meet and learn*

> Kentucky's public library facilities are over 500,000 square feet short of minimum standard, and more than 78 of the existing buildings

are over 20 years old. As major institutions for bringing communities together, libraries need more and better space to address an information-driven economy and a bewildering array of educational, cultural and social challenges facing all of us. It would take nearly 95 million dollars just to address the minimum standard shortage. Using local government bonding capacity, the department could accomplish 25% of this unmet need in the biennium with $1 million in fiscal year 2007 and $2 million in fiscal year 2008.

Library Science Scholarship Fund, *KRS 171.303–educating professional staff for 21st century information services*

Kentucky ranks 45th in the number of librarians with master's degree education. Nationally, it is estimated that over 46% of librarians will retire by the year 2008. Clearly, the need for recruiting and educating new professional librarians to work in Kentucky is vital to the public interest. To accomplish this, the department is requesting a modest beginning for this program of $50,000 in fiscal year 2007 and $100,000 in fiscal year 2008. At $5,000 per scholarship, these funds would support 10 scholarships in 2007 and 20 scholarships in 2008, which would help Kentucky meet its growing need for a new and diverse professional library workforce.

Mobile and Virtual Access Programs–*serving the information and knowledge needs of a geographically diverse population*

Kentucky is still primarily a rural state and its people are spread over a broad geographic region. To provide library services to rural citizens, the department is requesting restoration of funds historically used within the Bookmobile Program. The program needs $275,000 annually to overcome the problems associated with an aging bookmobile fleet. Of the existing 101 bookmobiles, 6 are over 17 years old, and another 29 are between 10 and 16 years old.

Additionally, the department provides grant support to the Kentucky Virtual Library (KYVL), which serves all Kentuckians by providing access to information databases. KYVL is a critical resource for teachers and students in P-16 education programs. The department is requesting $111,100 annually to restore funding previously cut from this program in recent budget reductions.

This approach to matching the "ask" from the KPLA Legislative Committee with the KDLA Budget Overview helped all the stakeholders in the budgeting and appropriations game understand the needs of our public library community. It also demonstrated that the state agency and the library advocacy group were on the same page and asking for the same things. It clearly demonstrated the strong collaboration between these two statewide library groups.

During the same session, the KPLA Legislative Committee also began what may be the most significant advocacy effort in the long run–the establishment of a public library caucus in the House of Representatives. This concept was based on what the Kentucky Arts Council had done in the US House and the reason to begin it on the House side is because that is where the budget issues are generated. The concept is to also do this on the Senate side, but at this point it was determined to begin on with the House. In Kentucky, and in most other legislative venues, the House of Representatives is a much broader and more "democratic" legislative chamber and that helps to make the caucus concept more likely to find legs. Following is the concept paper which was developed to communicate just what the caucus would do and to help sign up members.

KENTUCKY PUBLIC LIBRARY ASSOCIATION
LEGISLATIVE COMMITTEE
JULY, 2005

Concept Paper

Kentucky General Assembly Public Library Caucus

> The Kentucky General Assembly Public Library Caucus is a bipartisan organization for members of the Kentucky House of Representatives who support public libraries through state initiatives. The Public Library Caucus will be well-informed elected officials and a proactive and clear voice when issues affecting our cherished public libraries arise. The people of the Commonwealth stand to benefit from efforts of the Public Library Caucus.
>
> The major objective of the Public Library Caucus is to support legislation and budget initiatives in the Kentucky General Assembly that strengthen and advance the important public library agenda.

Specifically, Caucus members will advocate for (1) full funding of the public library improvement and equalization legislation (HB 825) passed in 2000; and, (2) securing capital funding to help communities build necessary facilities; and, (3) restoring bookmobile grants to serve every Kentucky family.

In addition, the Caucus will support opportunities through legislative efforts to help public libraries deliver services and programs to citizens, provide information through technology, partner with community organizations for children and youth activities, serve as a community anchor, and welcome and assist visitors.

Members of the Public Library Caucus participate in press conferences in support of public libraries, may testify before key committees in support of statewide public library initiatives, speak with and to colleagues about the positive impact of public libraries, and participate in the annual Public Library Day in the Kentucky General Assembly.

Members of the House of Representatives shall be invited by Public Library Legislative Committee members and approved by the co-chairs to participate as a member of the Public Library Caucus. The Legislative Committee of the Kentucky Public Library Association shall be the liaison to the Caucus, providing opportunities for members to become more fully informed about public library issues, and seeking occasions for Caucus members to speak about the importance of public libraries.

The Legislative committee shall also comply fully with Kentucky legislative ethics law and Commission regulations with respect to expenditure reporting requirements.

Membership on the Public Library Caucus shall be for a one year period (General Assembly session), modeled after similar formats in Congress. Each year, members will be asked to "sign on" to support public library initiatives.

The co-chairs of the caucus are the majority party caucus chair and the minority party caucus chair in the House. This is very appropriate because the basic nature of what these individuals do is negotiate various salient issues in the normal course of legislative duties. This initial group is made up of nineteen members–eleven Democrats and eight Republicans, all known to be strong library supporters.

With the development of the caucus and the thematic "Libraries Build Communities" serving as a foundation for advocacy efforts in the 2006 General Assembly, the KPLA Legislative Committee made significant progress in organizing itself and its efforts to build upon in the coming years. Clearly, this movement will only serve well if supported and sustained–advocacy efforts need to be ongoing and connected.

Since all politics are local, it's also critical that the statewide advocacy effort has local connections. To that end, the committee has assigned itself contacts to stay in touch with local libraries and to make sure those libraries understand statewide themes, but, more importantly, that they maintain regular contact with their legislators and "friends of the Governor" where possible. The bottom line is that these kinds of efforts only work if various individuals take on responsibilities and leadership to the important details of advocacy.

The other initiative the KPLA Legislative Committee is working on is to have several of its meetings around the state and invite local library representatives to meet with members. The obligation would only be to agree to work locally; if any local library representative wants to become involved with the statewide work, he or she would be welcomed to the committee's overall efforts.

Collective and Collaborative Results

So, have all these efforts to blend marketing and advocacy in Kentucky had any real impact on the condition and/or sustainability of public libraries in this state? The answer is yes; but mainly as a foundation-building exercise. Some direct results can be found in increased public awareness and library membership/attendance increases in those counties where the libraries were involved in the institute. The billboard campaign in Scott County got major attention for its "Smart Card" campaign, including having the coach of the girls' high school basketball team (featured on one billboard) ask if the girls could come back to the library and work with kids' reading programs. In one county, the library director was prepared to change careers, but she got so inspired by the Institute that she literally recommitted herself to the profession and the library where she worked.

The Advocacy piece did help raise awareness in the hot public arena of the Kentucky Legislature and that resulted in additional state aid appropriations to be able to fund the per capita section of the formula at the 2000 Census level while holding all counties harmless regardless of population loss. In fact, it even allowed for a small distribution increase statewide. Several bills which would have been harmful to local public libraries never made it out of committee and cuts suffered by other programs didn't hit the public libraries quite so directly.

The public library construction program got a small increase, $600,000, but the new construction formula which allows for KDLA to match debt payments for local libraries allowed this small amount of money to grow to nearly $8 million on the ground using local debt capacity.

The formula allowing this was established in the Public Library Facilities Construction Fund, one of the legislative goals of the KPLA Legislative Committee in a previous legislative session. In that same session, the Public Library Services Improvement and Equalization Fund was established and while that was not funded, it received much attention. This fund was modeled after the public school fund which helps equalize state assistance in the rural areas. There was an additional $250,000 for bookmobile grants in 2006 session as well.

The key to success in these joint efforts to move forward with greater awareness of the value libraries contribute to Kentucky and a stronger advocacy effort will be the ongoing commitment of the key players. The Public Awareness Institute is budgeted to continue and is being promoted at state library meetings to keep the interest sharp. The advocacy group remains consistent and committed while gearing up to build on its own organizing capacity and advancing the development of the Library Caucus in the coming months. Both marketing and advocacy, working in tandem, jointly connected through the two statewide organizations and carrying a common message will demonstrate that mingling the concepts and practices of these key issues in a collaborative context can sustain library services in the Commonwealth for years to come.

NOTES

1. Public Agenda. Long Overdue: A Fresh Look at Public and Leadership Attitudes about Libraries in the 21st Century. New York, NY: Americans for Libraries Council, 2006, 20.
2. Ibid., 13.
3. Ibid., 30.
4. Ibid., 36.
5. American Marketing Association (2006). *Marketing Definitions*. Retrieved July 24, 2006 from the World Wide Web: <http://www.marketingpower.com/content4620.php> 1 of 1.
6. *Marketing*.Wikipedia (2006). Retrieved July 24, 2006 from the World Wide Web: <http://www.wikipedia.org/wiki/Marketing> 1 of 7.

7. NPAction (2006). *Lobbying Versus Advocacy: Legal Definitions*. Retrieved July 24, 2006 from the World Wide Web: <http://npaction.org/article/articleview/76/1/248> 1 of 3.

8. Ibid., 1 of 3.

9. Kentucky Department for Libraries and Archives (2002*). Background of the KDLA@yourlibrary Project.* Retrieved September 15, 2006 from the World Wide Web: <http://kdla.ky.gov/onlinepubs/kdla@yourlibrary/bkgrd.htm> 1 of 2.

10. Kentucky Department for Libraries and Archives (2002). *Case for Support of Our Public Libraries.* Retrieved September 15, 2006 from the World Wide Web: <http://www.kdla.ky.gov/onlinepubs/kdla@youlibrary/@youlibrary/support.htm> 1 of 4.

11. Kentucky Department for Libraries and Archives (2002). *Kentucky Public Libraries–Values.* Retrieved September 15, 2006 from the World Wide Web: <http://www.onlinepubs/kdla@youlibrary/@yourlibrary/values.htm> 1 of 2.

12. Gibbons, Judith. "We Lobbied Legislators with 70 Bookmobiles." *Marketing Library Services*. 20.3 (May/June 2006):1-3, 9.

doi:10.1300/J118v25n01_09

Politics and Advocacy: The Role of Networking in Selling the Library to Your Community

Charles R. McClure
Sari Feldman
Joe Ryan

SUMMARY. Current research conducted by the Information Use Management and Policy Institute, Florida State University, identifies the characteristics of the successfully networked public library (SNPL) and in particular explores the impact of technology on both library advocacy and networking in the political system. This paper identifies the factors that are critical to a public library's success in advocacy, community support, government relations, and ultimately the perceived importance of the library in the community. This perspective on the SNPL is reinforced by the examination of Cuyahoga County Public Library's program to use the strategies of the SNPL. doi:10.1300/J118v25n01_10 *[Article copies available for a fee from The Haworth Document Delivery Service:*

Charles R. McClure is Professor of Information Studies and Director of the Information Institute at the College of Information, Florida State University (E-mail: cmcclure@mailer.fsu.edu).

Sari Feldman is Executive Director, Cuyahoga County (Ohio) Public Library (E-mail: sfeldman@cuyahoga.library.org).

Joe Ryan is Senior Research Associate at the Information Institute at Florida State University (E-mail: jryan@mailbox.syr.edu).

[Haworth co-indexing entry note]: "Politics and Advocacy: The Role of Networking in Selling the Library to Your Community." McClure, Charles R., Sari Feldman, and Joe Ryan. Co-published simultaneously in *Public Library Quarterly* (The Haworth Press, Inc.) Vol. 25, No. 1/2, 2006, pp. 137-154; and: *Current Practices in Public Libraries* (ed: William Miller, and Rita M. Pellen) The Haworth Press, Inc., 2006, pp. 137-154. Single or multiple copies of this article are available for a fee from The Haworth Document Delivery Service [1-800-HAWORTH, 9:00 a.m. - 5:00 p.m. (EST). E-mail address: docdelivery@haworthpress.com].

Available online at http://plq.haworthpress.com
© 2006 by The Haworth Press, Inc. All rights reserved.
doi:10.1300/J118v25n01_10

1-800-HAWORTH. E-mail address: <docdelivery@haworthpress.com> Website: <http://www.HaworthPress.com> © 2006 by The Haworth Press, Inc. All rights reserved.]

KEYWORDS. Advocacy, government relations, networking, political system, sustainable support

INTRODUCTION

The laundry list of factors that can determine the overall success of today's public library is daunting. Public library directors have such a long list of factors to address that it is often difficult to know which should be priorities. Clearly, however, one of the key factors to address is working the local political system as a means of advocating for the library. Two key phrases in the previous sentence, "working the local political system" and "advocating for the library" are the key to this paper.

Local public policy decision-making and the role of the library in that process may vary from community to community due to local and state laws and the local personalities involved in the process. Public policy making is essentially a socially agreeable way or collaborative process used to make decisions. *Stakeholders*, the people affected by a social problem or *issue*, recognize that policies and decisions may be developed to deal with a particular library issue. Stakeholders often have conflicting value systems and differing objectives in the resolution of an issue. Public policy decisions and issues are usually the subject of ongoing discussions. Politics, and working the local political system, is the process by which public policy decisions and policies are made.

Recent research by Bertot, McClure, Jaeger, and Ryan (2006) suggests that working the local political system is essential for advocacy and for becoming a successfully networked public library (SNPL). Public libraries now exist in a complex and ever-evolving electronic networked environment in which services and resources are often provided via a national, state, regional, or local networked environment (Courtney, 2006). Local governing boards and residents may not understand the extent to which information technology and the networking environment are now the backbone of public library services and the basis for being "successful." Without a high quality technology information infrastructure and network, public libraries simply cannot compete in the information marketplace.

Advocacy has many meanings and uses. Generally, as used in public librarianship, the term suggests organizing community residents and others to promote the library, its services, and its overall importance in the community. Often the goal of such advocacy is to obtain additional resources to support public library services. *Library Advocate's Handbook* (ALA) is a good example of this type of advocacy. Indeed, the American Library Association offers a broad range of resources and tools in support of such advocacy.[1]

While such advocacy clearly is essential for public libraries, this paper agues that a better linking of working the local political process and advocating for the library–orchestrated by library managers–may also pay significant benefits for the library. Indeed, this paper argues that advocacy without working the local political system may have less impact than desired by library managers and local community members. More specifically, key themes in this paper include:

- Library directors must be able to work the local political process to successfully advocate for the public library.
- A picture or vision of what constitutes a successfully networked public library in a particular community is essential for local politicians, governing boards, and residents to then advocate to reach that vision.
- Local situational factors have to be identified, understood, and considered in the advocacy plan for the library to reach a vision of being successful.

Advocacy and working the political process have to be done in the context of accomplishing specific goals and working toward a vision of what a successfully networked public library in a particular community would be. But if there is no clear vision of what a successful library should be in a particular community, it will be impossible to reach such a vision.

In a recent study, *Long Overdue: A Fresh Look at Public and Leadership Attitudes about Libraries in the 21st Century*, (2006), key findings included the following:

- Community Soldiers Could Fight for Libraries: These champions for libraries may not be aware of the financial vulnerability of the library and need to be educated;

- Computers and Internet Access Are Priorities: While traditional services are still needed, community residents expect better and more information technology from their library; and
- A Public Unaware of What Could be Lost: Although the local community values its public library, libraries must proactively start to orchestrate financial support for the library.

These and other findings support findings from the Bertot, McClure, Jaeger, and Ryan study, *Public Libraries and the Internet 2006: Survey and Site Visit Results and Findings* (2006) in terms of the importance of having a successfully networked public library.

This paper provides a perspective on politics and advocacy and how the concept of a successful library can serve as a vehicle to promote advocacy. Moreover, the paper stresses that advocacy and aspects of a successful public library can be important tools that can be used to obtain additional resources and support for the library. In addition, the paper offers one example of successfully working the political environment for local advocacy. The paper is not intended to be a literature review of topics such as advocacy, planning, technology deployment, etc. Rather, it offers one perspective on how the concept of a successful public library can assist library managers to better engage in the local political and advocacy environment.

SUCCESSFULLY NETWORKED LIBRARIES

Becoming Successfully Networked Public Libraries is a portion of the *2006 Public Libraries and the Internet* national, biennial study[2] conducted by Florida State University, College of Information, Information Use Management and Policy Institute.[3] The 2006 study is funded by the Bill and Melinda Gates Foundation[4] and the American Library Association.[5] The phrase "successfully networked" is used broadly to include public library computing, Internet, networks, telecommunications, integrated library systems and other related electronic resources, services, and support. The findings go beyond networked aspects of the library and covered a much broader scope–as it turned out. The study included five state visits in the winter and spring of 2006. Five State Library agencies, nineteen public libraries, and 84 library managers were interviewed. Details on the study method can be found in the final study report (Bertot, McClure, Jaeger, and Ryan, 2006).

KEY FINDINGS

In 2006, a successfully networked public library provides high quality *traditional* library services as well as networked services. Library managers may find it helpful to focus on three service areas: networked services offered within the library; the library's virtual branch, meaning Web-based external services; and the infrastructure needed to support both. In brief, factors describing these libraries in 2006 include:

Networked Services Within the Library

- SNPLs offer public access copiers, fax, printers, scanners, public access computing workstations, and may lend a variety of equipment including digital cameras, GPS equipment, ipods, MP3 players, and even telescopes. Often, SNPLs provide the first introduction to new information technology (IT) and serve as the access point of first and last resort for their communities and visitors.
- SNPLs offer an integrated library system (ILS) including an online public access catalog (OPAC) of library materials.

Library's Virtual Branch

- SNPLs view their Website as an additional branch, or a virtual branch.
- They seek to offer the same or equivalent services as those offered within the library in addition to those only available virtually.
- Provision of virtual branch management, staff, resources, and budget equivalent to a traditional branch may not yet be in place.
- Virtual branch evaluation is done, but data are not integrated with physical branch results.

Network Infrastructure

- SNPLs have addressed the IT staff issue: having dedicated IT staff who may make certain types of networked library services possible and can save the library money. They conduct extensive, continuous, formal and informal network service planning.
- SNPLs have enough bandwidth and offer or plan to offer wireless connectivity, but anticipate future need for additional bandwidth as video, music, and large file transfers become more common.

- SNPLs have enough public workstations but know they may never meet peak demand.
- SNPLs provide enough IT (including software) and training so that all staff members are proficient at their jobs.
- SNPLs have built, or are considering building, facilities better tailored to the networked environment.
- SNPLs recognize and capitalize on the potential of the Internet as a shared information infrastructure where hardware, software, resources, and services and staff expertise may be shared.

Advocacy

SNPLs engage in a wide range of advocacy strategies for continued public library and networked services support. The following is a summary of SNPL advocacy efforts:

- Proactive: A distinguishing characteristic of all of the SNPLs visited when compared to other public libraries is their proactive approach. SNPLs proactively partner with local and state governments and non-profits for mutual benefit. SNPLs actively look for opportunities to show what the library was already doing to address local, state, and regional issues, and actively seek partners and funding to address these issues. SNPLs do not wait to be invited to the table.
- Leadership: The public library director is a leader both in the library and in the local community. The director, while not wanting to be on the "bleeding edge" of innovation, is on the leading edge.
- Opportunistic: The SNPL managers are masters at perceiving an opportunity to make the library's worth visible to others and to obtain funding or support, particularly when the source doesn't mention libraries but doesn't exclude them either. SNPL managers all recognize that financial support is only one of many types of support that successful libraries need.
- Prepared: SNPLs are often, but not always, better prepared than peer government agencies to make their potential contribution known and to make their funding case. Part of the preparation includes assembling relevant evidence and arguments based on the evidence.
- Relationships: SNPL managers have a year-round positive relationship with elected and appointed officials and government agency and nonprofit leaders as well as community opinion makers. SNPL managers are not meeting strangers when they go to the annual library budget hearing.

In Search of Sustainable Support

What types of support do these libraries need? Have public libraries found ways to generate new, sustaining revenue due to their success in providing network services to their communities? The research revealed several interesting approaches to obtain sustainable support:

- Stable funding is key. Stability is a prerequisite to becoming a successful library because it enables realistic multi-year planning.
- The library conducts continuous, semi-systematic environmental scans seeking to match need, information technology, and funding opportunity.
- Most libraries are transitioning to increased local support of networked services.
- Support for library services is not limited to money–shared hardware, resources, staff and staff training, and other benefits are equally important.

Next Steps

Successful public library directors recognize and celebrate the significant achievement of connecting most public librarians in the U.S. to the Internet. Many librarians believe it is now time to focus attention on two areas:

- Network public library brand: Develop a convenient, easy-to-use collection of content, resources, and services that the public highly values, that most public libraries offer, and that the public recognizes as coming from public libraries. One element of such a public library brand now in place is that the public knows to look for a public library if it needs access to the Internet. One element not in place is convenient, easy-to-access public library content. Existing potential elements of public library-branded content such as OPACs and subscription databases are too cumbersome and time consuming when compared to free, commercial equivalents such as Google.
- Network efficiencies: Successful libraries recognize the potential to improve public library efficiency using a network and extending a range of public access computing services such as the rapid development of virtual reference services. But the use of networks is still new with many unanswered questions. Will local public library users accept remotely delivered services? How will content,

resources, and services be jointly developed, coordinated, funded, and evaluated?

All libraries visited recognized that a connection is not enough. All are looking for library branded content and services that will establish the library in the networked world and as a leader in the local community.

LINKING SUCCESSFUL LIBRARIES TO POLITICS AND ADVOCACY

The above description of a successfully networked library in 2006 also identified that the libraries visited had a vision and set of goals that they could "sell" to local government officials, the governing board, and community residents. To some extent this description of the library served as a base from which a range of other library services (both traditional and networked) can be provided. But without this vision, the technology infrastructure, and perceived importance of that vision, the library could not be a leader in the provision of information services and resources in the community.

Library directors were actively engaged in the local political environment and advocacy through a number of activities. First, they proactively promoted external relationships with units of local government, state government, local civic organizations, other libraries, and members of the private sector. These relationships often take years to build but are essential if library managers are to be visible and demonstrably involved in local civic activities and be knowledgeable about the local political environment.

Second, All of the libraries visited were aware of the findings of the OCLC Environmental Scan (OCLC, 2003) and the Perceptions study in the fall of 2005 (OCLC, 2005) and the need for branding of the library within the local community. The study suggested that today's Internet users rarely thought of the library when meeting their information needs. The most successful (both in traditional and network service provision) of the successful public libraries agreed on the following points:

- There is a need for public library branded, Internet based content and services on par with the best Internet content and services currently offered. The goal: when people (young and old) use the Internet, that they will be aware of and use the high quality and probably free content and services offered by the public library;

- At present, the principal, networked public library content consists of digitized local special collections (audio, video, photographs, maps, historic documents). Local public libraries are very interested in making more local digital content available. Often the material is made available without attention to national standards and cataloging, thus making statewide, national aggregation difficult. Branding such material may be difficult in any case;
- At present, the principal networked public library service is virtual reference, which is in its infancy–particularly in usage; and
- In general, the libraries were disappointed with licensed, subscription, vendor offerings particularly when compared to such free Internet services as Google <http://www.google.com/>. Many of the libraries are paying for some of these services such as *Discovering Collection* using local funds. Google's search engine is far superior to anything offered by subscription services *or* by OPAC vendors. Federated search engines are only a partial solution at best. Enough library users (as well as non library users) prefer convenience and speed (Google) over peer-reviewed quality (subscription databases) to make the library quality argument moot.

In short, there is a need to both brand the local public library as the place for information services and to educate members of the local political environment as to the changing nature of libraries in a networked environment. There is also a need to find competitive equivalents to Google which also offer the quality associated with library services.

Third, traditional methods of advocacy are still important, but ... The library manager must rally local residents, organizations, and government in support of the library and that rallying cry must include the importance of traditional library services and how the library can meet those information needs. But the message must now also address the role of the public library in a networked, high-speed, technologically sophisticated environment and offer a vision (an exciting vision!) of goals for how the library can operate in that environment yet still provide high quality traditional services. Thus, advocacy goals to support the public library must go beyond the importance of reading, literacy, and circulation of mystery books.

Fourth, any strategy that incorporates the concept of a successful library to promote working the political system and advocacy must take into consideration a host of local situations and conditions. Clearly, one size does not fit all communities when it comes to developing an advocacy plan. Prior to implementing such a plan the authors recommend a quick political audit that asks:

- Who are the most important players in the local political environment, what type of power do they have, and to what degree can they influence others in the community?
- Who are the supporters of the library and to what degree are they part of the political process in the community? Can they become more active and successful in that political process?
- How is the library director perceived by key players in the local political environment and by library supporters?
- To what degree is the public library seen as a solver of community problems and a player in the local political process? How can the library become more involved?

These are but a few of the key questions that one can consider in conducting a political audit of a local community. The audit is best done informally by developing a set of questions and probes and administering them via informal interviews to key leaders and stakeholders. Additional questions and factors, depending on that community, its history, its form of government, and the nature of individuals involved in that community (among other factors) will also need to be considered.

Finally, the library manager who is successful in the local political process does so with subtlety, informality, persistence, and perhaps most importantly with current and accurate information about who the players are, what they believe, how they might be persuaded to better support the library, and the current hot issues in the community and how the library can assist in solving those issues. The last point is especially important; the library must be positioned as an organization that can be a problem solver–not problem maker–in the local community. Increasingly, a number of community issues and problems that can be solved *could* include the library.

ONE EXAMPLE OF A SUCCESSFULLY NETWORKED PUBLIC LIBRARY

Cuyahoga County Public Library (CCPL) serves 47 suburban communities outside the City of Cleveland.[6] The population of approximately 630,000 is economically, ethnically, educationally, and racially diverse. The Library is consistently ranked as one of the ten best, according to the Hennen's American Public Library Ratings (Hennen, 2006), and ten busiest, according to the Public Library Association statistics ranking libraries in the United States serving over 500,000 in population. Dedicated state funding through personal income tax combined with a local property tax has ensured Cuyahoga County Public Library one of the highest per capita spending thresholds in the United States.

This strong support is typical in the State of Ohio but recent state level threats to the Library and Local Government Support Fund and proposed Tax Expenditure Limination (TEL) amendment, coupled with local property tax payer fatigue, brings recognition to the need for advocacy and "working the political system" in order to sustain the current level of services constituents have come to expect.

There are some issues for Cuyahoga County to consider in some of the traditional advocacy efforts typically in use:

- Meet and greet events with government officials, board members, and citizens are an effective method to gain recognition; however, with 16 state legislators, 3 county commissioners, 45 mayors and councils, and 2 township trustees and clerks, this becomes a daunting task.
- Education programs such as PLA's "The Smartest Card," conducted as a sole advocacy effort, may reach only traditional library supporters without touching non-users and impacting government relations.
- Attending political fund raisers, having a library presence at community days, and providing library meeting space to non-partisan government meetings will increase visibility of the library, but may not make a real impact on decision makers.

These, and other traditional efforts–such as marshalling local support into political action–may still be useful strategies; other strategies and approaches, however, can also be considered.

BECOMING A SUCCESSFULLY NETWORKED PUBLIC LIBRARY

The findings from the Bertot, McClure, Jaeger, and Ryan (2006) research suggest additional approaches to public library advocacy and government relationships or working the political system. By developing quality, visible, networked services, the Library achieves a significant place in community development and growth. Cuyahoga County Public Library exemplifies such quality services.

Networked Services Within Cuyahoga County Public Library (CCPL)

- Offering public access to public access copiers, fax, printers, computer workstations, and making available individual and group instruction to support customers in the community. Even with approximately 80% of the Library's constituents having a personal PC and Internet connection available either at home or work, the quality and speed of the Library's bandwidth attracts people at all economic levels to public library branches.
- Offering wireless access at all branches has increased the number of non-traditional library users including home-based business owners in the branches.
- Offering an integrated library system (ILS) including an online public access catalog (OPAC) of library materials. CCPL also provides direct customer access to the OhioLINK collections, a consortium of over 85 colleges, universities, and the State Library of Ohio. In 2006, CCPL worked with others to establish SearchOhio, direct access to the collections of four other large public libraries in the state. Daily delivery brings materials directly to branches for customers from both resource sharing programs.

Library's Virtual Branch

- Recently the CCPL's Website was completely redone in a content management system to improve maintenance, navigation, and customer satisfaction.
- Through the new Website, CCPL has attempted to maximize the customer's ability to receive full service in a virtual place by offering the online library card application, holds, renewals, e-commerce, eBooks, audio eBooks, and downloadable music, reference, program registration, and Web casting.
- CCPL continues to seek new opportunities for online services, realizing that customer convenience is critical to the Library's survival. In May 2006, the Library began text messages as a means of library-to-customer communication.
- The IT division has been reorganized to provide stronger support and leadership for the Website and virtual services.

Networked Infrastructure

- CCPL has dedicated IT staff, a T-3 line to Library headquarters, and a T-1 line to each branch.
- There is extensive, continuous, formal and informal network service planning. IT staff receive support for training and skill development.
- CCPL currently has enough bandwidth but is well aware of its future bandwidth needs and cost implications. CCPL has been an early adopter of the regional OneCommunity project (formerly OneCleveland) that is making a high-speed fiber network available to not-for-profit organizations. Through an IMLS grant and a distance learning project with The Cleveland Museum of Art, CCPL has been able to connect two branches to the OneCommunity network.
- While there are never enough workstations to satisfy public demand, wireless access has enabled the branches to supplement desk top PCs with tablet devices, increasing the number of access points per building. Wireless service and laptops or tablets allow for any and every meeting room space to be converted to a computer instruction lab without dedicating valuable building real estate.
- A partnership with Cuyahoga Community College increased the amount of on-going software training for all staff. This is a continuing training contract with qualified instructors.

Advocacy

- Proactive: CCPL has served on the County Invest in Children (early childhood) planning committee, Blue Ribbon Task Force on Economic Development, and Universal Pre-K project. CCPL took a leadership role with the County, Cities, and Libraries during the 2005 state budget process.
- Leadership: CCPL is a founding member of OneCommunity, a spokesperson for the project, and has membership on the board. CCPL worked with Cleveland Public Library to provide training and education on the new electronic voting prior to the May 2006 primary. CCPL worked with My Medicare Matters to support older adults with online support services to select a prescription drug plan.
- Opportunistic: CCPL has received County Funding for its "new baby kit," a kindergarten kit, computer labs, homework centers, and special summer programming for children and teens as part of

the County's initiatives on early education and quality out-of-school time for youth.
- Prepared: CCPL is continuously updating data and is well positioned to communicate evidence on customer need and use of services. CCPL takes its communication program seriously and has a dedicated and professional marketing department that includes public relations and graphics.
- Relationships: CCPL managers work to establish and maintain relationships with mayors and township trustees. They actively work within their communities and are visible at community events. CCPL administration and board members communicate with mayors on system-wide issues and as needed to support regional efforts. CCPL administration and board members are deliberate in their efforts to reach out to County Commissioners and State Legislators. CCPL has offered available bandwidth to local communities to expand wireless access beyond the library walls. To date, two cities have made community space wireless in partnership with the Library.

Next Steps

The above suggests a number of areas that CCPL targets for being involved in the political process and working the political system. But some of the next steps include:

- Build buildings designed to use wireless service and maximize customer convenience. CCPL has just concluded a series of meetings with a community advisory group of government, business, education and civic leadership to recommend "best practice" in capital projects to the Library's board.
- Increase the number of branches on the OneCommunity network, build the brand of high speed access, and use the broadband for distance learning and kiosk downloads of audio and video on demand.
- Convert the Library's Intranet to a content management system to improve communication and resources for staff.
- Introduce a PC management system to maximize community access to computer services.
- Continue collaborations with public libraries in Ohio and nationally to increase resource sharing, virtual reference services, new software applications for improved customer service, and e-learning opportunities for staff and customers.

- Continue proactive leadership that positions CCPL as a community change agent and decision maker. Examples include: developing a project with City and County workforce development to develop a "virtual gateway" to public, private, and library services that supports job seekers and links directly to County and State goals and collaborating with Cleveland Public Library and Cleveland State University's Maxine Goodman Levin College of Urban Affairs to host the Urban Libraries Council's 2007 Partners for Successful Cities Conference.
- Strengthening the Library's Foundation and seeking other unique funding to reduce dependency on state funding.
- Ensuring that Trustees and Friends members are active in new models of advocacy.

As funding pressure increases in the State of Ohio, Cuyahoga County Public Library will continue to position itself as a networked public library, using both its virtual network resources to build community and its new network of collaborators and partners to build service models that support community priorities.

BEING MORE SUCCESSFUL IN THE POLITICAL PROCESS AND IN ADVOCACY

The degree to which public libraries are successful in the local and state political process and accomplish a range of advocacy goals will have a direct relationship to the overall success of the public library. There are a number of practical steps that the library director and staff can take to increase the library's involvement in the political process and in advocacy.

A key beginning point is to understand first that there are many factors that contribute to the success of the public library. Traditional measures of outputs, outcomes, and a range of performance measures can help keep the library on track and provide excellent diagnostics to monitor various library services, programs, resource use, and electronic services. But all libraries, ultimately, are local. That is, the personal strengths of the director, staff, trustees, friends, the make-up of local government and its personalities, community demographics, and a host of other factors make each library's situation different.

The library administration will need to become informed and knowledgeable about political activism, the details of how local government works–both formally and informally–and also about what areas in the local community have the best opportunities for the library administration and staff to get involved. The same holds true with advocacy, why it is important, how to do it, and how to set specific strategies for successful advocacy. The findings reported above provide a beginning point for becoming knowledgeable, plus there are many excellent sources with detailed information about working the political process and advocacy.

Earlier, the paper suggested the importance and need to conduct a political audit in the local library community. Other types of audits are also useful–such as determining the strengths and weaknesses of staff, identifying the degree to which local leaders can become strong supporters of the library, assessing the success with which local resources (including private sources) have been tapped for the library, and understanding what library services, programs, and resources can be best "sold" in the local community. Taking stock of the library's strengths in working the political system and promoting advocacy is an important first activity. Determining what will be a SNPL in *your* situation and articulating that vision is essential.

These various audits then provide input for the library's planning process. There are numerous planning approaches available to support the library, but it may be less important *which* process is used than that *some* process is in place. Regardless of the planning process in use (see, for example, McClure et al., 1987; and Himmel and Wilson, 1997), the library will need to develop goals, objectives, action steps, and performance indicators related to the success with which the library is involved in and works the political process, the degree to which advocacy is accomplished, and the degree to which factors related to becoming a successfully networked library are being accomplished.

Another key step for the library administrators to take is to educate the staff, the trustees, the friends, and other key stakeholders associated with the library about the importance of being involved and working the political process and how ongoing and successful advocacy can significantly improve the overall quality of the library. These can be done formally through workshops and training, and informally, by example. Educating key stakeholder groups about these topics is ongoing and will be a constant effort on the part of the library administrators (and staff).

Investing in a clear and consistent message that tells the library story is critical for all library communication. As key stakeholders develop relationships to build political capital for the library, it is essential that the library values and offerings are a "brand," distinguishing the institution in the community as well as in the virtual community. When the local library comes to mind, there should be a key message or picture of the library that residents recall.

Building relationships with other libraries, government, business, and other organizations to strengthen service and to identify efficiencies is an important element for the successfully networked public library. Library administrators, trustees, etc., need to foster collaboration and partnerships with policy makers and politicians for efficient service and libraries can bring excellent examples to their attention. The local library can be especially "successful" if it is seen as solving community problems. Such an approach may bring both tangible results and political capital.

Working the political system and improved advocacy, in and of itself, will not be a cure-all for improving the success of the library. Multiple other factors and strategies also certainly play a part in being a successfully networked public library. But findings from recent research conducted by the authors, and real-life activities at CCPL make it clear that these two factors–working the political system and improved advocacy–are key components to becoming a successful public library.

NOTES

1. See, for example <http://www.ala.org/ala/issues/issuesadvocacy.htm>.
2. *Public libraries and the Internet studies* <http://www.ii.fsu.edu/plinternet.cfm>.
3. Florida State University, College of Information, Information Use Management and Policy Institute <http://www.ii.fsu.edu/>.
4. Bill and Melinda Gates Foundation <http://www.gatesfoundation.org/Libraries/>.
5. American Library Association <http://www.ala.org/>.
6. For additional background information see <http://www.cuyahogalibrary.org/>.

REFERENCES

American Library Association (2006). *Library Advocate's Handbook*. Chicago: American Library Association.

Bertot, J. C., McClure, C. R., Jaeger, P. T. & Ryan, J. (2006). *Public libraries and the Internet 2006: Study Results and Findings*. Tallahassee, FL: Florida State University, College of Information, Information Use Management and Policy Institute, available at <http://www.ii.fsu.edu/plinternet>.

Courtney, N., ed. (2006). *Technology for the Rest of Us: A Primer on Computer Technologies for the Low-Tech Librarian*. Westport, Connecticut: Libraries Unlimited.

Hennen, T. J. Hennen's American Public Library Ratings, available at <http://www.haplr-index.com/>.

Himmel, E., and Wilson, W. J. (1997). *Planning for Results: A Public Library Transformation Process.* Chicago, American Library Association.

Long Overdue: A Fresh Look at Public and Leadership Attitudes about Libraries in the 21st Century (2006). New York: Americans for Libraries Council, available at <http://www.lff.org/long_overdue061306.html>.

McClure, C. R., Owen, A., Zweizig, D. L., Lynch, M. J., and Van House, N. A. (1987). *Planning and role setting for public libraries: A Manual of options and procedures.* Chicago: American Library Association.

OCLC, (2003). *2003 OCLC Environmental Scan: Pattern Recognition.* Columbus, OH: OCLC, Inc., available at <http://www.oclc.org/reports/escan/default.htm>.

OCLC, (2005). *Perceptions of Libraries and Information Resources.* Columbus, OH: OCLC, Inc., available at <http://www.ala.org/ala/issues/issuesadvocacy.htm>.

Ohio Library Council (2006). *Community Engagement Toolkit.* Columbus, Ohio: OLC. Available at <http://www.oclc.org/communityconnections.asp>.

doi:10.1300/J118v25n01_10

Creating Advocates for Public Libraries

Kathleen R. T. Imhoff

SUMMARY. While public libraries in the United States vary widely by size and location, they all serve a common purpose: to provide information, education, and recreation for all people in their service areas. To continue to serve this purpose, especially in the midst of the current shrinkage of public funding, public libraries need advocates who believe in them strongly and are willing to speak publicly on their behalf. doi:10.1300/J118v25n01_11 *[Article copies available for a fee from The Haworth Document Delivery Service: 1-800-HAWORTH. E-mail address: <docdelivery@haworthpress.com> Website: <http://www.HaworthPress.com> © 2006 by The Haworth Press, Inc. All rights reserved.]*

KEYWORDS. Advocate, advocacy, American Library Association, bond issue, Friends of the Library, library foundation, radio, testimonials, Board of Trustees, funding

INTRODUCTION

Each of the 17,046 public libraries across the United States is unique, but they have some things in common. Each library provides information, education, and recreation for people of all ages in its service area.

Kathleen R. T. Imhoff is Executive Director/CEO, Lexington Public Library, 140 East Main Street, Lexington, KY 40507 (E-mail: kimhoff@lexpublib.org).

[Haworth co-indexing entry note]: "Creating Advocates for Public Libraries." Imhoff, Kathleen R. T. Co-published simultaneously in *Public Library Quarterly* (The Haworth Press, Inc.) Vol. 25, No. 1/2, 2006, pp. 155-170; and: *Current Practices in Public Libraries* (ed: William Miller, and Rita M. Pellen) The Haworth Press, Inc., 2006, pp. 155-170. Single or multiple copies of this article are available for a fee from The Haworth Document Delivery Service [1-800-HAWORTH, 9:00 a.m. - 5:00 p.m. (EST). E-mail address: docdelivery@ haworthpress.com].

The libraries of America have varied levels of support; they vary in building size and resources. But regardless of size, public libraries have in common the need for good advocates, committed people who believe in the library and are willing to go to bat to keep or increase library service. When Salinas Public Library in California was closing its doors due to lack of funds, people in the community as well as people across the county united to urge the elected officials to fund the library so it could reopen. Whether in Westchester, New York, or Austin, Texas, groups of library supporters have banded together to promote good library service.

Because of the growth of the Internet, there are an ever-increasing number of homes with computers, and people are questioning the need for public and school libraries. If everyone has instant access to millions of Web sites, blogs, mashups, RSS feeds, and podcasts, why fund outdated repositories of the printed word? Who will answer these questions? Library employees could, but they might be viewed as only protecting their jobs when they speak up for increased funding for public libraries and expansion of services.

Non-librarian advocates, people who are ready, willing, and able to speak up are crucial in telling the library story and sharing the importance of libraries with political leaders and legislatures.

WHAT IS A LIBRARY ADVOCATE?

An advocate is a person who: (1) espouses a cause, (2) is an upholder, (3) pleads for or on behalf of another, (4) supports and urges, (5) defends, (6) recommends publicly; and an advocate is, (7) You. Let's investigate further advocates and their roles.

A library advocate is a person who espouses the library cause, a person who turns "The Library" into "My Library," a person who is committed to the importance of public libraries in a democracy and is willing to tell others. Since the majority of public libraries are run by a group of trustees of the library, this group of trustees, by agreeing to be appointed to the Library Board or to run for election to the Library Board, is making a public statement that they espouse a cause, the Public Library. By agreeing to serve, trustees are dedicating a portion of their time and talents to their library.

An advocate is also an upholder. A library advocate is an upholder of the Library Bill of Rights (http://www.ala.org/ala/oif/statementspols/statementsif/librarybillrights.htm). A library advocate upholds that the public library is open to all people coming into its doors or through its Website. A library advocate upholds the right of all to find different points of view in the library. Library advocates step up to the front line when the library or intellectual freedom is challenged. Many Library Boards face difficult decisions in defining community standards and deciding what should be included in the library when individual books are challenged. A library advocate is always willing to speak out and uphold the values and selection policies of the library. Every public library has its own vision and mission. A library advocate upholds the mission of that public library. Some public libraries print the library's mission on the back of the Library Trustees' business cards so it is handy for them to share.

An advocate is a person who pleads for or on behalf of another. A library advocate pleads on behalf of the library. Library advocates can be more effective in many cases than the library staff can be. An effective library advocate represents community interests. The advocate can talk about the benefits of the library. The advocate has first-hand knowledge of the economic impact of the library in the community–the help a library gives in creating an educated workforce, instilling the joy of reading, helping kids who read to succeed, providing a community gathering place, and teaching literacy. An effective library advocate can make a plea for more services, renovated, expanded, or new buildings, a larger budget, and more staff. An effective library advocate can tell the library story so that it isn't a sad plea but rather an articulate plea to improve the community and its people by improving the public library.

An advocate supports and urges. A library advocate supports the Library and urges others to help in its sustainability and/or expansion. A library advocate talks at every opportunity about the library. A library advocate doesn't wait until the week before the library budget will be up for discussion at the City Council. A library advocate talks about the library all year round.

The Richland County Public Library (RCPL) in Columbia, South Carolina, received twenty-seven years of consecutive budget increases. In 2006, RCPL received its largest budget increase in more than twelve years, a 13.2 percent increase in funding. "Community support and an active Library Board of Directors and Friends Group made it possible for RCPL to receive its full funding request this year," said C. David Warren, Executive Director. He went on to say, "Library users in Richland County are not shy about vocalizing their support to the county council. That level of support has been the driving force behind 27 years of consecutive budget increases."[1]

A library advocate does not wait until a problem comes up at the library which could cause dissension in the community. Through constant, up-to-date communication with key people and decision makers, library advocates urge people to support the library. The library advocate goes many extra miles, attends city meetings, talks about the library at lunch, and volunteers to be part of the city's Speakers Bureau, ready to talk about the library at a moment's notice.

An advocate defends a position or idea. A library advocate defends the library's position or stance. Library advocates are critical to the defense of the library's budget, both when increases are requested and when there is a potential loss of revenue. Due to the increased competition for the public dollar, library advocates are more important than ever in defending support for the Public Library.

A library advocate often is called upon to defend various library policies. If the Library Board has made an unpopular decision, library advocates can help the community understand the Board's decision. The only exception to this is personnel decisions. Personnel decisions should not be discussed since they are dealt with in closed sessions. However, library advocates can still be helpful by projecting a positive attitude through statements such as, "The Board takes its responsibilities seriously; I'm sure there are good reasons for its decision." Another helpful and defusing comment might be, "Many decisions are difficult for the Board because there are valid points on both sides; however, I'm sure after careful consideration, the Board made the best decision."

A library advocate is often called to defend challenges against the library's Internet Policy, filtering, use of MySpace, and a variety of constantly changing issues. At issue could be the latest Harry Potter book, use of the library's meeting rooms for religious services, or library service to undocumented immigrants. A library advocate should be kept well informed by the library staff and/or Library Board so they understand the issue and can help defend the challenge or issues and can help defend the challenge.

An advocate is someone who recommends publicly. A library advocate is someone who publicly tells the library story. Although every library advocate may not be comfortable or effective speaking to large groups, all advocates are spokespeople when they speak to people at work, in religious or education groups, or to their neighbors or relatives.

In a few extreme cases, library advocates have had to work hard to help a library threatened with closure. The 52-branch Buffalo and Erie County Library (B&ECPL), New York is one such case. In late 2004, the city threatened to cut 75 percent of its operating funds. Even at a time when B&ECPL was the busiest in its 168-year history, the severe economic problems of Erie County led to this action. Friends, library users, board members, and people throughout the county made their voices heard. Although the entire budget could not be restored, the decrease was reduced from 75 percent to 11 percent. The advocates' voices were heard and their message received.[2]

A person may advocate formally or informally. One advocate might be best to speak to the PTA or PTO about potential partnerships between the schools and the public library, while another library advocate might be most persuasive and comfortable talking to a friend in a grocery store line about reasons to support the library's upcoming bond issue. Some long-time advocates like the challenge of live talk radio shows, while others are skillful in writing op-ed pieces for the local paper or community newsletter. Some library advocates can be helpful blogging about library issues, while others may have extensive email lists they could use to distribute news about the library. There are as many ways to publicly advocate for the public library as there are kinds of public forums.

In a unique move to call attention to the funding plight of the Kingsteignton Public Library in Devon, England, the Friends of the Library had an eye-catching poster made up and distributed throughout the area showing them tastefully arranged "in the buff" behind the library shelves. Needless to say, this tactic did bring attention to their plea for more money for their library.

A Library advocate is not afraid to speak up but must keep current on library issues at all times, in order to be effective. Anyone can be an advocate; anyone can be a library advocate. The most convincing library advocates have taken a personal inventory, know their strengths and unique skills, and can capitalize on those skills in a way that makes them helpful to maintaining, improving, and expanding public library service in their area, state, or country.

WHO ARE LIBRARY ADVOCATES?

Library advocates can be anyone, but they typically are composed of several groups of people. Many library advocates are members of the library's Friends of the Library groups or they are literally a "Friend" of the library but unaffiliated with a specific group. Library advocates often are trustees, past trustees, or Advisory Committee members. Library advocates are library users, library partners, community leaders, people involved in education, library staff, current and past, and potentially everyone.

Library Friends make excellent library advocates. Most Friends of the Library groups have similar missions. The Lexington Public Library's Friends of the Library articulates advocacy as its mission:

> In appreciation of the role the Library plays in the quality of life in this area, the friends of the Lexington Public Library provides non-essential financial and volunteer services to the library, and functions consistently with the goals and objective of the Lexington Public Library and its Board of Trustees.

Many Friends groups are involved in some type of fundraising activity, selling used books and running gift shops being the most popular. People who volunteer their time to work collecting, sorting, and/or selling books in order to raise money are very likely to be spending time in the library. They do it because they believe in the library's mission. They are proud of their role in helping the library provide more services than the library would have been able to provide without the Friends' help. One example of the fundraising power of this type of library advocate is the Friends of the Hunterdon County Library in Flemington, New Jersey. They hold an annual weekend book sale in the local National Guard Armory. They use armored tanks to display the booksale signs. This year there were more than 158,000 used books and other materials for sale. This hard working Friends group raised $95,000 that will be used for new laptop computers and public computer training class.[3]

Friends are the citizen representatives of the library to the community. By investing their zeal and volunteering their time, they are telling their friends and neighbors that the library and its services are vital to an information-literate nation. Don't assume that they know all of the library issues and concerns. Consider doing an orientation so these volunteers stay up-to-date on the library needs and plans for the future. Nurture your Friends of the Library, recognize them during National Volunteers Week or National Library Week, and continually thank them for their help.

One of the strengths of uniting with your Friends of the Library members is that they are already in place. They have declared themselves ready by joining the Friends and/or volunteering their time. In most parts of the country there are many volunteer opportunities. The fact that your Friends of the Library members have chosen the library as the institution and service to which they donate their time and money indicates that they are already supporters and could be willing to take a more specific advocacy role in addition to being a Friend.

Most Friends groups are almost self-recruiting, because helping with the book sales or other fundraising activities is enjoyable, provides socialization, and is personally worthwhile. Friends tell their friends about the library. The more successful your Friends group, the more other people want to join and participate. Friends make the most successful advocates if they are kept current all through the year, not just when there is a crisis. Consider having a staff liaison to the Friends group. This person also can encourage the Friends in their many and varied advocacy roles.

Don't overlook the Library Friends who haven't joined the formal Friends of the Library group. Some people aren't joiners and/or don't have time to volunteer. They still may consider themselves a "Friend" of the Library. Consider having a mailing list of people interested in the library and those who would like to be kept up-to-date. "Never underestimate the power of a single individual to change the world. It has always been so," said Margaret Mead.

Current and past Library Trustees and Library Advisory Board members have connections in the community that make them effective library advocates. If the Library Trustees stand for election, don't overlook those not elected as people who could be library advocates. People who are willing to serve on Public Library Boards and Advisory Committees generally understand the importance of providing free access to information in a democratic society. They know the critical role libraries and librarians play in bridging the digital divide, in navigating and authenticating information, and in helping to stabilize the community in times of economic downturns and disasters.

Since library advocacy must be tied to the library's overall goals, the Trustees and Advisory Committee members are the people who can make this connection most easily. Successful advocacy plans do not just happen. In order to be successful, people need to know for what they are advocating. Goals must be identified, a plan developed, tasks assigned, and progress evaluated. Trustees and Advisory Committee members are knowledgeable and experienced in the political arena. They can be very helpful in developing plans and strategies and in recruiting others.

Although Board and Committee members are appointed and/or elected, remember to recruit past Trustees and potential Trustees as advocates. Sometimes the past members have more free time available to them.

The strength of Library Trustees and Advisory Committee members is their vast knowledge about the library. Many members have long tenure and understand the history and culture of the library in the community. Others are well connected and know instinctively whom to contact when a problem arises. This group of individuals is charged with representing the best interests of the library and as such has great influence in the community.

Funding for Texas libraries was $30 million less in 2004 than in 2002. The impact of the cuts was devastating to communities and schools across Texas. The Texas Library Association, in coordination with the Planning Committee of the 2005 Texas Library Association, in an unprecedented move, planned a rally to send this united message to lawmakers: "Libraries are an investment that works and library funding must be restored!" (see Figure 1).

Complete with 100 drums, 2,000 "Texans Love Libraries" fans, 150 placards, and several large banners, the 2,500 library supporters in attendance were so energized–chanting "get libraries out of the red"–that legislators actually came out from inside the Capitol to tell them that they could be heard underground and on the House floor. One librarian reported that a couple of well-dressed lobbyists joined the librarian festivities and said they could hear the rally from two blocks away. They came to see what the fuss was about and were astonished to learn that the members of the loud, spirited group were librarians and library supporters.

The rally garnered over two hours of broadcast time in local and state TV and radio. TLA has a videoclip of the rally available as streaming

FIGURE 1. April 6, 2005, over 2,500 Texas library supporters on the steps and front lawn of the State Capital in Austin for the "Rally for Texan Libraries."

Printed with permission. Texas Library Association.

video. For a sense of "being there," view the video clips on the 2005 conference page: <http://www.txla.org/conference/conf05/conf05.html>.

People who use the library and its services play a key role in advocacy efforts. People describing to others how the library changed their life is a very powerful advocacy tool. Adults who have learned to read at the library can be dramatic advocates. Testimonials about life changing information found at the library command serious attention from decision makers. The story of Ernest and Julio Gallo finding the key information for their wine making success at the Library, the story of the new immigrants who can communicate on-line with their family members left behind, the story of the child who improved his or her reading skills at the library by reading to a therapy dog are more powerful than the most impressive statistics about the library.

The strength of library users as advocates is their first-hand knowledge of the vital role of the library in their community. Stories often touch the heart strings and emotions of the people hearing them in a way that circulation figures and pie charts do not.

There are many ways to recruit library users to become library advocates. Most just need to be asked. When the American Library Association (ALA) sponsored the "Libraries Change Lives" contest, it provided a model for libraries to use. Some libraries regularly sponsor similar story contests. Other libraries have blank cards on the information desks for people to fill in with their success stories. Collecting stories from thank-you letters and front-line staff encouraging library users to write down the stories they relate while they are in the library are two other ways to collect stories. Have your staff encourage library users to tell their success stories to others including those on the funding bodies. Several state libraries have gathered stories statewide and made them available for libraries to use.

Library partners, community leaders, and people who are involved in education, students, faculty, school and college administrators, and foundation officials are people to be involved in the advocacy network. Education partners particularly are useful as they often have goals similar to those of the Library. This group's strength is that their voices can often be heard at the highest levels. Leaders from forty-eight universities signed letters supporting the Federal Research Public Access Act of 2006 (FRPAA) which would require federal agencies with over $100 million in annual external research budgets to make that research available online within six months of publication. In addition to the university presidents and vice presidents that wrote to support this bill, a coalition of library groups announced their support.

Associate Executive Director of the Association of Research Libraries Prudence Adler said, "There are strong voices of support in diverse constituencies that will be actively working on this legislation." With the important backing of leaders of major universities and the vocal support of respected educational research organizations, this legislation has a better chance for passage.[4]

Library partners are like the Friends. They have already made a commitment to the library and its mission. They are already on board. Make sure partners are kept well-informed as they may have unique contacts from the other advocates.

Library staff members are library advocates every time they answer the question "Where do you work?" Whenever news articles appear about the library, their families and friends will ask staff questions. Staff can help enhance the public's understanding of the library and its role in the community. Like all the members of the library's advocacy team, the staff needs to have the information to fulfill their advocacy role. Each person, Friends members, Trustees and Advisory Committee members, partners, educators, students, library users, community leaders and staff all have slightly different roles in the library's advocacy efforts. It is up to each library to define these roles for its particular situation.

The strength of using staff in an advocacy role is the amount and extent of their knowledge about the library. A weakness in some situations is that it can appear to be self-serving to have staff advocating. The staff usually fills the advocate's role as upholder. The staff upholds the Library's Bill of Rights, the Library Board's policies, and the ALA's Right to Read and View. Staff is helpful in explaining these policies to the public. Many states or cities define the role of staff in lobbying laws.

The role of library staff as advocates should be clearly outlined for all staff at new staff orientation. Staff should be encouraged to repeat patrons' success stories and help explain Library policies to the public. Encouraging staff to share the library's message is an effective method of promoting it. Staff as members of a community Speaker's Bureau is another advocacy tool.

Although this article has reviewed some specific groups as potential players in your advocacy network, everyone in your community is a potential advocate. Brainstorm with staff according to your advocacy goals, to determine which people would make the best advocates. In specific instances, celebrity advocates can be helpful. When the Broward County Library in Fort Lauderdale, Florida, was working to pass a building bond issue it recruited local celebrity tennis champ Chris Evert,

Dave Thomas of Wendy's, and football's Dan Marino for its Better Libraries for a Better Broward campaign.

WHEN DO YOU USE THE ADVOCATES?

Library advocates need to be current on what's happening at the library at all times. They need to know about potential problems before they hear or read about them from the media. No one likes to be surprised. Library advocates are no exception. A well-informed library advocate is an effective advocate. There will be times the library will need the advocacy network to be proactive. If a piece of legislation or ordinance is being discussed and likely to affect the library, it is necessary to have your advocates ready to urge support or defeat for the library's position. Arm them with a position synopsis, a question and answer sheet, some clear sound bites, and a uniform message. Make sure each staff member has the same information. Most of the time the library uses the advocates to build, maintain, and sustain support for the library. However, sometime the library needs to mobilize the advocates in time of crisis.

Some potential crises can be anticipated. People continue to challenge the inclusion of specific materials in libraries. All public libraries should have a plan in place to deal with potentially negative situations that can be anticipated. Natural disaster or crime cannot be anticipated, but library advocates can play an important role in a quick and positive response. Each public library should determine how to most effectively use its library advocates.

AN EXAMPLE OF SUCCESSFUL USE OF ADVOCATES

In early 1999, Broward County Library, Ft. Lauderdale, Florida had only seven weeks from the date of approval to have a $139.5 million dollar library bond issue on the ballot until the date people would be voting. It was imperative to have citizens involved if the bond issue had any chance of passing. Library Director Samuel F. Morrison called on the Broward Public Library Foundation (BPLF) for help. BPLF created a citizen-led committee of high-profile people; the committee included a political consultant and pollster, experts in public relations, a direct mail consultant representative from the Friends of the Library, Foundation members, and staff. A speaker's bureau led by the well respected former library Director, Cecil Beach, made more than 170 presentations to community groups.

Following is a list of decisions that led to the bond vote's success and demonstrates the diverse advocates working on the project:

1. The committee focused their activities on the supervoters, people who constantly vote in primaries and mid-year elections.
2. Staff were able to act as advocates and provide information about the bond issue to the public because the County Attorney ruled it was not a conflict of interest.
3. Committee members used their contacts to secure the celebrity endorsements.
4. Through letters and personal phone calls, committee members and staff secured endorsements from colleges and universities in the county, unions, homeowner and condo associations, and Chambers of Commerce.
5. Committee advocates encouraged city officials to issue Resolutions of Support, and promote the measure to their citizens.
6. The Committee Chair and the Library Advisory Board Chair wrote guest editorials for the *Ft. Lauderdale Sun-Sentinel* and the *Miami-Herald*.
7. The League of Women Voters and Friends of the Library helped staff information tables at all 35 libraries.
8. The county's bus system agreed to have bus signs on the outside of the buses.
9. A billboard company was convinced by a library advocate to provide billboard space at a reduced rate for billboards with the message, "Better Libraries for a Better Broward. Vote yes for libraries on March 9."

On election night, committee members and staff watched the poll results come in at the library's auditorium. Over the intense seven-week period, camaraderie developed among the various advocates. They all celebrated the resounding 72.45% yes vote. This overwhelming positive vote would not have been possible without strong advocate support.

WHERE DOES THE LIBRARY START?

Most public libraries are required by their funding source or their state library agency to have a strategic multi-year plan that outlines the library's goals and objectives. Library advocacy goals must be tied into the library's overall goals. In order to develop an effective advocacy campaign, the library must develop an action plan with clear goals and objectives. A major part of the plan will be the development of a clear message and a training plan both for the staff advocates and other advocates.

The starting place before the plan is developed is determining what it is that the library needs. Is it passage or defeat of a specific piece of legislation or ordinance? Is it more money? Is it a change in the local or state funding allocation? Is it approval of a bond referendum? Most public library advocacy initiatives center on increasing funding, approval of a bond issue for a new or renovated building, and/or proposals to change library funding mechanisms.

When public librarians participated in the May 2006 National Library Legislative Day in Washington, D.C., they were armed with several messages: gratitude for LSTA dollars but caution over threats to open and equal access to information. The most important starting point is, knowing exactly what you want. The American Library Association (ALA) in its *Library Advocate's Handbook* provides an excellent outline for getting organized:

1. Define goals and objectives.
   Identify desired outcomes: New legislation, more funding, greater visibility.
2. Assess the situation in targeted areas based on your objectives.
   Identify barriers/opposition/strengths/potential supporters.
3. Identify critical tasks.
   Key areas include:

   – Steering committee
   – Budget
   – Volunteers
   – Coordination of activities with ALA/state association
   – Fundraising

4. Develop a communication plan.
   Key elements include:

   – Defining the key message
   – Targeting key audiences
   – Identifying communication strategies and resources needed

5. Develop a work plan with tasks, assignments and deadlines.
   Monitor progress regularly.

6. Document and evaluate results.
   This is how you learn to do it better next time.[5]

There are other excellent resources available at the Advocacy Resource Center of the American Library Association <www.ala.org/ala/issues/issuesadvocacy.htm>.

An on-line advocacy training program is particularly helpful to advocates and staff who are unable to attend training sessions. There is an extensive list of resources on this site as well as directions on how to subscribe to an electronic advocacy discussion list and contacts to provide support.

WHERE DOES THE LIBRARY GO FROM HERE?

Public libraries have a long tradition of advocating for their needs. When ALA President Pat Schuman rallied libraries and librarians in 1991-92 to become advocates, she asked them to support better funding and draw attention to the funding plight across the nation. The public library advocates stepped up to the plate. The late Arthur Curley, Director of the Boston Public Library, Pat Woodrum, Director of the Tucson Public Library, Bob Croneberger, Carnegie Library of Pittsburgh, and Mitch Freedman of the Westchester Library System in New York all joined "The Charge for Library Advocacy Now!" They appeared on TV, spoke on radio talk shows, and wrote op-ed pieces in newspapers. They spoke unceasingly about the value of public libraries as the cornerstone of democracy.

After years of dwindling funds for public libraries and the threatened closure of some libraries, and years of advocacy training for staff, Trustees, and Friends, ALA began preparing advocacy materials and developing regular training sessions in 1999. The first advocacy position was added to ALA's Public Information Office in 2001. The "@ your library" campaign was launched to begin a national branding program in April 2001 in Washington, D.C., with First Lady Laura Bush (see Figure 2).

Public libraries enthusiastically embraced the advocacy campaign. They saw the evolution of their tried and true Friends of the Library groups which always have been advocacy groups with the Friends of the Library name, morph into true advocacy groups. Over the next several years after repeated advocacy training across the country, the number of bond referendums that passed slowly began to increase. Several major new public libraries were approved, funded, and built–Seattle, Salt Lake City, and Minneapolis. Californians grew tired of the poor library services that developed as a result of tax cutting Proposition 13, and a series of local bond referendums to improve and expand library service were passed. All the battles to reduce hours and cut public library funding weren't won, but the ever-expanding downward spiral had been stopped. Several ALA presidents who are public librarians have made advocacy their top priority. Carole Brey-Casiano and Leslie Burger both worked tirelessly to advocate for the importance of advocacy.

In the fall of 2004 the Public Library Association unveiled the @ your library campaign, "The Smartest Card. Get it. Use it. @your library" (see Figure 3). This campaign includes a complete tool kit to help public

FIGURE 2. Library Advocacy Poster

Printed with permission. American Library Association.

FIGURE 3. Smartest Card Logo

Printed with permission. American Library Association.

librarians and public library advocates help the public understand the value of public library services and to use them.

Public library advocates are like a salad. Each lettuce leaf or spinach leaf stalk is like each individual library advocate. It is only a single ingredient in a rather bland, unmemorable salad. Adding more ingredients, the carrots, celery, black olives, green pepper, onions, pine nuts, and broccoli are as single ingredients less tasty but all together they create a powerful mix. Add the dressing, the advocate's message, and carefully toss it among and over all the ingredients and you have a memorable, filling salad or a successful advocate's network. Working together with a unified message, advocates can transform libraries and the services they offer and help transform communities.

NOTES

1. "Good Budget News for Richland County PL." Library Hotline, vol. XXXV, No. 31 (August 7, 2006): 2.
2. "Buffalo Library System Saved But Must Reduce Service, Staff." Library Hotline, vol. XXXV, No. 31 (January 3, 2005): 1.
3. "Friends of the Hunterdon County." Library Hotline, vol. XXXV, No. 31 (August 28, 2006): 4.
4. "Public Access Bill Gains Support of 48 Universities." Library Hotline, vol. XXXV, No. 31 (August 21, 2006): 6.
5. "American Library Association." Library Associate's Handbook, Revised 3rd edition, (2003): 7.

doi:10.1300/J118v25n01_11

Developing an Outreach Program Based on Freedom Songs

Leslie A. Acevedo

SUMMARY. The Flint Public Library developed the grant funded program, "The Power of Song: Ain't Gonna Let Nobody Turn Me 'Round," to provide young people with in-depth exposure to the creative and purposeful aspects of the protest traditions of African-American freedom songs. The project used the resources of the Library to promote individual student and community research. doi:10.1300/J118v25n01_12 *[Article copies available for a fee from The Haworth Document Delivery Service: 1-800-HAWORTH. E-mail address: <docdelivery@haworthpress.com> Website: <http://www.HaworthPress.com> © 2006 by The Haworth Press, Inc. All rights reserved.]*

KEYWORDS. Outreach, civil rights movement, protest music, freedom songs, choir, Title I, Dr. Bernice Johnson Reagon

INTRODUCTION

The Flint Public Library recently designed an outreach project, "The Power of Song: Ain't Gonna Let Nobody Turn Me 'Round," to expose students and the Flint community to the enriching aspects of the protest

---

Leslie A. Acevedo is the Young Adult Programs and Services and Lead Librarian at the Flint Public Library, Michigan and Project Coordinator of "The Power of Song: Ain't Gonna Let Nobody Turn Me 'Round."

Address correspondence to: Flint Public Library, 1026 East Kearsley Street, Flint, MI, 48502 (E-mail: lacevedo@fpl.info).

[Haworth co-indexing entry note]: "Developing an Outreach Program Based on Freedom Songs." Acevedo, Leslie A. Co-published simultaneously in *Public Library Quarterly* (The Haworth Press, Inc.) Vol. 25, No. 1/2, 2006, pp. 171-179; and: *Current Practices in Public Libraries* (ed: William Miller, and Rita M. Pellen) The Haworth Press, Inc., 2006, pp. 171-179. Single or multiple copies of this article are available for a fee from The Haworth Document Delivery Service [1-800-HAWORTH, 9:00 a.m. - 5:00 p.m. (EST). E-mail address: docdelivery@haworthpress.com].

Available online at http://plq.haworthpress.com
© 2006 by The Haworth Press, Inc. All rights reserved.
doi:10.1300/J118v25n01_12

172   CURRENT PRACTICES IN PUBLIC LIBRARIES

traditions of African-American freedom songs. Over a six-month period, Dr. Bernice Johnson Reagon shared her extensive knowledge with the Title I Children's Choir and Verse Chorus, an after-school program founded 21 years ago by the Flint Community Schools, and their directors. Using the resources at the Flint Public Library, the children learned about the Civil Rights Movement and the role of protest music in the movement. The project culminated in a concert on April 14, 2005, where the Title I Choir performed protest songs with Dr. Reagon and other young musicians in a free public concert to over 700 people. In a desire to give the project funders full documentation and the concert members a keepsake, a CD studio recording of the concert was made in December 2005.

BACKGROUND

How Do You Feel When You Sing? When Did You First Know That You Wanted to Sing? Were You Ever Afraid to Sing? How Old Are You? Are You Married?

Confident, curious and animated, members from the Title I Children's Choir posed these questions to Dr. Bernice Reagon at a video teleconference on October 28, 2004. Dr. Reagon was in Reston, Virginia and the young people were in Flint, Michigan at Mott Community College's Regional Technology Center. The video teleconference kicked off a very special project between the Flint Public Library and the Flint Community Schools. The project was called *The Power of Song: Ain't Gonna Let Nobody Turn Me 'Round*, whose title was inspired by a well know civil rights song. Generously funded by the Ruth Mott Foundation, the "Power of Song" project was designed to expose students and the community to the enriching aspects of the protest traditions of African-American freedom songs. The library felt this was going to be a powerful project, but did not have any idea how powerful this outreach project would be.

Outreach is a strong and invaluable tool for libraries working in communities where the libraries, colleges, government entities and other institutions of learning are seen with unease or discomfort. Not only do libraries have vital resources that can change and improve their citizens' lives; inside libraries are resources that can entertain, motivate, excite, and bring back memories and fill in holes forgotten as its citizens leave public school.

In this library outreach project, designed and conceived in partnership with the Flint Community Schools, with the Title I Children's Choir and Verse Chorus as the major recipients, the staff of the library developed and called upon its community partners and hired a professional producer/musician of African-American musical history to develop the musical presentation. Dr. Bernice Johnson Reagon selected the musical compositions made famous during the movement and then created a narrative that provided a historical framework of the movement for the young singers. Dr. Reagon had participated in the Civil Rights Movement as a founding member of the *Student Nonviolent Coordinating Committee (SNCC) Freedom Singers* and brought with her an authenticity few others could bring. In the early design of the project, the songs and script, which wove the protest songs together, were to be presented in a concert in April 2005 for the Flint community and each choir member would also be required to develop an "artistic expression of learning" that would be exhibited at the library in April 2005. Later, encouraged to enter the recording studio and document the concert, representative members of the Choir, the narrators, the soloists, and Dr. Reagon recorded an archival CD of the project.

BUILDING A UNIFIED CONCEPT

The first major task was developing a collective concept of how this project was designed to convey the role of protest songs in the civil rights movement and how members of the project would work together toward the concert and the children's exhibits. A library project team consisting of three staff members was selected to implement the project. The project's coordinator was the liaison between all the project partners. The team worked with the choir and its musical directors, with Dr. Reagon, with the library's community partners and within the library to develop and coordinate the resources needed for a successful project.

Introducing and developing a shared vision of the project to the various administrators became the next task. The Choir directors, the library staff, and the coordinator of the young narrators met to discuss the project together in August 2004 before the choir was in session. Selecting dates for introducing the project to the choir youth and the October Video Teleconference led the project team forward in the fall 2005. Building consensus and trust from the beginning aided the project team during crucial times when difficult or timely decisions were needed.

Not satisfied with developing a concert with the 100 + member choir, the library invited two special musicians to participate in the concert. Flint home-town son, Antwaun Stanley, had sung to great acclaim at the library's annual Martin Luther King, Jr. celebration and had been performing locally at weddings, gatherings, and other local venues for years. The library saw him as a role model for the Flint choir members so they might envision for themselves careers in music. If Antwaun could make it into the University of Michigan, School of Music and devote his career to music, maybe there is a future there for other young Flint singers too.

Gareth Johnson, a featured violinist of Detroit's Sphinx Organization, also added a special element to the project. Not only was his background in a classical string instrument performance, the violin, but Gareth was already on track pursuing a professional musician career on a national level. As Gareth expressed to our staff during April rehearsals: ". . . didn't have an African American, classical violinist for a role model to motivate me, but maybe I can be that for other young, African American children someday."

The final component was inviting a local organization, the Gamma Delta Kudos and the Kappa Leadership League, to narrate the evening's civil rights journey. Dr. Reagon wove the protest music of the civil rights movement into a cohesive piece by writing a narrative component that introduced and gave the background stories, thus setting the scene for each song. This narration had to be clear, fluid, and expressive. Four young Flint high school men were chosen from the organization, and were coached by their mentor and coach, John Rhymes, to narrate the performance while the choir would sing the songs.

INTRODUCING THE CONCEPT AND COMPONENTS TO THE CHOIR

In October 2004, the library staff introduced the project to the choir and introduced the concept of conducting and participating in a video teleconference from Flint, MI, with Dr. Reagon who would be in Virginia, to the choir members and their families. The library team traveled to Gundry Elementary School several times on choir rehearsal days and spoke with the 100 + member choir about the project. A requirement of the Flint school's Title I funding was that these "at-risk" students receive some academic component as part of their choir activities. Therefore, the choir worked on homework or worked with a tutor for 45 minutes and then the choir rehearsed for 1.5 hours twice a week.

During our visits we provided the basic historical background of the American Civil Rights Movement using library resources including clips from several video documentaries and a library storyteller. There was an introduction to Dr. Bernice Johnson Reagon and her expertise, using video clips of program interviews and her concerts; we also introduced the resources (CDs, books, song sheets, videos and DVDs) from the library that would be available to them as they studied both protest music and the Civil Right Movement; and we spoke with them about possible suggestions of "artistic expressions of learning" they could think about choosing for their exhibit at the library in April 2005.

The library team members continued to visit the choir periodically throughout the fall of 2004 not only to enjoy hearing them sing, but also to continue to build a relationship with the choir and their families and to draw attention to the resources of the library.

FIRST INTRODUCTIONS

The October video teleconference was another moment to pause for evaluation of the impact of this project on the choir and the Flint community. The choir in Flint, MI was being introduced to an internationally acclaimed musician and historian who would develop this project and sing with them in a community concert, via modern, state-of-the-art technology, in almost real-time, in Reston, Virginia. Few of the members involved in the project had ever participated in a video teleconference and indeed few in the Flint community ever had.

The students were not only able to introduce themselves and ask Dr. Reagon questions about her life as a singer/songwriter, author, historian, and civil rights activist, but were also able to develop a bond of sorts with her, making the projects less abstract and more real via the teleconference. It helped them envision how the music affected those who participated in the movement.

FACE TO FACE

By the time January 2005 grew near, the choir had learned more than half the songs they would perform in April; they had met with Dr. Reagon via the teleconference and from the library staff presentations; and they had done private civil right research during the tutorial time on Choir rehearsal days.

On January 12, 2005, Dr. Reagon arrived in Flint for the first face-to-face rehearsal with the choir and other members of the project. Nervous and excited, the choir arrived for this event after practicing diligently for months; they were ready for this meeting. The connection with Dr. Reagon and the choir was electric and almost immediately visible. They understood her command of the material and her inherent understanding of both what it means to be singer and the power that music and lyrics can have on sending a message to the greater community. It was beautiful! They gave Dr. Reagon 200% and she challenged them to give her even more.

This was also the first introduction for Antwaun Stanley and the narrators to Dr. Reagon and to the Choir. It was the first time anyone would hear what before this moment was just a concept, the narration and the songs performed together. While there was still much work to be achieved before the project was ready for performance, the concept was unfolding with each part understanding how they fit into the whole. Everyone left the rehearsal very satisfied and enthusiastic about the coming concert–optimism was the fuel for the momentum for the last leg of preparations for the performance.

MOVING FORWARD

During the early months of 2005 before the concert were more rehearsals; choosing the concert hall; developing the evening brochure; having everyone from the choir come visit the library and updating their patron card records; and producing and exhibiting the choir's artistic expressions of the project. Each piece was seen as pivotal to the success of the whole with quality always being the standard to which we measure our readiness.

At the beginning of April the library hosted the Title I Children's Choir and Verse Chorus "Remembering the Civil Rights Movement" Artistic Expressions Exhibit at the library. The exhibit consisted of poems, collage, drawings, protest posters, songs, and raps from the choir juxtaposed with photographs and commentary from Flint's Alfred P. Sloan Museum's collection of Flint's historical civil rights photos. This collaboration of old and new, historical and contemporary art expressions spanning over three generations of Flint citizens was enthusiastically acclaimed by the local community who came to view the exhibit.

Young students with parents and grandparents viewed the civil rights movement exhibit side-by-side each explaining his or her understanding/memories of this historical period. It would be difficult to judge who had a better understanding of this historical movement, as the choir members, thanks to the extensive work supported by the project and Dr. Reagon, had evidenced by their expressive works, a deep understanding of the civil rights movement and the role that protest music played in the movement.

FINAL PREPARATIONS

On April 12, 2005 the choir, Dr. Reagon, Tenor Antwaun Stanley, and the Sphinx Organization violinist, Gareth Johnson met to rehearse. Everyone was anxious and wondering if we were prepared. In two days, what had been worked on for over 9 months was going to be executed and over in little more than an hour-long performance. Did everyone know their words, their parts; were they singing on key; did we have enough water for the choir; did the parents know when and where to bring the children on Thursday, the concert day? What had we forgotten?

THE CONCERT

On Thursday, April 14 in the early afternoon the library project staff, Antwaun Stanley, Gareth Johnson, Dr. Bernice Johnson Reagon, and the choir directors waited for the choir members to arrive. The Concert was scheduled to begin at 6:00 p.m., giving just enough time for parents to finish work and arrive on time. Dr. Reagon hoped to have a short rehearsal before the concert.

At 6:15 p.m. over 700 people were gathered in the church and the narration began: *"Music has always been integral to the African American struggle for freedom. The music of the Civil Rights Movement was shaped by those who participated in the rallies, the marches, those who went to jail, those who marched to the courthouse to register to vote; –as they marched–they sang."* These memorable words, now etched forever in the minds of all who participated in or witnessed the project, began a concert that would be a testament to the power of teamwork, the power of outreach, and power of collaboration in Flint, Michigan. A reception, to celebrate a job well done, followed the concert.

THE RECORDING STUDIO, THE CD AS DOCUMENTATION, THE WEBSITE AND MEDIA KITS

With a desire to give each participant a keepsake of the evening and toward fulfilling the grant requirement of full documentation of the project, Dr. Reagon stressed the need of going into the recording studio shortly after the school year began. She hoped to complete the CD before the New Year while the inspiration of the concert was still in everyone's memory.

With this tool (CD) the library is able to develop media kits that can transmit a fuller picture of the project. Included in the kits are: CD, a full script of the evening concert, song lyrics, a timeline of the project, and a list of resources at the library on protest music, civil rights movements, stories of the Civil Rights Movement, and information on important persons in the Civil Rights Movement.

We have also developed a Website which gives the overview of the project elements, the concert script, and printable song lyrics. You may listen to song clips from the CD, and view photographs of the project and evening concert. The site also includes a timeline of the project, background notes on the participants, a list of the community partners, a bibliography of protest music, freedom songs, the Civil Rights Movement, and more. The Web site is <www.fpl.info/powerofsong>.

> *The struggle of the Civil Rights Movement, the culture of the struggle, the singing, the coming together of people to call their country to higher ground, is important not only as a history lesson, but in contemporary times it is crucial that we try to understand the importance of organizing, the importance of non-violence, the importance of our individual responsibility in the practice of good citizenship.*–Dr. Bernice Johnson Reagon (from concert narrative)

RESULTS–THE POWER OF OUTREACH

Dr. Reagon was so pleased with the outcome of the project that she has inquired about and supported making it a model for other communities to follow. Consider the following:

- Approximately 700 people attended the *Power of Song: "Ain't Gonna Let Nobody Turn Me 'Round"* concert of Dr. Reagon, the Title I Children's Choir and Verse Chorus, Antwaun Stanley, Gareth

Johnson and the narrators who provided drama to the history of the movement.
- The Library received a total of $28,000 in funding including $25,000 from the Ruth Mott Foundation for expenses related to the project.
- Thirty-five music teachers and choir directors attended a workshop, presented by Dr. Reagon, entitled "African American Pioneering Gospel Music Composers."
- More than 75 people listened attentively as Dr. Reagon spoke about her life as a singer and composer.
- More than 145 people attended a public lecture by Dr. Reagon.
- More than 400 people visited the Library to view an exhibit of artwork, poems, and essays created by the Title I Choir.
- Dr. Bernice Johnson Reagon stated the following: "For me . . . this has been a unique and deeply moving experience and one that I will treasure always. I thank the visionary work of this Library which stretched the meaning of its work to create such a wonderful opportunity of sharing . . . with its community through the voices of its children."
- Finally, perhaps the most important outcome of this project was that this in-depth interactive experience significantly increased the knowledge of the Civil Rights Movement for its participants. The project also fueled intergenerational discussions among family and community members.

For further information on this project, photographs, and music clips of the concert, printable lyrics and the concert script, or for contact information to learn more details on creating a similar project go to the Flint Public Library's *The Power of Song: Ain't Gonna Let Nobody Turn Me 'Round* Website: <http://www.flint.lib.mi.us/powerofsong/about.shtml>.

From Literate to Information Literate Communities Through Advocacy

Carol A. Brey-Casiano

SUMMARY. Public libraries have long played an active role in creating literate communities, and we must now take steps to create *information literate* communities. Librarians and library stakeholders can use reliable advocacy techniques to strengthen information literacy in their own communities. doi:10.1300/J118v25n01_13 *[Article copies available for a fee from The Haworth Document Delivery Service: 1-800-HAWORTH. E-mail address: <docdelivery@haworthpress.com> Website: <http://www.HaworthPress.com> © 2006 by The Haworth Press, Inc. All rights reserved.]*

KEYWORDS. Literacy, information literacy, advocacy

THE PATH FROM LITERATE TO INFORMATION LITERATE COMMUNITIES

It has been more than five years since the American Library Association introduced the concept of "Building Information Literate Communities,"

Carol A. Brey-Casiano is currently serving as Director of the El Paso Public Library System. She holds a Master's degree in Library Science from the University of Illinois, and a Bachelor's degree in Music from Illinois State University. She also served as the President of the American Library Association from 2004-2005.

Address correspondence to: Carol A. Brey-Casiano, El Paso Public Library, 501 North Oregon, El Paso, TX 79901 (E-mail: breycx@elpasotexas.gov).

[Haworth co-indexing entry note]: "From Literate to Information Literate Communities Through Advocacy." Brey-Casiano, Carol A. Co-published simultaneously in *Public Library Quarterly* (The Haworth Press, Inc.) Vol. 25, No. 1/2, 2006, pp. 181-190; and: *Current Practices in Public Libraries* (ed: William Miller, and Rita M. Pellen) The Haworth Press, Inc., 2006, pp. 181-190. Single or multiple copies of this article are available for a fee from The Haworth Document Delivery Service [1-800-HAWORTH, 9:00 a.m. - 5:00 p.m. (EST). E-mail address: docdelivery@haworthpress.com].

Available online at http://plq.haworthpress.com
© 2006 by The Haworth Press, Inc. All rights reserved.
doi:10.1300/J118v25n01_13

under the leadership of President Nancy Kranich (2000-2001). At that time a new ALA Special Presidential Committee on Information Literacy and Advocacy was formed to focus on building public awareness of what it takes to be literate in the 21st Century. And in 2001, ALA issued an Action Pack entitled "A Library Advocate's Guide to Building Information Literate Communities."

I must confess, I had partially forgotten about this important effort on the part of Past President Kranich and ALA, until I was invited last spring to speak on the topic of Information Literacy for a conference to be held in Greece. A literature search brought up the 2001 Action Pack on Building Information Literate Communities.[1] I was struck by how relevant this toolkit was to my own work–both as ALA President (2004-2005) with the grassroots advocacy initiative "Stand Up and Speak Out for Libraries," and in my community where I serve as the Director of the El Paso (TX) Public Library. I knew that advocacy was critical to the success of libraries everywhere, and particularly in El Paso–where one in three adults is functionally illiterate. I very much wanted to share the ALA Action Pack, and what I knew about building information literate communities from my own experience, with my colleagues in Greece. But would others find these ideas relevant, particularly across the Atlantic?

In an introductory letter to the Action Pack, Past Presidents Kranich and Pat Schuman wrote that "librarians help to ensure a society where everyone is information literate. That is the story that librarians, trustees, Friends of Libraries and all library advocates must tell if we are to increase support for all libraries. By speaking out, loudly, clearly and with one voice, library advocates can make a difference." Through the Advocacy Institutes that ALA has been holding across the country, we have brought large numbers of library stakeholders together to learn basic and advanced advocacy skills–creating action plans that will enable local communities to build necessary support for libraries and information literacy.

INFORMATION LITERACY–A DEFINITION

So that we are all in agreement regarding what we mean by information literacy, I turned to yet another ALA source for a definition, the *Presidential Committee on Information Literacy: Final Report*[2] published by the Association of College and Research Libraries in 1989. This report states that, *"to be information literate, a person must be able* to recognize when information is needed and have the ability to locate, evaluate, and use effectively the needed information." In short, "*Information literacy is the ability to find and use information*," as summarized in Information Power[3] published by the American Association of School Librarians.

This definition seems clear, but how do we as public librarians communicate the importance of information literacy to our communities? We know that information literacy forms the basis for learning in life, and can help individuals obtain critical information that satisfies a wide variety of personal and business needs. But even more important from my perspective as an urban public library director is the idea that people have the *right* to information that will improve their quality of life. Even as librarians, who generally know how to find information, we have experienced the frustration of solving a problem when we don't have access to the right information. Imagine what the situation would be like for someone who is trying to find the best care for an aging parent, yet doesn't have the ability to find the necessary information or worse yet, can't read and understand the instructions issued by the parent's physician.

This is often when another phenomenon emerges: seeking the information one needs from a neighbor or family member. The ACRL Report indicates that "most people have become dependent on others for their information. Information prepackaging in schools and through broadcast and print news media, in fact, encourages people to accept the opinions of others without much thought."[4] How can we in public libraries turn this trend around? The sheer volume of information available is enough to make people run to their libraries for clear answers. How many of us have had this experience at the reference desk: a father and his 10-year-old son approach regarding the son's assignment, to do a report on a particular variety of cactus. Upon typing the word "cactus" into Google on their home computer, the father receives 26,700,000 hits and promptly decides to head to the library for help in refining his search. Good idea! But how many people would accept the first few sources received as reputable sources, and happily write the report–content with their "research"?

FAST INTERNET FACTS

In the year 2000, the Web consisted of 2.7 billion Web pages for the public, and that number has continued to grow each year since then– with over 76 million domain names in existence today![5] Yet it has been reported that as much as 70% of health and medical information on the Web is wrong or misleading–a sobering amount. Debra Jones once stated that "trying to find information on the Web is like walking into a library after an earthquake, with the books strewn all over the floor."

We all know that the local public library is often the most convenient access point for essential information, and certainly the best resource for lifelong learning. Not only do our libraries provide people with the necessary knowledge to make effective use of available resources, but the Library is also the best defense against the control of information! As the poet John Ciardi once said, "The public library is the most dangerous place in town."

PUBLIC LIBRARIES AND BASIC LITERACY: STRIVING TOWARDS INFORMATION LITERACY

Of course, the public library is also a great place to gain the basic literacy skills that form the basis for information literacy. Clearly, one must be able to read before adopting effective information literacy skills. We should not overlook the public library's role in this area either.

U.S. public libraries currently provide the following support for local basic literacy efforts:

- Up-to-date information about literacy programs (94%)
- Appropriate meeting and studying space for tutors and learners (84%)
- Interesting and timely materials for tutors and learners (84%)
- Library tours for adults, children and families (68%)
- Classes for adult literacy students (30%)
- Computer classes (26%)

The public library serves as "the people's university," based on the library's historic role in support of public education. This is all well and good, but recent studies indicate that the general public may not be turning to their libraries for assistance with information, or information literacy. How can we–as librarians, library workers, and library stakeholders–broadcast our role as the ultimate source for information literacy? The answer, of course, is: advocacy.

BUILDING INFORMATION LITERATE COMMUNITIES–HOW TO MAKE IT HAPPEN!

A Library Advocate's Guide to Building Information Literate Communities lays out a clear plan for making your community aware of the library's role in promoting information literacy. Readers can view the complete toolkit on the ALA Website,[6] but I have included the most important steps here along with some examples shared by libraries around the world.

DEVELOP AN ACTION PLAN

In our Advocacy Institutes, as well as most advocacy training presented by ALA, we encourage participants to develop an advocacy action plan that they can take home and implement. One of the most critical elements of the action plan is the overall purpose–what is it that the advocacy plan will accomplish? Perhaps it is heightened awareness of the public library's role in terms of information literacy, the creation of an information literacy training program, or more general awareness of the public library's programs and services.

What does a more information-literate community look like? The *Guide to Building Information Literate Communities* outlines several goals that should be inherent to any awareness campaign related to information literacy:

- Communities enjoy a high quality of life;
- Workers have the skills and competencies they need;
- Students graduate with the skills and competencies they need;
- Libraries of all types receive increased support; and
- Librarians are recognized as information experts and key players in the education process.

THE ACTION PLAN: KEY MESSAGES

In advocacy training, we know that formulating the key message(s) of the campaign is critical. This can also be the most fun part of the process, as participants think about making these messages clear, concise and memorable. One example from the Guide: "Information literacy is a critical skill in today's information jungle. Libraries and librarians can help you find your way." Or, my personal favorite: "The ultimate search engine is your librarian."

How you develop your message, and deliver it to most effectively make your case, is also critical. Think of stories from your own experience that truly illustrate the importance of information literacy. It could be a story about a disadvantaged teen who, upon the librarian's encouragement, applied and was accepted to Harvard University. Or perhaps you have a story about a difficult medical case where the librarian saved the day. My personal favorite is the story of Mr. and Mrs. Juan Rosales, patrons at the Clardy Fox Branch of the El Paso Public Library. When Mr. and Mrs. Rosales retired, they sought an activity to fill their free time and decided to achieve their lifelong dream of becoming American citizens. After attending citizenship classes at their local library branch, they so enjoyed the relationship they had developed with the Clardy Fox Branch staff that they decided to pursue their education and attended classes in preparation for taking the GED exam. Both of them passed the exam, of course! Sadly, Mrs. Rosales passed away recently, but Mr. Rosales is still taking English-as-a-Second Language (ESL) classes at the Branch–a great example of how the library can assist its users to better their lives and pursue lifelong learning.

DELIVERING THE MESSAGE

How you deliver your message is also important, in order to reach a broad range of current and potential supporters. You can start at home by providing an orientation session for library staff regarding your new advocacy campaign. You might host a "working lunch" for potential partners, or schedule short meetings with community leaders and others in power. The support of Library Friends Groups and the Library Board is also invaluable. If you don't have a Friends Group, start one, or revitalize the one you have. Keith Michael Fiels, Director of the American Library Association, puts it this way: "When it comes to library advocacy, one board member is worth ten librarians and one Friend is worth ten board members." In other words, those who hold your library's purse strings are more apt to listen to a member of the community–because the librarian appears to have a vested interest in library funding.

POTENTIAL PARTNERS IN INFORMATION LITERACY

With increased challenges to Library funding, it is essential to have partners in the community who can share the load and bring synergy to your efforts. The first step, of course, is to identify potential partners who can assist you with a wide variety of library programs–including information literacy. Depending on how much you have worked with these potential partners, it might be wise to develop a strategic plan for your efforts and create a vision for the future together. As you work with new partners, remember to keep an open mind, stay flexible, and be willing to negotiate. You may not get everything you want from the partnership at first, but experience has shown that successful partnerships will eventually surpass your original plan. The key is maintaining regular communication, expressing appreciation along the way, and evaluating your effort periodically.

One example of a successful partnership is that formed by the El Paso Public Library with El Paso Community College (EPCC) in 2002, when we embarked on our first joint-use library partnership. EPCC was building a new library at its Northwest Campus, and we worked with campus officials to develop a partnership that resulted in one of our librarians being placed permanently there to create a "Children's Corner" and provide programming for children and young adults. We also provided funds for books and resources that would appeal to the community at large. Four years later this partnership has succeeded beyond our wildest dreams, and we are taking it to the next level–with plans to renovate 12,000 square feet at another EPCC site to create a second community branch that will serve students and the general population. This partnership has succeeded because of good, positive communication on a regular basis between all parties, as well as expressions of appreciation (here is another one–thank you, EPCC!) and periodic evaluations–at least semi-annually.

SAMPLE MESSAGES FOR POTENTIAL PARTNERS

The Business Community

If you are trying to draw in potential partners, it doesn't hurt to share sample messages that will appeal to them. The toughest partner to attract in many communities seems to be the business community. You can start by joining the local Chamber(s) of Commerce–El Paso Public Library has joined all three here in our community. Attend meetings and "Business After Hours" events, take your business cards, and listen to what the business owners tell you about their needs. You can share your important message too, which could be something like, "You know, Joe–sound business decisions depend on good information, and we can help you with that at the El Paso Public Library. Why don't you stop by on Monday and see one of our reference librarians for help with that information you need about expanding your business?" Another important message is how critical literacy and information literacy are to a competitive workforce. Many corporations have their own literacy programs, but small business owners may not realize that their employees could become literate by attending free classes at the local public library.

Community Leaders

You can appeal to community leaders with a set of tailored messages as well, emphasizing that "Leaders know the importance of having citizens who are information literate." Even if your community struggles with high rates of illiteracy as we do in El Paso, a good leader will recognize the importance of libraries as centers for information, culture, and lifelong learning. Other leaders who are not as effective may not recognize these important qualities of libraries, but you are there to remind them!

BUILDING YOUR LIBRARY NETWORK

Once you have identified a wide variety of potential partners in your community–business leaders, educators, Library board members, Friends– it is time to build your library network. Think about "who you know" that can help you support the Library, and start building a list of email addresses, phone numbers, and other information so that you can easily reach your network when you need it. You might need assistance from your network during the Library's budget presentation, or a funding crisis–or maybe to help you create your new advocacy campaign. Whatever you are trying to accomplish, you can never have too many partners.

PARTNERSHIPS WITH THE MEDIA

The local news media can also be an effective partner. We often think of the media as adversaries, but members of the media can prove to be your biggest supporters. Most reporters and others associated with the news media believe in intellectual freedom, which creates a common ground from which to start. Newspapers and other printed media also recognize the importance of literacy, and nearly every media outlet will attest to the importance of information literacy–even if the quality of some media reports make that hard to believe. To effectively work with the local news media, start by researching the media outlets in your area. Who are the news editors at the local newspaper office, radio and television stations? Does your local newspaper have a community or perhaps even a literary page? Find out who is in charge, call them, and go visit them personally. Tell them about the great programs and services at the library and find out where to send your press releases. Find out the deadlines for various types of stories, as well as the kinds of stories the news outlet likes to cover. Offer to write an Op-ed piece for the newspaper, and add all the people you have met to your mailing list in order to invite them to upcoming events. Remember, reporters are people too!

SUCCESS STORIES: BUILDING INFORMATION LITERATE COMMUNITIES

Greece and the Campaign for the World's Libraries

So how did my presentation on "Building Information Literate Communities" go over in Greece? The Greek Library Association has asked to translate several of ALA's advocacy resources into Greek, and subsequently I heard from several Greek librarians who are pursuing their own advocacy campaigns. This is not unlike the experiences I, and countless other advocacy trainers have had around the world. When it comes to library advocacy, those of us who believe in libraries and want to support them speak a common language. That is why tools like the *Campaign for America's Libraries*[7] and the *Campaign for the World's Libraries*[8]–with the ever-popular @your library logo–have resonated so well with advocates everywhere. Consider these Core Messages from the *Campaign,* which still resound after five years:

- Libraries are changing, dynamic places
- Libraries are places of opportunity
- Libraries bring you the world

The American Library Association wants to hear from you regarding your needs when it comes to promoting information literacy. The "Building Information Literate Communities" Action Pack is due to be updated, and ALA Advocacy Officer Marci Merola is asking for input from the library community. You can send your comments to her at: mmerola@ala.org.

THE ULTIMATE GOAL: GLOBAL INFORMATION LITERACY

One of the most important things I learned during my ALA Presidency was the commonalities librarians experience all over the world. This led me to believe that we should create a *world-wide* network of library advocates who can share ideas, resources and much more. With the many resources available to us here in the United States, provided by ALA and other organizations, we can build information literate communities in every corner of the world, which provide a better quality of life for the people who live there.

NOTES

1. A Library Advocate's Guide to Building Information Literate Communities. Chicago: ALA, 2001. <http:www.ala.org/ala/advocacybucket/informationliteracy.pdf>.
2. Presidential Committee on Information Literacy: Final Report. Chicago: ALA, 1989.
3. Information Power: Building Partnerships for Learning. Chicago: American Library Association and the Association for Educational Communications and Technology, 1998.
4. Presidential Committee on Information Literacy: Final Report. Chicago: ALA, 1989.
5. Domain Tools, <http://www.domaintools.com/internet-statistics/>.
6. A Library Advocate's Guide to Building Information Literate Communities. Chicago: ALA, 2001. <http:www.ala.org/ala/advocacybucket/informationliteracy.pdf>.
7. *Campaign for America's Libraries Website*, <http://www.ala.org/ala/pio/campaign/campaignamericas.htm>.
8. *Campaign for the World's Libraries Website*, <http://www.ifla.org/@yourlibrary/index.htm>.

doi:10.1300/J118v25n01_13

A Literacy Center Where?
A Public Library Finds Space to Promote and Provide Family Learning Activities

Tony Petruzzi
Mary Frances Burns

SUMMARY. In the past, mid-sized public libraries left the literacy needs of their patrons to other agencies in the community, preferring to focus on the traditional library roles of being a center in the community for popular materials, community information, reference assistance, life-long learning, etc. As the literacy levels in the community weakened and began to affect both the status of a community and children's ability to learn, traditional services and literacy can be combined into a successful program that benefits all who participate. doi:10.1300/J118v25n01_14 *[Article copies available for a fee from The Haworth Document Delivery Service: 1-800-HAWORTH. E-mail address: <docdelivery@haworthpress.com> Website: <http://www.HaworthPress.com> © 2006 by The Haworth Press, Inc. All rights reserved.]*

Tony Petruzzi is the Coordinator of the Open Book Family Literacy Center at Morley Library, the public library located in Painesville, Ohio. He received his B.S. in Education and his Masters in Library Science from Kent State University (E-mail: tpetruzzi@morleylibrary.org).

Mary Frances Burns is the Director of Morley Library, and received her B.A. from Immaculate Heart College in Los Angeles in psychology, and her M.A.L.S. from Dominican University in River Forest, Illinois (E-mail: mfb@morleylibrary.org).

[Haworth co-indexing entry note]: "A Literacy Center Where? A Public Library Finds Space to Promote and Provide Family Learning Activities." Petruzzi, Tony, and Mary Frances Burns. Co-published simultaneously in *Public Library Quarterly* (The Haworth Press, Inc.) Vol. 25, No. 1/2, 2006, pp. 191-197; and: *Current Practices in Public Libraries* (ed: William Miller, and Rita M. Pellen) The Haworth Press, Inc., 2006, pp. 191-197. Single or multiple copies of this article are available for a fee from The Haworth Document Delivery Service [1-800-HAWORTH, 9:00 a.m. - 5:00 p.m. (EST). E-mail address: docdelivery@haworthpress.com].

Available online at http://plq.haworthpress.com
© 2006 by The Haworth Press, Inc. All rights reserved.
doi:10.1300/J118v25n01_14

KEYWORDS. Literacy, collaboration, public libraries, tutoring, reading skills, library skills, children

INTRODUCTION

In the Fall of 2003, as Head of Children's Services in a mid-size library district serving 45,000 people I asked the director for a room to provide a family learning center in our new library. This center would be dedicated to strengthening families through learning, reading and sharing. Learning would be experienced at the center by tutoring and teaching activities, while reading would be encouraged by all kinds of story activities and sharing with programming provided by area agencies.

Morley Library was in the process of working with Meehan Architects to provide a new 62,000 sq. ft. building for our Lake County Library District that consisted of a small city, a large suburban township, and several small villages. Morley Library is situated in the city of Painesville, the county seat of Lake County, located in northeastern Ohio. The City School District consists of five elementary schools, and ever since the Ohio Department of Education (ODE) started proficiency testing in the mid '90s, most of the schools were in academic emergency or academic watch, which meant a low score in reading, among other subjects, according to ODE scoring standards.

Painesville is the county seat, and therefore provides convenient services to transient families and families needing assistance through county government agencies located in the city. Many families come and go in and out of the school system as they move along the economic scale. Recent Mexican immigration has also pushed the Hispanic school population over 30 percent. Painesville City and some of the surrounding areas needed help with providing reading and language skills to many of their newest and youngest citizens.

Morley Library had a strong history of collaboration with the local schools. Class visits to the library were plentiful. Schools were actively involved in the library's summer reading clubs, and competed for awards for having the most readers. The Children's Room also collaborated with area schools in bringing published children's authors to local schools and the library for over 10 years.

In 1999, Morley Library began to reach out to assist the Painesville City Local Schools (PCLS) with literacy support by applying for and gaining an OhioReads Community Grant. This renewable grant was an Ohio Department of Education initiative to improve the reading scores of school districts with low reading test scores. Money was available for books and for coordinating a one-on-one tutoring program. Each year Morley Library applied in conjunction with the PCLS to provide this tutoring for elementary age children in the library after school. The School District identified children in need of this service, provided transportation to and from the Library, and measured the students' reading progress. The Library recruited, trained, scheduled, and supervised the tutors. It also provided refreshments and reading materials for the children.

This grant and the activities involved in providing a structured reading program gave me the opportunity to make personal contact with school district personnel from the superintendent to individual teachers.

With these two successful programs in place, the concept of starting a literacy collaborative to assist area families with reading and language activities beyond the traditional story time programs was within reach. The need was there. While adult literacy help was provided by the Painesville Adult Basic Literacy Education (ABLE), and assistance was available to preschoolers through Head Start and EvenStart, nothing addressed the needs of elementary-age students or the family as a whole.

Soon another collaborator surfaced. Lake Erie College (LEC) is a small liberal arts college within walking distance of Morley Library. It has a College of Education that provides many new teachers to the local schools and surrounding area. John Meehl, a new member of the Education Department, had been very successful developing a literacy collaborative in a neighboring county before he left his position as Assistant Superintendent to work part time at LEC. Meehl and I had the good fortune to meet and discuss the need for a literacy collaborative in Lake County.

The Greater Painesville Area Literacy Council (G-PAL) was born from our conversations in the fall of 2001. Area agencies that promoted reading and education were approached to form a collaborative that would provide cooperative programming and services. These entities, representatives from ABLE, EvenStart, Painesville City Local Schools, Lake Erie College, Crossroads (a local mental health agency), and Head Start formed the Council. Fortuitously, this occurred as Morley Library passed a bond issue for a new building.

MAY I HAVE YOUR SPACE?

When Department Heads started meeting with the architect to plan a new building, the Children's Room homework center that I envisioned soon turned into a whole new concept needing a much larger area. In order to move forward, The Greater Painesville Area Literacy Council needed space to provide its joint programming, and needed one contact point to introduce the services provided by the different agencies to citizens in need of them.

The Morley Library Board of Trustees, Library Director, and Department Heads discussed the concept of a literacy center at a retreat in 2003. The Board and Administration were very supportive of the concept. Despite the fact that construction of the new building had progressed past the framing stage, money was found for change orders to create the area that would become the Morley Library Open Book Family Learning Center. The concept was that Morley Library would provide the space and approximately 15 hours a week in staff time, but that grants and the agencies in the G-PAL Council would provide programs, materials, and services. The Center became a reality when the new building opened in November, 2004.

HOW CAN WE PAY FOR THESE SERVICES?

A new building brings new expenses. How could Morley Library pay for new positions and services? Asking the Library to provide more money was not financially realistic at this time. Funds needed to be found in other areas. The G-PAL Council and I started looking and planned fundraising events and collaborative grants.

Two *Murder Mystery* events were planned and implemented by G-PAL members. The first was held at Lake Erie College and profits made from the event provided additional tutoring materials for elementary students. The second murder mystery was held in the new library on the main floor and was an even bigger fund raising success. The funds from this were earmarked to pay for a new preschool tutoring program called Alpha Books.

As the Morley Library Outreach Coordinator of the Open Book Family Learning Center, one of my tasks has been to write grants to fund it. A Library Services Technology Act Grant was awarded in 2005 that provided the Center with eleven Dell PCs, a SmartBoard, and LeapFrog diagnostic testing and reading materials. A local Wal-Mart Literacy Grant and a local City of Painesville Improvement Grant provided funds to pay for planning and implementation of programming. We have also been fortunate that the Center has been the recipient of some memorial donations. Fundraising for the Center continues to be a time-consuming and ongoing process.

Lake Erie College provided through a work-study program a graduate student who eventually became the Assistant Coordinator in the Center. The Assistant Coordinator has a degree in Education with a specialty in reading instruction. Her position is divided into two major roles. She helps plan and implement many of the on-going activities in the center, and coordinates the activities provided there by other G-PAL members. She also serves as the Reading Specialist, doing diagnostic testing and evaluation for the Center's students. Small local grants mentioned above have been used to help pay for an Assistant Coordinator's salary once the work-study funds ended. The Morley Library Board of Trustees also approved a procedure for charging customers fees for special tutoring help through the Center that falls beyond the scope of the OhioReads project. Since the Assistant Coordinator's salary comes completely from grants and fundraising, the additional tutoring fees make up the difference needed to provide her salary.

WHAT ACTIVITIES TAKE PLACE IN THE OPEN BOOK LEARNING CENTER?

The original OhioReads tutoring program that was the impetus for the OBFLC will continue as long as funding is available. Because the collaboration with the Library has demonstrated results in improved reading and library skills, the Painesville City Local Schools have expressed a desire to continue a similar program using other federal and state funds if necessary. Students from the 2004-2005 OhioReads Tutoring Program on average improved one reading level according to the LeapTrack testing performed at the end of the year. Students also demonstrated their knowledge of library resources by showing growth in library skill post tests and by increased use of the library. Therefore, on-going tutoring, library instruction, and family programming will most likely continue in the OBFLC and at the Library in the future.

G-PAL Agencies are asked to provide programs in the Open Book Family Learning Center that promote literacy either by using the space in the Center to hold informational programs that invite participation in their programs, such as a Head Start *Parent Round-Up,* or by using the space to do family literacy programs such as EvenStart's on-going *Parent and Child Together* programs.

Of special interest is the Alpha Book program, mentioned above. It was our first fee-based program. Students at the local preschool run by the Painesville City Local Schools were individually tested for knowledge of letter recognition and phonemic awareness in the late spring of 2005. From the test results, it was shown that many students needed more instruction in these areas, as well as in decoding skills.

Parents were given the opportunity to enroll their child in a six week, one day a week summer program at the Library. Parents were charged a fee of $10 per session to cover some of the costs involved. Fees were waived for parents who could not afford to pay, or reduced it they had multiple children in the program. The support for this program came from the fundraisers and small local grants.

Parents were responsible for dropping off and picking up their child in the Center. Parents stayed in the library during the tutoring sessions. Some parents went to the adult area to find adult materials and some parents went to the Children's Room with younger or older siblings and picked out books for them. The Alpha Book program children were read stories and did story extensions. These activities also happen in our story time sessions. However, *unlike* what happens during our story time sessions, Alpha Book children were given specific reading skill instruction and activities to take home. After the 30 minute program, students were walked upstairs to the Children's Room to meet parents and then staff assisted them in selecting age- and skill-level appropriate books to take home.

As mentioned above, the Assistant Coordinator uses her reading expertise to keep struggling students on track by helping them to use age-appropriate and level-appropriate reading materials. This is an important factor in the success of the program.

Besides focusing on specific reading skills, all programs in the OBFLC provide students and parents with important library skills. Students from preschool to middle school are introduced or reintroduced to how to use a library card responsibly, how to use the online catalog, how to use online databases, and how to select a work of fiction or nonfiction based on individualized reading skills. The library skills activity is usually done by myself or another MLS Librarian on staff. The Assistant Coordinator has also gained knowledge and skills in teaching library skills by observation and by instruction.

The results of this six week program were encouraging. Many children could find books they liked to "read" by themselves. Some advanced in pre-reading skills as evidenced by the post tests given. Most importantly, many parents expressed a new awareness of the value of the public library. They now use the library for all the family reading needs and said they felt more comfortable in finding age-appropriate materials.

WHAT DOES THE FUTURE HOLD FOR THE MORLEY LIBRARY OPEN BOOK FAMILY LEARNING CENTER?

The Alpha Books program for preschoolers, mentioned above, is a successful example of what we hope to keep providing in the OBFLC. Currently we are in the process of applying for grants in order to add more Alpha Book programs. We are also planning to provide a self-esteem and literacy program called the *Omega-5 Program* for youths 14 to 16 years old. The Omega-5 program was the idea of a local community member and an area church. This program wishes to reach out to at risk youth in order to help provide goal setting skills and other work force related skills that will insure success in school and in future work places. It is a faith-based non-denominational program that G-Pal agencies help support by making referrals and by providing curriculum ideas and materials. This new program is still in the planning stage.

As funding continues to grow, the Center will also offer area parents and students a low-cost tutoring program two evenings a week and on Sunday afternoons. Offering free informational programs that help parents with academic discipline, literacy skills, and life-coping skills will also be part of the evening and Sunday tutoring programs. Many of these will be provided by other G-PAL agencies. Parents will be encouraged to continue to use the Library for information and recreational literacy needs along with their children.

So, if you had extra space to provide service to your eager learners or struggling readers, what would you create?

The Personal Touch:
A Case for a Small, Independent Library

L. Susan Hayes

SUMMARY. Small city libraries often face pressure to join county systems, but the flexibility of being independent permits opportunities for service that bigger entities cannot offer. In addition, the personal touch helps distinguish libraries from other information providers such as book stores or internet services. Programs can be developed and offered on a few days' notice, without a lengthy approval process. Individual attention, such as delivering books to the doorstep of a shut-in patron, is routine. This article makes a case for independent libraries to remain that way. doi:10.1300/J118v25n01_15 *[Article copies available for a fee from The Haworth Document Delivery Service: 1-800-HAWORTH. E-mail address: <docdelivery@haworthpress.com> Website: <http://www.HaworthPress.com> © 2006 by The Haworth Press, Inc. All rights reserved.]*

KEYWORDS. Personal service, small libraries, independent libraries

INTRODUCTION

Imagine buying, cataloging, and processing a book for a patron in a few hours. Yes, that's hours, not days, or weeks. This type of personal service from small libraries is not only not unusual, it's the norm.

L. Susan Hayes, MSLS, is Director, Wayne State University, Parkland Library, 6600 University Drive, Parkland, FL 33067 (E-mail: shayes@cityofparkland.org).

[Haworth co-indexing entry note]: "The Personal Touch: A Case for a Small, Independent Library." Hayes, L. Susan. Co-published simultaneously in *Public Library Quarterly* (The Haworth Press, Inc.) Vol. 25, No. 1/2, 2006, pp. 199-203; and: *Current Practices in Public Libraries* (ed: William Miller, and Rita M. Pellen) The Haworth Press, Inc., 2006, pp. 199-203. Single or multiple copies of this article are available for a fee from The Haworth Document Delivery Service [1-800-HAWORTH, 9:00 a.m. - 5:00 p.m. (EST). E-mail address: docdelivery@haworthpress.com].

Available online at http://plq.haworthpress.com
© 2006 by The Haworth Press, Inc. All rights reserved.
doi:10.1300/J118v25n01_15

Personal service is the most often-cited advantage of being in a small library. We know we give up some economies of scale in purchasing power, training, and resources, but the ability to offer customized service keeps most of us happily in the ranks of the small.

"Library 2.0," much discussed in recent months, suggests this is the new library service model: improved customer-driven offerings. But for small municipal libraries, it has been the practice for our entire existence, with or without the technology focus. While running a library is certainly different than running a business, there are some "new rules" in the business arena that affirm this idea. According to *Fortune* magazine, the customer, rather than the shareholder, is king [Morris 2006]. A recent *Library Journal* article describes Library 2.0 as having "user-centered change" at its heart [Casey and Savastinuk 2006]. The focus of many municipal libraries (the term is often used interchangeably with city libraries) and other small libraries is on being agile in response to patron requests. It's what makes us different, and it's the old-fashioned as well as the new-fashioned way we work.

The library discussed here is a city-based library in a small community of just under 25,000 people. We have chosen to remain independent of the county-wide system in our area, and the community is willing to support us with its tax dollars. This article will describe some of the services we offer that we think make it worthwhile to remain a small, independent place. We draw upon other libraries in similar circumstances to provide additional descriptions.

Home delivery of library materials through the mail has been a practice for many years. Small library staff members can be found driving to a patron's home to deliver an item in person. In our case, this usually happens with an elderly person who either isn't feeling well enough to come to the library or who doesn't want to drive in bad weather. We've had offers to sit down at the home for a cup of tea, and although that is always declined, it shows the comfort level our patrons have with our staff.

Being in Florida, many of our patrons spend the summers "up north." Audio books are popular with those who face 10-20-hour drives. If the northern stay is for a month or so, we will adjust the normal 3-week loan date. For longer stays, we sometimes provide self-addressed envelopes so the people can return the books after arriving at their destination. Adjusting the due date happens from time to time for other reasons as well, such as when the people are not able to phone us or the online renewal period will be too short to cover their absence. Obviously, loan policies and other policies are in place for a reason, but small libraries have the flexibility to waive the policies on an ad hoc basis to meet a customer need.

Other examples of such flexibility can be observed at small libraries nation-wide. For example, most libraries have policies about unattended children, but tribal libraries in Northern Wisconsin have a different philosophy of service, representing Native American values. Everyone is considered part of the larger "family," so if a child is in the library alone, the staff will keep an eye on him or her for a parent who may be running an errand or is otherwise away from the building.

Instructional activities are similarly flexible. Our local school district prohibits teachers from offering private tutoring on school grounds. However, our city commission has decided that our children's education is a very high priority, so the teacher-tutors are permitted to use library space. One of our staff members is a retired math teacher, so she offered to develop a program of free math tutoring at a more advanced level than the private tutors were offering. While the attendance was small, we have one student who is still receiving help nearly 2 years later. When we teach our computer-use classes, the opportunity for extensive individual follow-up is available in person or over the phone. Some individuals have received 3-4 hours of staff help in the days or weeks after attending a class. We haven't yet found students to take over this process, although we know other places do it that way. When we added DVDs to our collection, we provided instruction to one patron on the proper use of his remote control, which he had brought to the library, in order to view the movies.

CUSTOMER DRIVEN PROGRAMS

Story programs are the area where we have been the most flexible. Since our story room space is small, we require advance registration for the weekly programs. A couple of years ago, as we were registering children for the 12-to-24-month age group, several parents pointed out that if they attended the program with the child of that age (as we require), a younger or older sibling would be unattended, so they couldn't register their child. Therefore, on the spot, we created a sibling program, so that several children of varying ages could attend together. We opened the registration immediately and designed a modified program during the week before the sessions began. The children who attended the new program were 6 months to 34 months old, and their caregivers were thrilled that we could offer this accommodation. This fits another of the

Fortune magazine article's new rules: agile is best. The next part of the saga is that for our current cycle of story times, no one signed up for the sibling class. Repeating our previous move, within 24 hours, we had deleted that session and added an additional one for another age group where there had been a waiting list.

Customer-driven programs are easy to produce when the decisions are made locally. In addition to the library-based programs, we often travel to other venues, especially to provide cultural experiences that are not available in our service area. Our Fort Lauderdale area patrons, along with several staff members, travel by chartered bus to the Miami International Book Fair. Another Fort Lauderdale area library, Lighthouse Point, offers bus trips to theaters in Miami and to the Kennedy Space Center, some 150 miles distant. The library in New Port Richey, Florida purchases an annual pass to a museum and then checks it out to cardholders on a single-day basis.

New Port Richey also offers a Summer Reading Program that rivals a camp: full-day programs Monday through Friday on such topics as arts and crafts, a mad science lab, and Website mania. Lunch, movies, and special performers enhance the story times, in addition to the more standard reading log program. Our library encourages adults to set a good example by having a summer reading program for grown-ups. Why should the kids have all the fun?

Who has ever had a free massage, manicure, or waxing at their local library? Local businesses team up to participate in offering such pampering services in the annual Women's Nite Out in New Port Richey. Add a fun book, and the perfect relaxation event is set. This is one more example of a new rule: create something new.

Family events are often hosted at our library: planting a butterfly garden, circling the city by bicycle on our extensive trails, how to care for your pet horse, and building gingerbread houses. The latter became the subject of a local newspaper editorial by the publisher who found a special connection with his children that day. While these events may seem like pure entertainment, we find increased book circulation on related topics directly tied to the themes.

As these examples show, whether using a business model with "new rules," a library model for a "2.0 version," or just the old-fashioned way we have traditionally been operating, a small, independent library can be a place for flexible and personal patron service. Smallness offers flexibility not available to larger organizational structures, and can result in innovations that might be more widely adapted in larger contexts.

REFERENCES

Casey, Michael E. and Laura C. Savastinuk. 2006. Library 2.0. *Library Journal* September 1: 40-42.
Morris, Betsy, 2006. The New Rules. *Fortune* v. 152, n. 2 July 24: 70-87.

doi:10.1300/J118v25n01_15

Mentoring GenX for Leadership in the Public Library

Gail Doherty

SUMMARY. Mentoring relationships have typically reflected the hierarchical world of which they were a part. Now the metaphor of the web, with its connections and decentralization of power, has blurred the lines between managers and workers. Mentorship within a web-like structure of connections can help to ensure that the public library evolves and thrives in a world that is flatter, looser, and fond of multi-tasking. doi:10.1300/J118v25n01_16 *[Article copies available for a fee from The Haworth Document Delivery Service: 1-800-HAWORTH. E-mail address: <docdelivery@haworthpress.com> Website: <http://www.HaworthPress.com> © 2006 by The Haworth Press, Inc. All rights reserved.]*

KEYWORDS. Leadership, mentoring, mentorship, peer mentoring, organizational storytelling

---

Gail Doherty is the Coordinator of Library Information Services and New Initiatives at Winnipeg Public Library in Canada, 251 Donald Street, Winnipeg, Manitoba, R3C 3P5, Canada (E-mail: gdoherty@winnipeg.ca). During her career she also has worked as a children's librarian, branch manager, and head of acquisitions, and led a variety of project teams. She obtained her M.L.S degree from Dalhousie University in Halifax.

[Haworth co-indexing entry note]: "Mentoring GenX for Leadership in the Public Library." Doherty, Gail. Co-published simultaneously in *Public Library Quarterly* (The Haworth Press, Inc.) Vol. 25, No. 1/2, 2006, pp. 205-217; and: *Current Practices in Public Libraries* (ed: William Miller, and Rita M. Pellen) The Haworth Press, Inc., 2006, pp. 205-217. Single or multiple copies of this article are available for a fee from The Haworth Document Delivery Service [1-800-HAWORTH, 9:00 a.m. - 5:00 p.m. (EST). E-mail address: docdelivery@haworthpress.com].

Available online at http://plq.haworthpress.com
© 2006 by The Haworth Press, Inc. All rights reserved.
doi:10.1300/J118v25n01_16

BACKGROUND

The mentorship of a younger, less skilful person has a long established human history. Until recently, such relationships usually reflected the hierarchical world of which they were a part. But as businesses employed a variety of computer technologies, the ways in which knowledge is shared within organizations changed. A wired world, where a broad range of information is easily accessible to workers or managers, means that the old patterns of "who knows what" have blurred. This has implications for mentoring a new generation of managers, as well as negotiating the ways in which "information" can evolve into "organizational wisdom."

A LOOK BACK

When women gathered and men hunted, mentorship involved a transfer of knowledge that was closely related to physical survival. In time this grew to include other skills important for the development of a community, whether they related to the duties of kinship or the necessities of economic growth. In the time of the Greeks, Homer wrote that Mentor taught Telemachus, son of Odysseus, the responsibilities of his role as a king's son. The great mediaeval guilds of masters and apprentices built the castles and cathedrals that fostered urban expansion.

In many ways, this world clearly defined the role of all participants. The protégé eventually took his or her rightful place as a leader, and the whole process started again, with protégé now assuming the role of mentor to a new generation. Traditionally the mentor shared a well-defined body of knowledge, whether it was the inside track on how to be a young Greek warrior about town or the trick to making a buttress really fly.

The obvious beneficiary in these relationships was the protégé, who gained admission to a world that might otherwise remain mysterious or even closed. The benefits that accrued to mentors were real, but less apparent. Mentors used their connections, expertise, and authority for the good of the protégé. In return, the protégé projected the mentor's influence forward.

The process of mentoring might be based in hierarchical notions of power or expertise, but it was still easy to see its relationship to organic ideas of community, growth, and human connection. It was only later, when the Industrial Revolution promoted a more mechanistic view of the value of a person's work, that organizations of people were described in the language of the factory and the machine. These powerful metaphors coloured perceptions of organizational life. The language used in the professional world to delineate and catalogue work not only describes what is done, but helps to embody and create its reality.[1]

THE NEXT EVOLUTION IN MENTORING

Now another metaphor has become significant. It is the concept of the Web, with its connections, its decentralization of power, and its blurring of the lines between managers and workers. The term itself interestingly merges organic ideas of finely spun and spidery connection with the technological networks that are its backbone. To carry the metaphor further, we all know that our "spidey senses" tingle at the challenges that come with Internet access in our branches![2]

The wide acceptance of this Web metaphor has many implications for how knowledge is shared and transmitted within organizations. The concepts we employ to explain and describe what we do and create have a significance that can't be discounted. Once the narrative structure changes, the reality of work life also changes. We could learn a lesson from Charlotte, that great friend and consummate Web spinner. Her wonderful and succinct story of Wilbur rescued him from a probable future as a pork chop. The stories that we tell may save our bacon![3]

This article will discuss how mentorship within a Web-like structure of connections can help to ensure that the public library evolves and thrives in a world that is flatter, looser, and fond of multi-tasking. It also will discuss briefly the generations of staff in the workplace and their different expectations. These dynamics affect how and why mentoring will be successful and why some of its approaches will shift to accommodate the changing requirements of the organization.

But while the methods may evolve, effective mentoring still enhances library functions and services, provides opportunities for transmitting both practise and values, improves understanding and human interactions, and gives participants a way to give back to the profession.[4]

The pace of change may be chaotic, but the library still exists for longstanding goals of public good. It promotes open access, democracy, diversity, and intellectual freedom. The public widely recognizes the library's dedication to these virtues. This understanding, an implicit contract between users and staff, informs the work of all public libraries.

Many public libraries now take customer satisfaction as an end goal in very tangible ways. This gives all staff, whether they provide internal services or serve the public directly, opportunities to see their work as part of an organic whole. Staff members see the many interconnections between what they do and the experience of the user. In turn, this changes interactions and communication between divisions and sections of service. The customer service "story" makes it possible to see a commonality of goals and provides opportunities for a variety of mentoring experiences.

The skills that can be learned and shared in a mentoring relationship fall into several broad categories. These include tangible, practical day-to-day skills, as well as the development of leadership and management abilities. The practical lessons often involve the "what" we do and "how" we do it questions, while the management and leadership areas often involve the "why," "when," and "where" of the profession. Of course, there is some overlap between these skill sets, as well in the mentoring methods that can be used to teach and coach about them.

MENTORING SKILLS IN THE PUBLIC LIBRARY

The library's role in life-long learning makes mentoring a natural act for many library staff. The general milieu encourages teaching and the interchange of ideas, although the managerial hierarchy sometimes seems to discourage it. This discouragement may be a clash of styles rather than active disparagement. While it is not good to generalize, people in the Boomer, Generation X, and Millennial age groups, to offer three examples, bring some different perspectives to their work, with differences in "communication styles, approaches to objectives, and value systems."[5]

Younger staff members, more comfortable with technology, often have a natural propensity to challenge entrenchment. This is an uncomfortable prospect for those who are used to their authority being a given. For some administrators, it can be rather like signing on as a Jane Austen character, but ending up in a William Gibson novel. Imagine Fanny Price blogging, or Lizzy Bennet spamming Mr. Darcy. It is too alarming, although Mrs. Bennet, with her nefarious schemes for marrying off five daughters, is obviously ripe for multi-tasking. The point is that younger staff members, who are immersed in the digital world and collaborative methods, bring different kinds of knowledge to the Box Hill picnic.[6]

While it is popular to employ a vague term such as "learning organization" without much understanding of the term's implications, the library's history and values make it a good candidate for transmitting and teaching its internal norms to guide decision-making in the future. In order to do this well, administrators must recognize that people need to learn throughout their working lives. Creating an environment where learning can cross boundaries and levels and be available to all employees is a crucial factor in an organization's success.[7] So the public library's need to transmit and share knowledge about policies and procedures, leadership, and management brushes up against the Web metaphor of distributed understanding.

PEER MENTORING

Traditional mentoring relationships provide a protégé with career direction and support, and give the mentor the personal satisfaction of assisting a new colleague. These top-down relationships can still play an important role in an organization. But practical mentoring that transmits everyday skills is crucial to the provision of front-line service. Peer mentoring provides an informal method for those at a similar level in an organization to learn from each other. Staff themselves often will identify a need to learn a skill and locate a person that can teach it to them. This need will usually be based on a requirement to provide improved service. A peer mentor may be one of a multiple number of mentors. If the library wants to create an internal learning culture, then this is an effective way to accomplish the task, since peer mentoring is non-hierarchical.[8] In some of these relationships a staff member may play the role of protégé, in others that of mentor. Always ahead of the curve, Geoffrey Chaucer created one of the first descriptions of this type of mentoring in his *Canterbury Tales*. The character of the Clerk embodies the skills of the peer mentor: "and gladly would he learn and gladly teach."[9] This ability to give and receive information on a variety of levels and in a flexible manner is an embodiment of the virtues of a Web of connections.

An opportunity to observe peer mentoring in action occurs at any public service desk with staff of different ages. More than ever, public service requires a broad range of skill sets. These range from knowledge of traditional reference resources and the ability to solve challenging technology problems to the ability to negotiate win-win deals when patrons battle over Internet computers. Younger staff members are more comfortable with seeming less expert and trying different methods to respond to a question. Older staff may be used to their status as "experts" and more invested in a particular path. This can be a big issue as people work together at a desk since the experiential and direct can be interpreted as smart-alecky and abrasive. There is potential for conflict and discomfort between older staff members and younger ones unless opportunities for mutual teaching and mentoring are made.

THE CUSTOMER SERVICE "STORY"

My experience in supervising a large reference desk at a central library is that staff members are drawn together in service of the customer. This important focus can defuse potential conflict. If there is an acknowledgement that all make a significant contribution and can help each other to serve the customer better, then skill sharing is more likely to occur. We have seen this evolve over a number of years as new staff came into a department that had seen little turnover for a period of time. Some of this informal learning was about how things work in a large organization. Some was about the greater use of technology as a key component in providing excellent customer service. Discussion involved everything from practical matters such as organizing Web bookmarks to interchanges about the evolving nature of communities on the Internet. As a supervisor, there were some opportunities to guide new staff members, but I was consistently struck by how much I learned rather than imparted in my meetings with them! It might start out as practical information about blogs, but turn into recognition about the different perspective that these staff members brought to their work and how it could help us to provide better service.

An environment of peer mentoring and more open communication percolates through an organization. People come to appreciate the talents of others with whom they have contact and conversation. Those rewarding experiences that occur when a team comes together and executes its tasks in flawless fashion often start from a combination of cross-functional talent. Each person brings his or her own experience, focus, and particular strengths to the issue. Often the project starts out as a problem-solving exercise, but the initial free-form discussions to delineate the issue sometimes uncover the things that are going well. Sometimes these are set aside as interesting, but not germane. But if conversations about the key values and future of the organization have occurred, then people are more open to seeing strategies with new eyes.

One of the more successful ideas that Winnipeg Public Library implemented was a customer service program that brought together cross-functional groups of staff and provided the opportunity to discuss service from a variety of perspectives.[10] For some staff, it was the first time they had sat down in an environment of equals to discuss how their everyday work affected each customer's experience of our service. Through these discussions, staff came to a clear understanding that they were part of the whole, even if they worked behind the scenes processing materials or in a shipping department. The discussions we had with each group about what was going well in the organization were sometimes very inspiring. Long after the tangible skills such as dealing with difficult customers had been absorbed, the connections fostered in those sessions worked to the long-term benefit of the library. Staff members who felt validated and respected during those customer service discussions now recognized the value of their perspectives and were willing to bring them to other tasks. To offer one example, in 2000, when the library decided to implement a computer booking system, a team of librarians, branch heads, circulation staff, and systems staff worked to implement the software. We sat together in our computer training room and really were a Web of connection.

MENTORSHIP TO DEVELOP LEADERSHIP AND MANAGEMENT SKILLS

Another important mentoring role is to provide opportunities for staff to gain exposure to concepts of leadership and management. The public library, in common with many other organizations, expects to see a big turnover of staff in the next few years. Much of this turnover will occur at the senior level, leaving a lack of managerial and leadership skills. Those conversations about what is key to carry forward need to take place.

When computer technology first began to operate on a large-scale in the library world, some staff members grasped the future in a full-throttle embrace while others lamented the card catalogue's disappearance with a heartfelt *sic transit Gloria mundi*. Some of this armed camp hostility was based in conflicting ideas about what technology would bring. Some staff felt isolated from the entire process. Fears about the denigration of skills, intoxication with the glamour of being first to implement, the rush of excitement over potential new roles, uncertainty about what these would be and how individuals would fit in, contempt for "tekkies," disdain for "non-tekkies," and discomfort with chaos were all evident to some degree in most libraries. Now, with technology an integral part of public library services, it is important to be sure that a common leadership vision is fashioned from the talents of all staff that are in the organization.

Merging the styles of the soon to be departing "Boomer" managers and the younger "Gen-X" staff members that have already begun to replace them in leadership and management positions is an issue that needs to be addressed. One of the hardest tasks is to persuade members of the Gen-X generation of the wisdom of taking a position when, from their perspective, it presents a huge challenge to their accepted ideas about work/life balance. Also, Gen-Xers' direct communication style can be seen as almost confrontational. On the opposite side, one has to consider what behaviour current managers are modelling since Gen-Xers are quick to note any discrepancy between the "walk" and the "talk."

Succession planning is of major concern in all libraries. The 8Rs Research Team recently produced a document called *The Future of Human Resources in Canadian Libraries*. This document surveyed over 2,000 librarians and administrators and identified the provision of management and leadership training as a more significant need than the replacement of technical skills or knowledge. The report highlighted the need to create an environment where leadership is a key role of every position, as well as to model the leadership qualities the organization expects, and communicate these to staff.[11]

In public libraries, this transfer of leadership skills must not only embody the values with which the institution has long been associated, and which remain consistent in the face of technological change, but also concepts such as a tolerance for ambiguity and intelligent risk-taking.[12]

The 8Rs report suggests that one excellent way to provide exposure to norms and values is through mentoring experiences. A traditional mentoring relationship gives a senior colleague the opportunity to mentor a junior one for a period of time that sometimes lasts several years. But greater workforce mobility, the increased specialization of skill sets, and the press of unending workplace demands make it less likely that a mentor can model all roles for a protégé.

Leadership and management are two areas where the knowledge that needs to be transferred is often the undocumented, tacit type that exists in people's heads. These intangibles of knowledge are the most difficult to translate into formal training programs or staff documentation since they often inform specific situations in a variety of ways that involve an understanding of the patterns behind them.[13]

Intangible knowledge that is accumulated in an unstructured way can sometimes, surprisingly, be learned and distributed using flexible, unstructured methods. Sometimes just by doing his or her job and modelling the organization's values, a leader can transfer knowledge about what is important, with no intention of teaching. Of course, this depends on the delineation of a clear set of values, consistently promoted through congruent behaviour, with organizational rewards granted to those that model them.

LEARNING STYLES AS THEY AFFECT MENTORSHIP

Younger library staff members have an interest in and preference for experiences as a teaching tool, as well as a belief that collaborative methods are the way to work, and an unwillingness to give unthinking loyalty to any organization. They are not interested in layers of bureaucracy and can be frustrated with what they see as roadblocks to getting a job done. They may not see themselves moving into traditional administrative positions. This may be a function of either not seeing the virtues they value reflected in higher positions within the organization, or not understanding that the skills they bring are important in leadership roles within the library. While many "Boomer" managers struggled through the changes that have occurred in the library profession in the past twenty years, Gen-X staff members view technology and gadgetry as something fun and challenging. They enjoy that spur-of-the-moment problem solving that induces sweaty palms in staff who do not consider themselves fluent with the changing technology.[14]

While young staff members offer many technology and task-oriented skills in the workplace, they also may be less fluent with managing people or large projects. This can be especially difficult if they supervise older employees who may have completely different attitudes to the value of long-term experience within an organization and who may see the new manager's comfort with constant change and ease with technology as threatening. It is also easy to take the confident manner of young staff members at face value and not see the support they need to step into a leadership role.

Current administrators must be clear about what to carry forward as leadership values in the library world and to appreciate what can be learned and adapted from younger staff. Since Gen-X staff members want those opportunities to self-develop and also enjoy working in a climate of reassurance and feedback, mentoring represents a good way to develop their leadership abilities. But it also needs to be a two-way street.

HOW CAN MENTORING BUILD REQUIRED SKILLS?

Mentoring must offer exposure to the difficulties of managing a wide variety of personalities and work styles and ways to promote more tolerance about the fears that can accompany change. Since younger staff rush towards experience and are willing to "play" their way towards solutions, they need to acquire more understanding of how to make these skills work for them in delineating long-term goals and cultivating patience with what seems to be the glacial pace of effecting any real lasting change. They need to learn the benefits of listening instead of immediately leaping in to problem-solve. In turn, Boomer managers must learn more flexibility for the process of how something is done. While I am a firm believer in reading the instruction manual, younger staff will often use the "dump-it-all-on-the-floor" approach. Each side can become enraged by the other's methodology, when the end product will likely be the same. Opportunities to frame responses to ethical issues also are important. When there is massive change, clarity about what is significant becomes key. It is important to remember that the skills that younger staff members bring, adapted and polished by exposure to the best principles of older manager/leaders, will eventually become the norm. Then a new set of skills will be brought in by another generation of managers.[15]

What are some good ways to build these skills? I was fortunate to be able to mentor a younger colleague through a management development program at a local university. It offered us structured opportunities to reflect on issues, as well as giving her the chance to develop tangible project management skills. It was again one of those experiences in which I learned as much as she did. Our conversations allowed me to reflect as a manager on my own methods. Together we were able to frame and respond to questions about why certain decisions should be made, when we should make them, and where we could implement them. We would talk about what went well and what didn't and try to analyze why. And we told each other stories about some of our positive experiences.

To go back to an earlier analogy, Chaucer also realized that when you are thrown together, whether on a pilgrimage or in an organization, one of the things you do to break down barriers and create context is to tell each other stories. When the skills that a mentor is trying to impart are of the tacit variety, relating to management or leadership issues, it is much more likely that the transmission will contain a strong thread of narrative. Within an oral tradition there is the teller of the story and the listeners.

The teller and the listeners bring their own perspectives to what is being told. An organizational story contains a number of threads. On a very basic level, it provides valid information that can be or has been used to make decisions and that can be used as the basis to make other informed decisions in the future.[16] If the information that is transmitted is seen as the embodiment of compelling organizational values, if the teller brings human dimensions and compassion to his story, then this creates an environment in which listeners are able to make a heartfelt commitment to the narrative. Listeners then will "tell it forward," whether in a structured manner, in which they add their own dimension to the story, or by unconsciously assimilating the values of the story into their working life. The telling of the story changes it, and the changed story moves through an organization in unpredictable ways. This may seem like an inefficient method to promote and internalize an organization's values. And yet the metaphors and patterns in the story are assimilated and remembered in a way that the business plan may not be.

The blog phenomenon is one method of storytelling that can come as a surprise to managers unaccustomed to such informal sharing of experience. It is capable of carrying the perceived organizational message to a much broader audience, whether for good or ill. It's more common for young librarians to chronicle their workdays in blogs than their more established colleagues might think!

Informal storytelling is a powerful force within an organization, but it also is possible to harness it in a more structured way. Discussions about the organizational narrative are really stories about human beings and their longing to have meaningful conversations about the pursuits in which they are engaged. In fact, meaningful conversations are one way to engage them. Appreciative Inquiry, a system of study that links the organization's focus and scope for change with its positive energy and what it does well, grounds much of its work in structured dialogue about strengths and values.[17] In contrast to many management theories that concentrate their discussion on correcting the negative, Appreciative Inquiry wants to uncover "existing strengths, hopes, and dreams."[18]

The customer service program mentioned earlier in this article used some of the concepts of Appreciative Inquiry when it provided a place for staff members to talk about what was going well in the organization, and when it built appreciation for the roles that all staff played. Implemented well, in an environment that promotes a respect for differences and the willingness to manage them effectively, this management methodology could build bridges between various generations of staff by letting them share their particular strengths in the debate.

The older generation brings its organizational knowledge, sense of achievement, and seasoned creativity to add context to the discussion. The younger brings its desire for positive feedback, collaborative problem-solving skills, and willingness to question the existing structure.

CONCLUSION

The library world has changed rapidly in the past twenty-five years. Staff that began their career in the world of the card catalogue may end it starring in a personal blog. Technology has transformed the way in which we all work. Its changes confront us every day. Having survived, and often thrived in this environment, staff now face the challenge of teaching, modelling, and reframing the principles behind the public library's work. While methodologies may change, we still exist in service of the public. The Web metaphor of distributed skills and understanding is one way of thinking about the role we all play.

NOTES

1. Sally Helgesen, *The Web of Inclusion: A New Architecture for Building Great Organizations.* N.Y.: Doubleday, 1995: 187. The author talks of language as "generative," not merely "descriptive."

2. Helgesen, 16-17. The author discusses her idea of the organic nature of the Web versus the "rigid architecture of the machine."

3. E. B. White, *Charlotte's Web.* N.Y.: Harper Collins, 1952: 78. Charlotte's first attempt to describe Wilbur's uniqueness describes him as "Some Pig."

4. Staff Development Committee, Human Resources Section, Library Administration and Management Association, *Staff Development: A Practical Guide*, Third Edition. American Library Association, 2001. I have used some of the points from their discussion of the benefits of mentoring in Chapter 14: 79.

5. Pixie Ann Mosley, "Mentoring Gen X Managers: Tomorrow's Library Leadership is Already Here," *Library Administration and Management* 19, (Fall, 2005): 187.

6. Stephen Abram and Judy Luther, "Born with the Chip," *Library Journal*, 129 (May 1, 2004): 34-37. While the authors talk about patrons in this work, their points apply equally well to staff.

7. Mary Ann Mavrinac, "Transformational Leadership: Peer Mentoring as a Values-Based Learning Process," *portal: Libraries and the Academy* 5 (2005): 392.

8. Mavrinac, 398-400.

9. Geoffrey Chaucer, *The Canterbury Tales*, rendered into modern English by J. U. Nicolson. N.Y.: Doubleday, 1934, 10.

10. Our library worked with Dr. Lynda Pinnington of Pinnington Training and Development. Her company's Website is located at: <http://www.pinningtontraining.com/progserv.html>.

11. The 8Rs Research Team. *The Future of Human Resources in Canadian Libraries*, 2005: 17. As part of its research, the project team surveyed over 400 administrators and human resource professionals, over 2, 000 librarians, and close to 2, 000 paraprofessionals. Available at <http://www.Is.ualberta.ca/8rs/reports.html>.

12. Wendy Newman, "Mentor Alert! Please Share this with a Student or New Librarian," *Feliciter* 49 (2003): 5.

13. Walter Swap, Dorothy Leonard, Mimi Shields, and Lisa Abrams, "Using Mentoring and Storytelling to Transfer Knowledge in the Workplace," *Journal of Management Information Systems* 18 (Summer 2001): 96.

14. Mosley, 187.

15. Mosley, 190.

16. Thomas L. Moore, "Facilitative Leadership: One Approach to Empowering Staff and Other Stakeholders," *Library Trends* 53 (Summer 2004): 230-237. Moore discusses the core values that inform facilitative leadership and I have used these to talk about storytelling.

17. Diana Whitney and Amanda Foster-Bloom, *the Power of Appreciative Inquiry: A Guide to Positive Change*. San Francisco: Barrett-Koehler, 2003. I have based my comments on the definitions of Appreciative Inquiry they provide in Chapter 1.

18. Whitney, 15.

doi:10.1300/J118v25n01_16

Index

"A Library Advocate's Guide to Building Information Literate Communities," 182, 185
A National Plan for Public Library Service, 61
A Strategy for Public Library Change, 61
AAUP, 58
ABLE. *See* Painesville Adult Basic Literacy Education (ABLE)
Access to Public Libraries, 61
Acevedo, L., 3
Acevedo, L.A., 171
Acquisitions modules, for ILS, 101-102
ACRL Report, 183
Action Plan, of ALA, 182,185-186, 189-190
Adler, P., 164
Adult Basic Literacy Education (ABLE), Painesville, 193
Advocacy
  for CCPL, 149-150
  linking successful libraries to, 144-146
  marketing and, collaboration between, 117-135. *See also* Marketing, advocacy and, collaboration between
  in practice, 124-126
  principles of, 119-120
  public libraries role in, 151-153
  of SNPL, 142
  in transforming literate to information literate communities, 181-190. *See also* Information literate communities, from literate communities to, advocacy in

Advocacy Resource Center, of ALA, 168
Advocate(s), for public libraries
  creation of, 155-171
    introduction to, 155-156
    library's role in, 69f,166-170
  defined, 156-159
  described, 159-165,162f
  successful use of, example of, 165-166
  timing use of, 165
"African American Pioneering Gospel Music Composers," 179
ALA. *See* American Library Association (ALA)
Alfred P. Sloan Museum, 176
Alpert, P.S., 2, 91
Alpha Book program, 194-197
Amazon, 88
American Association of School Librarians, 183
American Civil Liberties Union, 58
American Civil Rights Movement, 175
American Historical Association, 58
American Library Association (ALA), 3, 6,7,24,45,58-60,65,139,140, 163,181-182, 186, 189,190
  Action Plan of, 182,185-186, 189-190
  Advocacy Resource Center of, 168
  Annual Conference of, 97
  Core Values Statement of, 59
  Council of, 65
  "Libraries: An American Value" of, 60
  "Libraries Change Lives" of, 163

Library's Advocate Handbook of, 167
Mission Statement of, Code of Ethics of, 65
Office for Research and Statistics of, 1,7,24
Policy Manual of, 64-65
Public Information Office of, 168
Right to Read and View of, 164
Small Business @ Your Library campaign of, 76
Social Responsibilities Round Table of, Hunger Homelessness and Poverty Task Force of, 67
Special Presidential Committee on Information Literacy and Advocacy of, 182
UDHR and, 64-65
Website of, 185
American Marketing Association, 89,119
American Medical Association, 58
American Public Library Ratings, 147
Apple, 68
Apple, M.W., 62
Armed for Action, 63
Ashton, R., 67
Association of College and Research Libraries, 182
Association of Research Libraries, 164
Automation, effect on public library collection development and technical services, 91-103
 budget allocation for, 92-93
 centralized/decentralized vs. best of both worlds, 96
 challenges of purchasing foreign language materials and, 94-95
 formats for, 92-93
 growing and changing community needs and, 93-94
 introduction to, 92
 outsourcing technical services, 97-98
 vendor negotiations for cataloging/processing and, 98-100
 vendor negotiations for online products and, 100-101

Baker, 95, 97
Basic literacy, public libraries and, 184
Beach, C., 166
Becoming Successfully Networked Public Libraries, 140
B&ECPL. *See* Buffalo and Erie County Public Library (B&ECPL)
Berry, J.N., III, 63
Bertot, J.C., 1, 27,138,140,147
Better Business Bureau, 87
"Better Libraries for a Better Broward" campaign, 165-166
"bibz.com," 97
Bill and Melinda Gates Foundation, 118,140
BIPC. *See* Business and Intellectual Property Centre (BIPC)
Blue Ribbon Task Force on Economic Development, 149
Booklist, 96
Books on Wings, 95
Boston Public Library, 61,63,168
"Both/and" world, 114
Bowker Annual, 62
BPLF. *See* Broward Public Library Foundation (BPLF)
Breck, L., 68
Brey-Casiano, C.A., 3,169,181
Brodart, 95, 97
Broward County Library, 164-165
Broward Public Library Foundation (BPLF), 165
Buffalo and Erie County Public Library (B&ECPL), 108-109,158-159
"Building Information Literate Communities," 181,189
Burger, L., 169
Burns, M.F., 3,191

Bush, L., First Lady, 168
Business and Intellectual Property
    Centre (BIPC), 86
"Business Assisting Services in
    Libraries," 83
Business community, in transforming
    literate communities to
    information literate
    communities, 187-188
Business Solutions Center
    of New York City, 83-84,86
    of SIBL of NYPL, 77

"Call Ahead," 78
Campaign for America's Libraries, 189
Campaign for the World's Libraries, 189
Carnegie Library of Pittsburgh, 168
Carroll County Public Library, 115-116
"Case for Support," 122
Cataloging/processing, vendor
    negotiations for, 98-100
CCPL. *See* Cuyahoga County Public
    Library (CCPL)
Center for Democracy and Technology, 58
Champion, D., 80
Change
    effects of, 106-107
    reasons for making, 107
Chief Officers of State Library
    Agencies (COSLA), 45
"Children's Corner," 187
Children's Internet Protection Act
    (CIPA), 35,58,68
Children's Room, 192-194,196
Ciardi, J., 184
CIPA. *See* Children's Internet
    Protection Act (CIPA)
City of Painesville Improvement
    Grant, 194
Civil Rights Movement, 3,173,175,177-179
Clardy Fox Branch, of El Paso Pubic
    Library, 186
Cleveland Museum of Art, 149

Cleveland Public Library, 149,151
Cleveland State University, Maxine
    Goodman Levin College of
    Urban Affairs of, 151
Coalition for a Closer Look, 67
Coco, C., 101
Code of Ethics, of ALA Mission
    Statement, 65
Code of Hammurabi, 63
Cohen, M., 2, 75
Collaboration, described, 112-113
"Collection Cataloging and Processing
    Manual," 98-99
Collection development, of public
    libraries, multiculturalism
    and automation effects on,
    91-103. *See also* Automation;
    Multiculturalism
College of Information, of FSU
    GeoLib Program of, 2
    Information Institute of, 3
    Information Use Management and
        Policy Institute of, 140
Community(ies)
    business, in transforming literate
        communities to information
        literate communities,
        187-188
    growing and changing needs of,
        effect of multiculturalism and
        automation on public library
        collection development and
        technical services and, 93-94
    information literate, from literate
        communities to, advocacy in,
        181-190. *See also*
        Information literate
        communities, from literate
        communities to, advocacy in
    literate, to information literate
        communities, advocacy in,
        181-190. *See also*
        Information literate
        communities, from literate
        communities to, advocacy in

selling library to, networking in, 137-154. *See also* Networking, in selling library to your community
Community leaders, in transforming literate communities to information literate communities, 188
"Community Soldiers," 118-119,125
Connection, described, 112-113
Contribution, described, 112-113
Core Values Statement, of ALA, 59
COSLA. *See* Chief Officers of State Library Agencies (COSLA)
County Invest in Children, 149
CRM. *See* "Customer relationship management" (CRM)
Croneberger, B., 168
Crossroads, 193
Curley, A., 168
"Customer relationship management" (CRM), 88
Customer service convenience, at SIBL of NYPL, 78-80
Cuyahoga County Public Library (CCPL), 3,137,146-147,151, 153
  advocacy strategies of, 149-150
  library's virtual branch, 148
  networked infrastructure of, 149
  networked services within, 148
  steps for, 150-151

Davis, D., 1
Davis, D.M., 5, 27
D&B International Million Dollar Directory, 81
D&B Million Dollar Directory Total US, 81
de la Pena McCook, K., 2, 57
De Prospo, E.R., 61
Deleting Online Predators Act (DOPA), 58,68
Dell, 194

Denver Public Library, 67
Department of Commerce, 86
Dictionary of Marketing Terms, 89
Doherty, G., 4
Donnelly, J., 63
DOPA. *See* Deleting Online Predators Act (DOPA)
Dowlin, K.E., 62
Durrance, J., 63
Durrani, S., 68

Educating the "Right" Way, 62
EIC. *See* Rohatun Electronic Information Center (EIC)
El Paso Community College (EPCC), 187
El Paso Public Library, 3,182,187-188
  Clardy Fox Branch of, 186
Emerging Markets, 80
Environmental Protection Agency, 58
EPCC. *See* El Paso Community College (EPCC)
E-rate, applying for, in study of factors contributing to quality services and resources in public access computing and Internet access for public libraries, 34-35,34f
EvenStart, 193, 195
Evert, C., 164

Facebook.com, 68
Federal Research Public Access Act (FRPAA), of 2006, 163
Federal-State Cooperative System (FSCS), 2, 45
  of Library Data, 8
Feldman, S., 3, 137
Field Services Division, at KDLA, 121
Fiels, K.M., 24, 186
"Financing Your Business," 86
Flickr, 87
Flint Community Schools, 172-173

Index 223

Flint Public Library, 3,171-172,179
Florida Atlantic University, 4
Florida State University (FSU)
   College of Information of
      GeoLib Program of, 2,47
      Information Institute of, 3
      Information Use Management
        and Policy Institute of,
        1,137,140
   Information Institute of, 29
   Resources and Environmental
      Analysis Center of, 2
Foreign language materials, purchasing
      of, challenges of, effect of
      multiculturalism and
      automation on public library
      collection development and
      technical services and, 94-95
Freedman, M., 168
Freedom songs, outreach program
      based on, development of,
      171-179
   building unified concept in, 173-174
   introduction to, 171-172
   study of, background of, 172-173
Friends of the Hunterdon County
      Library, 160
Friends of the Library, 166,182
   of Lexington Public Library, 160
Friends of the Library groups, 168
FRPAA. *See* Federal Research Public
      Access Act (FRPAA)
FSCS. *See* Federal-State Cooperative
      System (FSCS)
Ft. Lauderdale Sun-Sentinel, 166
Funding, public library, 2003-2005,
      impact of local operating
      revenue fluctuations on, 5-26.
      See also Public library
      funding, 2003-2005, impact
      of local operating revenue
      fluctuations on

Gallo, E., 163
Gallo, J., 163

Gamma Delta Kudos, 174
Gay, lesbian, bisexual, and
      transgendered (GLBT)
      persons, library services for,
      human rights and, 66
Gay Pride Month, 66
Geographic information system (GIS), 53
GeoLib Program, at FSU's College of
      Information, 2,47
Gibbons, J., 126
GIS. *See* Geographic information
      system (GIS)
GLBT persons. *See* Gay, lesbian,
      bisexual, and transgendered
      (GLBT) persons
Goals Feasibility Study, 61
Gonzalez, M., 87
Google, 87,145
G-PAL Council. *See* Greater
      Painesville Area Literacy
      (G-PAL) Council
Greater Painesville Area Literacy
      (G-PAL) Council,
      193-195,197
Greek Library Association, 189
Griffith, G.L., 105
Gundry Elementary School, 174
Gwinnett County Public Library, 67
Gwinnett County Public Library
      Board, 68

Harry Potter, 158
Harvard Business Review, 80
Harvard University, 186
Hassan, F., 80
Hayes, L.S., 4,199
Head Start, 193,195
Hennen, T.J., 147
Hewlett Packard, 88
Hillsborough County Public Library, 66
Homeless persons, library services for,
      human rights and, 66-67
House of Representatives, 66
Huff-Hannon, J., 68

Human rights, public libraries and, 57-73
  connection between, 61-64
  introduction to, 58-61
  threats to, examples of, 66-68
    access to information and filtering, 68
    immigration, 67-68
    library service to GLBT persons, 66
    poor and homeless persons, 66-67
    Spanish-speaking persons, 67-68
Hunger Homelessness and Poverty Task Force, of Social Responsibilities Round Table, of ALA, 67
Hunt, C., 87

Idea to Product Boot Camp, in New York City, 82-83
ILL. *See* Interlibrary Loan (ILL)
ILS. *see* Integrated Library System (ILS)
IMCPL. *See* Indianapolis-Marion County Public Library (IMCPL)
Imhoff, K.R., 3,155
Immigration, library services and, human rights and, 67-68
Indianapolis-Marion County Public Library (IMCPL), 2-3,107-110
Industrial Technology Assistance Corporation, 82
Information Institute, of FSU, 3, 29
Information literacy
  defined, 182-183
  goal of, 190
  potential partners in, 186-187
  sample messages for, 187-188
  striving toward, 184
Information literate communities
  building of, process of, 185
  from literate communities to advocacy in, 181-190

building library network, 188
business community in, 187-188
community leaders in, 188
delivering message in, 186
Internet facts in, 183-184
partnerships with media, 188-189
sample messages for potential partners, 187-188
goal of, 190
path for, 181-182
success stories, 189-190
Information Power, 183
Information Use Management and Policy Institute, of FSU, 1,137
Ingram, 97
Innovation and the Library, 61
Institute for Museums and Library Services, 121
Integrated Library System (ILS), acquisitions modules of, 101-102
Interlibrary Loan (ILL), 92
Internal Revenue Code, 120
Internet, access for public libraries, factors contributing to quality services and resources, 27-42. *See also* Public library(ies), public access computing and Internet access for, factors contributing to quality services and resources
"iPage," 97

Jaeger, P.T., 138, 140, 147
Johnson, G., 174, 177-179
Jones, D., 184
Jue, D.K., 2, 43

Kappa Leadership League, 174
KDLA. *See* Kentucky Department for Libraries and Archives (KDLA)

KDLA@yourlibrary initiative, 121
Kent State University School of
    Library and Information
    Science, 95
Kentucky Department for Libraries
    and Archives (KDLA),
    3,119,121,128-131
  Budget Overview of, 131
  Citizens' Forums of, 121
  Legislative Committee of, 131
  July 2005, 131-134
Kentucky General Assembly, 126
  Public Library Caucus of, 131-132
Kentucky Legislature, 133
Kentucky Library Association (KLA),
    124
  Board of Directors of, 125
  Public Library Section of, 124-125
Kentucky Public Library Association
    (KPLA), 119,125
  Legislative Committee of, 125-126
Kentucky State Advisory Council on
    Libraries, 122
Kentucky Virtual Library (KYVL), 130
King, M.L., Jr., 174
Kingsteignton Public Library, 159
Kirkus, 96
KLA. *See* Kentucky Library
    Association (KLA)
Koontz, C.M., 2,43,54
Kotler, P., 79,89
KPLA. *See* Kentucky Public Library
    Association (KPLA)
Kranich, N., 182
KYVL. *See* Kentucky Virtual Library
    (KYVL)

Lake County Library District, 192
Lake Erie College (LEC), 193-195
LBR. *See Library Bill of Rights* (LBR)
LCSH. *See* Library of Congress
    Subject Headings (LCSH)
Leadership, in age of chaos and
    complexity, 110-112,110f

League of Women Voters, 166
LeapFrog, 194
LeapTrack, 195
LEC. *See* Lake Erie College (LEC)
Lexington Public Library, 3
  Friends of the Library of, 160
Librarian Awards, 84
"Librarians at the Gate," 68
"Libraries: An American Value," of
    ALA, 60
"Libraries Build Communities,"
    126-128,133
"Libraries Change Lives," of ALA, 163
Library(ies)
  public. *See* Public library(ies)
  selling to your community,
    networking in, 137-154. *See
    also* Networking, in selling
    library to your community
  small, independent, case for,
    199-203. *See also* Small,
    independent library, case for
"Library 2.0," 200
Library advocate(s)
  defined, 156-159
  described, 159-165,162f
  timing use of, 165
Library Advocate's Handbook, 139
Library and Local Government
    Support Fund, 147
Library Bill of Rights (LBR), 61,64,156
Library Board, 186
Library Data, FSCS of, 8
Library Friends Groups, 186
Library Information Services and New
    Initiatives, at Winnipeg
    Public Library, 4
Library Journal, 89,96
Library network, building of, 188
Library of Congress, 95
  Madison Building of, 59
Library of Congress Subject Headings
    (LCSH), 95
Library Services Technology Act
    Grant, 194

Library's Advocate Handbook, of ALA, 167
Libros Sin Fonteras, 95
Literacy
 basic, public libraries and, 184
 information. *See* Information literacy
Literacy center, 191-197
 costs of, means of paying for, 194-195
 introduction to, 192-193
Literate communities, to information literate communities, advocacy in, 181-190. *See also* Information literate communities, from literate communities to, advocacy in
Local operating revenue fluctuations, impact on public library funding 2003-2005, 5-26. *See also* Public library funding, 2003-2005, impact of local operating revenue fluctuations on
London Development Authority, 86
Long Overdue: A Fresh Look at Public and Leadership Attitudes about Libraries in the 21st Century, 118, 139

Madison Building, of Library of Congress, 59
Mann, H., 59-60
Marino, D., 165
Marketing
 advocacy and, collaboration between, 117-135
 introduction to, 118-119
 in practice, 121-124
 principles of, 119-120
Marketing Library Services, 126
Massachusetts State Aid, 22
Massachusetts State Board of Education, 59
Maxine Goodman Levin College of Urban Affairs, of Cleveland State University, 151
May 2006 National Library Legislative Day, 167
McCarthy era, 64
McClure, C.R., 3,61,137-138,140,147
McDonough, K., 2,75
Mead, M., 161
Media, partnerships with, in transforming literate communities to information literate communities, 188-189
Meehan Architects, 192
Meehl, J., 193
Merola, M., 189
Miami-Dade Public Library System, 2,93,95,98-99,101
Miami-Herald, 166
Mid-Manhattan Central Library, 76
Mielke, L.J., 2,105,115
Miller, W., 4
Morley Library, 3,192-195
Morley Library Open Book Family Learning Center, 194,197
Morrison, S.F., 165
Mott Community College, Regional Technology Center of, 172
Multiculturalism, effect on public library collection development and technical services, 91-103
 budget allocation for, 92-93
 centralized/decentralized vs. best of both worlds, 96
 challenges of purchasing foreign language materials and, 94-95
 formats for, 92-93
 growing and changing community needs and, 93-94
 introduction to, 92
 outsourcing technical services, 97-98

vendor negotiations for cataloging/processing and, 98-100
vendor negotiations for online products and, 100-101
Murder Mystery events, 194
My Medicare Matters, 149
MySpace.com, 68,87,158

National Center for Education Statistics (NCES), 29,45
National Guard Armory, 160
National Library Week, 160
National Volunteers Week, 160
NCES. *See* National Center for Education Statistics (NCES)
Nelson, J.A., 3,117
Networking, in selling library to your community, 137-154
   being more successful in political process and advocacy in, 151-153
   introduction to, 138-140
   linking successful libraries to politics and advocacy, 144-146
"New Book Room," 96
New York City
   Business Solutions Center of, 83-84,86
   Small Business Services Department of, 83
New York Public Library (NYPL)
   Branch Libraries of, 80-81
   new mission of, 76-77
   SIBL of, 2,75-90. *See also* Science, Industry and Business Library (SIBL), of NYPL
New York Restaurant Association, 87
NYPL. *See* New York Public Library (NYPL)

OBFLC. *See* Open Book Family Learning Center (OBFLC)

OCLC, 94
OCLC Environmental Scan, 144
ODE. *See* Ohio Department of Education (ODE)
Office for Research and Statistics, of ALA, 1,7, 24
Ohio Department of Education (ODE), 192-193
OhioReads Community Grant, 192
OhioReads Tutoring Program, 195
OMB Watch, 120
Omega-5 Program, 197
OneCommunity, 149
Online products, vendor negotiations for, 100-101
Online public access catalog (OPAC), 141,148
OPAC. *See* Online public access catalog (OPAC)
Open Book Family Learning Center (OBFLC), activities in, 195-196

Painesville Adult Basic Literacy Education (ABLE), 193
Painesville City Local Schools (PCLS), 192-193,195-196
Parent and Child Together programs, 195
Parent Round-up, 195
PCLS. *See* Painesville City Local Schools (PCLS)
Performance Measures for Public Libraries, 61
Petruzzi, T., 3,191
Phenix, K.J., 2,57
PLA. *See* Public Library Association (PLA)
Planning and Role Setting, 61
Planning Committee, of 2005 Texas Library Association, 162
Planning for Results: A Public Library Transformation Process, 62
Policy Manual, of ALA, 64

Political process, public libraries role in, 151-153
Politics, linking successful libraries to, 144-146
Poor persons, library services for, human rights and, 66-67
Porter County Public Library, 67
Presidential Committee on Information Literacy: Final Report, 182
Principles of Marketing, 79
Project Gutenberg, 58
Public Agenda, 118
Public Awareness Institute, 134
Public Information Office, of ALA, 168
Public Libraries and the Internet 2006: Survey and Site Visit Results and Findings, 140
Public library(ies)
　advocates for, 155-171. *See also* Advocate(s)for public libraries
　basic literacy and, 184
　closure of, proactive management related to, research in facilitation of, 43-56. *See also* Public library facility closure, proactive management related to, research in facilitation of collection development and technical services of, multiculturalism and automation
effects on, 91-103. *See also* Automation; Multiculturalism
　funding for. *See* Public library funding
　human rights and, 57-73. *See also* Human rights, public libraries and
　introduction to, 1-4
　public access computing and Internet access for, factors contributing to quality services

and resources, 27-42
　introduction to, 28
　study of
　　applying for E-rate in, 34-35,34f
　　data analysis in, 31-37,31f-33f
　　data limitations in, 30-31
　　discussion of, 37-38
　　findings from, 31-37, 31f-33f
　　implications of, 37-38
　　methodology and research objectives in, 29-31
　　operating expenditure changes from 2002-2003 and bandwidth in, 35-37, 36f
　　recommendations from, 39-41
　　technology training for staff in, 31-34, 31f-33f
　　variables in, 29-30
"Public Library and Bookmobile Day," 126
Public Library Association (PLA), 58,61-62,147,169
Planning Process of, 61-62
Public Library Association (PLA) Conference (March 2006), 94
Public Library Facilities Construction Fund, 134
Public library facility closure, proactive management related to, research in facilitation of, 43-56
　introduction to, 44-45
　study of
　　discussion of, 52-55
　　methodology in, 45-48
　　recommendations for, 52-55
　　results of, 48-52,49t, 50t
Public library funding
　reductions in, 13-20,13t-19t
　status of, 6-7

2003-2005, impact of local
   operating revenue
   fluctuations on, 5-26
   executive summary of, 6-7
   increases in funding, 8-13,9t-12t
   introduction to, 7-24,9t-20t
   outlook for fiscal year 2006, 20,20t
   reductions in funding,
      13-20,13t-19t
   respondents reporting of, 20-24
   sample design in, 24-25
   selection for, 24-25
   study of, objectives of, 8
   survey methodology in, 24-25
Public Library Manifesto, of
   UNESCO, 69
Public Library Mission Statement, 61-63
Public Library Quarterly, 96
Public Library Services Improvement
   and Equalization Fund, 134
Publishers Weekly, 96
Pungitore, V.L., 61

Quality services and resources, public
   library public access
   computing and Internet
   access for, 27-42. *See also*
   Public library(ies), public
   access computing and
   Internet access for, factors
   contributing to quality
   services and resources

"Rally for Texan Libraries," 162,162f
Rangeview Library District, 2
RCPL. *See* Richland County Public
   Library (RCPL)
Reagon, B.J., 172-179
Reference USA, 76,81
Regional Technology Center, of Mott
   Community College, 172
"Remembering the Civil Rights
   Movement" Artistic
   Expressions Exhibit, 176

Research Institute for the Economy
   Trade and Industry (RIETI), 83
Research Libraries, 81
Resolution on IFLA, Human Rights,
   and Freedom of Expression, 65
Resources and Environmental Analysis
   Center, of FSU, 2
"Retain Essentials: How to Open and
   Run a Retail Store," 87
Rhode Island School of Design
   (RISDI), 82
Rich, F., 69
Richland County Public Library
   (RCPL), 157
RIETI. *See* Research Institute for the
   Economy Trade and Industry
   (RIETI)
Right(s), human, public libraries and,
   57-73. *See also* Human
   rights, public libraries and
Right to Read and View, of ALA, 164
RISDI. *See* Rhode Island School of
   Design (RISDI)
Rohatun Electronic Information Center
   (EIC), 78,80
Rosales, J., 186
Ruth Mott Foundation, 172,179
Ryan, J., 3,137-138,140,147

Salinas Public Library, 156
Schering-Plough, 80
School of Library and Information
   Sciences, of University of
   South Florida, 2
Schuman, P., 168,182
Science, Industry, and Business
   Library (SIBL)
   business classes of, 81,82f
   of NYPL, 2,75-90
      adding value at, 80-83,82f
      customer service convenience at,
         78-80
      founding of, 75
      historical background of, 76-77

new strategies of, 77-78
online information lists at, 79
partnering with, 83-86,85f
proactive approaches of, 87-89
serving all users, 86-87,88f
TOP of, 86-87
small business programs of, 84,85f
SCORE. *See* Service Corps of Retired Executives (SCORE)
Service Corps of Retired Executives (SCORE), 77,83-84
SIBL. *See* Science, Industry, and Business Library (SIBL)
Singer, P.M., 2-3,105
Small, independent library, case for, 199-203
introduction to, 199-201
Small Business@Your Library campaign, of ALA, 76
Small Business Services Department, of New York City, 83
Smallwood, E., 68
SmartBoard, 194
SNPL. *See* Successfully networked public library (SNPL)
Social Responsibilities Round Table, of ALA, Hunger Homelessness and Poverty Task Force of, 67
Spanish-speaking persons, library services for, human rights and, 67-68
Special Presidential Committee on Information Literacy and Advocacy, of ALA, 182
Sphinx Organization, of Phoenix, 174,177
SPSS. *See* Statistical Package for the Social Sciences (SPSS)
Stakeholders, described, 138
"Stand Up and Speak Out for Libraries," 182
Stanford Encyclopedia of Philosophy, 63
Stanley, A., 174,176-177

State Advisory Council on Libraries, 122,125
State Library in Florida, 100
Statistical Package for the Social Sciences (SPSS), 25
Stewart, T., 80
Student Nonviolent Coordinating Committee (SNCC) Freedom Singers, 173
Successfully networked public library (SNPL), 137,140-144
advocacy strategies of, 142
development of, 147-151
example of, 146-147
key findings in, 141-144
library's virtual branch, 141
network infrastructure in, 141-142
networked services within library, 141
next steps for, 143-144
sustainable support for, 143
"Swimming upstream," 105-116
described, 106
introduction to, 106-107

Tax Expenditure Limination (TEL) amendment, 147
Taylor, 95,97
TechAtlas technology, 29
Technical services
outsourcing of, effect of multiculturalism and automation on public library collection development and technical services and, 97-98
of public libraries, multiculturalism and automation effects on, 91-103. *See also* Automation; Multiculturalism
Technology Opportunities Program (TOP), of SIBL, 86-87
TEL amendment. *See* Tax Expenditure Limination (TEL) amendment

Tennant, R., 89
"Texans Love Libraries," 162
Texas Library Association, 162
The Americans for Libraries Council, 118
"The Charge for Library Advocacy Now!", 168
The New Planning for Results: A Streamlined Process, 62
The New York Times, 84
"The Power of Song: Ain't Gonna Let Nobody Turn Me 'Round," 171-179
The Public Library Mission Statement and its Imperatives for Service, 61
"The Resource Guide to Small Business Development in the Five Boroughs," 86
"The Smartest Card," 147, 169-170,169f
Thomas, D., 165
Thomas Register, 80
Thornton, A., 81
"Tips for Opening and Running a Restaurant," 87
Title I Children's Choir and Verse Chorus, 172-173
  CD of, 178
  concert of, 177
  face to face with, 175-176
  final preparations of, 177
  first introductions of, 175
  introducing concept and components to, 174-175
  media kits of, 178
  moving forward, 176-177
  power of outreach of, 178-179
  recording studio for, 178
  Website of, 178
"TitleSource3," 97
TOP. *See* Technology Opportunities Program (TOP)
Towson Theory, 63
Tucson Public Library, 168

"12 Ways Libraries are Good for the Country," 60
2004 Public Libraries and the Internet, 29
2005 Texas Library Association, Planning Committee of, 162
2006 Public Libraries and the Internet, 140
2007 Partners for Successful Cities Conference, of Urban Libraries Council, 151

UDHR. *See Universal Declaration of Human Rights* (UDHR)
United Nations Educational, Scientific and Cultural Organization (UNESCO), 62
  Public Library Manifesto of, 69
United Nations General Assembly, 65
Universal Declaration of Human Rights (UDHR), 2,57,63-66
Universal Pre-K project, 149
Universal Right to Freedom of Expression, 65-66
University of Michigan, 174
University of South Florida, School of Library and Information Sciences of, 2
Urban Libraries Council, 2007 Partners for Successful Cities Conference of, 151
U.S. Census Bureau, 93
US Department of Education, 45
USA PATRIOT ACT, 58

Vance, C., 118
Vendor negotiations
  for cataloging/processing, 98-100
  for online products, 100-101
Video Teleconference, 173

Wal-Mart Literacy Grant, 194

Warren, C.D., 157
Wendy's, 165
Westchester Library System, 168
Wilson, W., 106
Winnipeg Public Library, Library Information Services and New Initiatives at, 4

Woodrum, P., 168
Workshop in Business Opportunities, 82
World Wide Web, 81

Yankelovich, D., 118

For Product Safety Concerns and Information please contact our EU
representative GPSR@taylorandfrancis.com
Taylor & Francis Verlag GmbH, Kaufingerstraße 24, 80331 München, Germany

www.ingramcontent.com/pod-product-compliance
Lightning Source LLC
Chambersburg PA
CBHW060601230426
43670CB00011B/1912